asian

asian

Bath · New York · Singapore · Hong Kong · Cologne · Delhi · Melbourne

This edition published by Parragon in 2009

Parragon Publishing
Queen Street House
4 Queen Street
Bath BA1 1HE, UK

ISBN: 978-1-4075-4706-0

Printed in Indonesia

Designed by Terry Jeavons & Company
Additional text by Linda Doeser

Notes for the Reader
This book uses imperial, metric, and US cup measurements. Follow the same units of measurement throughout; do not mix imperial and metric. All spoon measurements are level: teaspoons are assumed to be 5 ml, and tablespoons are assumed to be 15 ml. Unless otherwise stated, milk is assumed to be whole, eggs and individual vegetables such as potatoes are medium, and pepper is freshly ground black pepper.

The times given are an approximate guide only. Preparation times differ according to the techniques used by different people and the cooking times may also vary from those given as a result of the type of oven used. Optional ingredients, variations, or serving suggestions have not been included in the calculations.

Recipes using raw or very lightly cooked eggs should be avoided by infants, the elderly, pregnant women, convalescents, and anyone with a chronic condition. Pregnant and breastfeeding women are advised to avoid eating peanuts and peanut products. People with nut allergies should be aware that some of the prepared ingredients used in the recipes in this book may contain nuts. Always check the packaging before use.

Vegetarians should be aware that some of the prepared ingredients used in the recipes in this book may contain animal products. Always check the packaging before use.

contents

introduction 6

soups, salads & vegetables 12

appetizers & accompaniments 142

meat & poultry 278

fish & seafood 440

vegetarian 590

index 716

introduction

The continent of Asia includes nearly 30 percent of the world's land mass and comprises many countries, billions of people, numerous languages and dialects, and myriad cultures. Even if the focus, as here, is on only the eastern and southeastern parts, the diversity is breathtaking—and this is as true of its culinary traditions as of everything else.

You have only to walk along the main streets of almost any Western city to see thriving restaurants serving Asian food, and preparing, say, Chinese or Thai dishes at home has become more and more popular and increasingly easy. The attraction is partly because of their great variety and partly because of what they have in common. Even in our modern global village, Asian food still has an air of the exotic, using ingredients such as lemongrass, wasabi, fermented shrimp paste, and Sichuan pepper that have

never featured in traditional Western kitchens. From Kyoto to Kuala Lumpur and from Beijing to Bali, food is prepared with assiduous attention to balancing flavors, colors, and textures, a subtle use of spices and other flavorings, an imaginative variety of ingredients, and delightfully appetizing presentation that, in some cases, almost amounts to a work of art.

Nevertheless, the cuisine of each country—even different regions of the same country—is unique. As a result, there are recipes to suit all tastes, occasions, and moods. If you love spicy food and hot chiles, look for the highly seasoned dishes of Chinese Sichuan or the colorful but very different curries of Thailand or Indonesia. Lovers of fish and shellfish will be thrilled with Japanese and Vietnamese specialties, while poultry, especially chicken, features in a huge variety of dishes across the region because traditional peasant communities could rarely afford the luxury of other meats. This, in turn, means that recipes for beef or lamb, for example, were often created for special occasions or rich families and are ideal for entertaining. The high price of meat and the fact that many people in Asia are Buddhist means that the array of vegetable and vegetarian dishes is immense.

Many of them are based on the soy product bean curd, created in China in the 2nd century BC and widely used in Japan since the 8th century. It took Westerners hundreds of years to catch up with this useful ingredient and the best recipes still come from Asia. An interesting misconception is that so-called fusion cooking is a modern Western fashion, but many classic dishes from Canton, Indonesia, and Vietnam, in particular, have a remarkable cosmopolitan quality as a result of trade or conquest. For those new to cooking Asian food, these could be a good place to start.

In fact, most Asian cooking is not, as a rule, difficult, although Japanese sushi chefs are apprenticed for many years before reaching the highest level of their craft. Stir-frying and broiling—both quick-cooking techniques—are very common because in many places fuel was scarce, but other familiar ways of cooking,

such as braising and deep-frying, are also frequently used.

The most important thing, however, is to try to buy authentic ingredients, although, of course, many recipes also call for items that are already familiar. Nowadays, supermarkets stock the most commonly used pantry items, such as soy sauce, Thai fish sauce, Chinese five-spice powder, canned bamboo shoots, canned coconut milk, and, of course, noodles and rice. They also offer a range of fresh ingredients, such as bean sprouts, bok choy, Chinese cabbage, daikon, and shiitake mushrooms. It may be difficult to find some rather more unusual items, such as tamarind, spring roll wrappers, galangal, and nori, but it is worth looking for Asian grocers and specialist stores.

When looking for authentic ingredients, make sure that you buy the right "nationality." For example, Chinese soy sauce has a much stronger flavor than Japanese, and Thai basil is more pungent than the Western herb so they are not interchangeable. Although it's always best to use authentic ingredients, it may sometimes be necessary to use a substitute—lemon juice instead of tamarind, bottled lemongrass instead of fresh, or dry sherry instead of Chinese rice wine.

soups, salads & vegetables

All these dishes may be served as part of a meal with a selection of other dishes, as they usually are in their countries of origin, or as a light lunch on their own. Soups, which range from delicately fragrant broths to more substantial bowlfuls, and salads also make great first courses if you want to serve them Western-style. You might even like to try serving miso soup for breakfast as they do in Japan.

We tend not to associate salads with Asian cuisine, but they are a revelation to the taste buds and to the eyes. They are characterized by fabulous contrasting flavors, exciting mixtures of texture, intriguing combinations of ingredients, and often striking presentation.

Vegetables form an extremely important part of the diet in most Asian countries and so they are prepared and cooked with considerable care, attention, and inventiveness. As a result, Asian vegetable dishes are among the most imaginative, interesting, and delicious in the world. They are very often served with a dressing, usually of contrasting flavors such as hot and sour, rather like a warm salad. They may feature familiar vegetables, such as broccoli or potatoes, but are given a special Eastern treatment,

or use more exotic greens, such as choi sum, also known as Chinese flowering cabbage. While they are all great served as part of an Asian meal, they also make superb accompaniments to plainly broiled meat, chicken, or fish—a clever way to encourage the family to eat more vegetables.

mushroom & noodle soup

ingredients

SERVES 4

1/2 cucumber

2 tbsp vegetable oil

2 scallions, finely chopped

1 garlic clove, cut into thin
    strips

2 cups flat or open-cap
    mushrooms, thinly sliced

2 1/2 cups water

1 oz/25 g Chinese rice noodles

3/4 tsp salt

1 tbsp soy sauce

method

1 Halve the cucumber lengthwise. Scoop out the seeds using a teaspoon, then slice the flesh thinly.

2 Heat the oil in a large preheated wok. Add the scallions and garlic and stir-fry for 30 seconds. Add the mushrooms and stir-fry for 2–3 minutes.

3 Stir in the water. Break the noodles into short lengths and add to the soup. Bring to a boil, stirring.

4 Add the cucumber slices, salt, and soy sauce, and let simmer for 2–3 minutes.

5 Ladle the soup into warmed bowls, distributing the noodles and vegetables evenly.

rice noodles with bean curd soup

ingredients

SERVES 4

7 oz/200 g firm bean curd, drained

vegetable or peanut oil, for deep-frying

4 cups vegetable stock

5 scallions, halved

1 yellow bell pepper, seeded and sliced

2 celery stalks, sliced

1 small onion, sliced thinly

4 kaffir lime leaves

2 tbsp Thai soy sauce

1 tbsp green curry paste

6 oz/175 g wide rice noodles, soaked and drained

chopped fresh cilantro, to garnish

method

1 Using a sharp knife, cut the bean curd into even cubes. Pour the oil into a wok to a depth of about 2 inches and heat. Deep-fry the bean curd, in batches, until browned all over. Remove with a slotted spoon, drain on paper towels, and set aside.

2 Pour the stock into a pan and bring to a boil. Add the scallions, yellow bell pepper, celery, onion, lime leaves, soy sauce, and curry paste, and let simmer for 4–5 minutes. Add the noodles and the bean curd and let simmer for 2–3 minutes. Ladle into warmed bowls and serve hot, topped with chopped cilantro.

bean curd & bean sprout soup

ingredients

SERVES 4–6

10 oz/280 g spareribs, cut into
    small pieces

5 cups water

2 tomatoes, seeded and
    coarsely chopped

3 thin slices fresh gingerroot

scant 1 cup bean sprouts

2 tsp salt

7 oz/200 g soft bean curd, cut
    into 1-inch/2.5-cm cubes

method

1 Bring a pan of water to a boil and blanch the spareribs for about 30 seconds. Skim the water, then remove the ribs and set aside.

2 Bring the measured water to a boil and add the spareribs, tomatoes, and gingerroot. After 10 minutes, remove the tomato skins from the water. Add the bean sprouts and salt, then cover and let simmer for 1 hour. Add the bean curd cubes and let simmer for an additional 2 minutes, then serve.

thai chicken-coconut soup

ingredients

SERVES 4

4 oz/115 g dried cellophane
    noodles

5 cups chicken or vegetable
    stock

1 lemongrass stalk, crushed

1/2-inch/1-cm piece fresh
    gingerroot, peeled and very
    finely chopped

2 fresh kaffir lime leaves,
    thinly sliced

1 fresh red chile, or to taste,
    seeded and thinly sliced

2 skinless, boneless chicken
    breasts, thinly sliced

1 cup coconut cream

2 tbsp nam pla (Thai fish
    sauce)

about 1 tbsp fresh lime juice

1/2 cup bean sprouts

green part of 4 scallions,
    finely sliced

fresh cilantro leaves,
    to garnish

method

1 Soak the dried noodles in a large bowl with enough lukewarm water to cover for 20 minutes, until soft. Alternatively, cook according to the package instructions. Drain well and set aside.

2 Meanwhile, bring the stock to a boil in a large pan over high heat. Lower the heat, add the lemongrass, gingerroot, lime leaves, and chile and let simmer for 5 minutes. Add the chicken and continue simmering for an additional 3 minutes, or until the flesh is poached. Stir in the coconut cream, nam pla, and most of the lime juice and continue simmering for 3 minutes. Add the bean sprouts and scallions and let simmer for an additional 1 minute. Taste and gradually add extra nam pla or lime juice at this point, if you like. Remove and discard the lemongrass stalk.

3 Divide the noodles among 4 bowls. Bring the soup back to a boil, then add the soup to each bowl. The heat of the soup will warm the noodles. To garnish, sprinkle with cilantro leaves.

chinese mushroom soup

ingredients

SERVES 4

4 oz/115 g dried thin Chinese
egg noodles

1/2 oz/15 g dried Chinese
wood ear mushrooms,
soaked in boiling water for
20 minutes

2 tsp arrowroot or cornstarch

4 cups vegetable stock

2-inch/5-cm piece fresh
gingerroot, peeled and
sliced

2 tbsp dark soy sauce

2 tsp mirin or sweet sherry

1 tsp rice vinegar

4 small bok choy, each cut
in half

salt and pepper

snipped fresh Chinese or
ordinary chives, to garnish

method

1 Boil the noodles for 3 minutes or according to the package instructions, until soft. Drain well, rinse with cold water to stop the cooking, and set aside.

2 Strain the mushrooms through a strainer lined with a dish towel and reserve the liquid. Leave the mushrooms whole or slice them, depending on how large they are. Put the arrowroot in a wok or large pan and gradually stir in the reserved mushroom liquid. Add the vegetable stock, sliced gingerroot, soy sauce, mirin, rice vinegar, mushrooms, and bok choy and bring the mixture to a boil, stirring constantly. Lower the heat and let simmer for 15 minutes.

3 Add salt and pepper, but remember that soy sauce is salty so you might not need any salt at all—taste first. Use a slotted spoon to remove the pieces of gingerroot.

4 Divide the noodles among 4 bowls, then spoon the soup over and garnish with chives.

chinese vegetable soup

ingredients

SERVES 4–6

4 oz/115 g Napa cabbage

2 tbsp peanut oil

8 oz/225 g firm marinated
   bean curd, cut into
   1/2-inch/1-cm cubes

2 garlic cloves, thinly sliced

4 scallions, thinly sliced
   diagonally

1 carrot, thinly sliced

4 cups vegetable stock

1 tbsp Chinese rice wine

2 tbsp light soy sauce

1 tsp sugar

salt and pepper

method

1 Shred the Napa cabbage and set aside. Heat the oil in a large preheated wok or skillet over high heat. Add the bean curd cubes and stir-fry for 4–5 minutes until browned. Remove from the wok with a slotted spoon and drain on paper towels.

2 Add the garlic, scallions, and carrot to the wok and stir-fry for 2 minutes. Pour in the stock, rice wine, and soy sauce, then add the sugar and shredded Napa cabbage. Cook over medium heat, stirring, for an additional 1–2 minutes until heated through.

3 Season with salt and pepper and return the bean curd to the wok. Ladle the soup into warmed bowls and serve.

sichuan pumpkin soup

ingredients

SERVES 4–6

4 cups chicken stock

1 lb/450 g pumpkin, peeled
and cut into small cubes

1 tbsp chopped preserved
vegetables

1 tsp white pepper

4 oz/115 g any leafy green
Chinese vegetable,
shredded

salt (optional)

method

1 Bring the stock to a boil, then stir in the pumpkin and let simmer for 4–5 minutes.

2 Add the preserved vegetables with the pepper and stir. Finally, add the green vegetable. Season with salt, if liked. Let simmer for an additional minute and serve.

vegetable & noodle soup

ingredients

SERVES 4

2 tbsp vegetable or peanut oil

1 onion, sliced

2 garlic cloves, chopped finely

1 large carrot, cut into thin
   sticks

1 zucchini, cut into thin sticks

1 small head broccoli, cut into
   florets

4 cups vegetable stock

1³/₄ cups coconut milk

3–4 tbsp Thai soy sauce

2 tbsp red curry paste

2 oz/55 g wide rice noodles

³/₄ cup mung or soy bean
   sprouts

4 tbsp chopped fresh cilantro

method

1 Heat the oil in a wok or large skillet and stir-fry the onion and garlic for 2–3 minutes. Add the carrot, zucchini, and broccoli and stir-fry for 3–4 minutes, until just tender.

2 Pour in the stock and coconut milk and bring to a boil. Add the soy sauce, curry paste, and noodles, and let simmer for 2–3 minutes, until the noodles have swelled. Stir in the bean sprouts and cilantro and serve immediately.

monk's soup

ingredients

SERVES 4

4 cups vegetable stock

1 stalk lemongrass, center part only, finely chopped

1 tsp tamarind paste

pinch of dried red pepper flakes, or to taste

5 oz/140 g thin green beans, cut into 1-inch/2.5-cm pieces

1 tbsp light soy sauce

1 tsp brown sugar

juice of 1/2 lime

9 oz/250 g firm bean curd, drained and cut into small cubes

2 scallions, sliced diagonally

2 oz/55 g enoki mushrooms, hard end of the stalks cut off

14 oz/400 g fresh udon noodles or thick Chinese egg noodles

method

1 Put the stock in a large pan with the lemongrass, tamarind paste, and red pepper flakes and bring to a boil, stirring until the tamarind dissolves. Lower the heat, add the green beans, and let simmer for 6 minutes. Add the soy sauce, brown sugar, and lime juice. Taste and stir in more sugar, lime juice, or red pepper flakes if liked.

2 Stir in the bean curd and scallions and continue simmering for just 1–2 minutes longer, or until the green beans are tender, but still with a bit of bite, and the bean curd is warm. Add the enoki mushrooms.

3 Pour boiling water over the udon noodles to separate them, then divide them among 4 large bowls and divide the soup among the bowls. The heat of the soup will warm the noodles.

spicy beef & noodle soup

ingredients

SERVES 4

4 cups beef stock

$2/3$ cup vegetable or peanut oil

3 oz/85 g rice vermicelli
    noodles

2 shallots, sliced thinly

2 garlic cloves, crushed

1-inch/2.5-cm piece fresh
    gingerroot, sliced thinly

8-oz/225-g piece fillet steak,
    cut into thin strips

2 tbsp Thai green curry paste

2 tbsp Thai soy sauce

1 tbsp fish sauce

chopped fresh cilantro,
    to garnish

method

1 Pour the stock into a large pan and bring to a boil. Meanwhile, heat the oil in a wok or large skillet. Add a third of the noodles and cook for 10–20 seconds, until they have puffed up. Lift out with tongs, drain on paper towels, and set aside. Discard all but 2 tablespoons of the oil.

2 Add the shallots, garlic, and gingerroot to the wok or skillet and stir-fry for 1 minute. Add the beef and curry paste and stir-fry for an additional 3–4 minutes, until tender.

3 Add the beef mixture, the uncooked noodles, soy sauce, and fish sauce to the pan of stock and let simmer for 2–3 minutes, until the noodles have swelled. Serve hot, garnished with the chopped cilantro and the reserved crispy noodles.

ground beef & cilantro soup

ingredients

SERVES 4–6

2 cups ground beef

6$\frac{1}{2}$ cups chicken stock

3 egg whites, lightly beaten

1 tsp salt

$\frac{1}{2}$ tsp white pepper

1 tbsp finely chopped fresh
    gingerroot

1 tbsp finely chopped scallion

4–5 tbsp finely chopped
    cilantro, tough stems
    discarded

marinade

1 tsp salt

1 tsp sugar

1 tsp Shaoxing rice wine

1 tsp light soy sauce

method

1 Combine all the ingredients for the marinade in a bowl and marinate the beef for 20 minutes.

2 Bring the stock to a boil. Add the beef, stirring to break up any clumps, and let simmer for 10 minutes.

3 Slowly add the egg whites, stirring rapidly so that they form into fine shreds. Add the salt and pepper and taste to check the seasoning.

4 To serve, place the gingerroot, scallion, and cilantro in the bottom of individual bowls and pour the soup on top.

clear soup with mushrooms & chicken

ingredients

SERVES 4–6

1/4 cup dried cèpes or other
    mushrooms
4 cups water
2 tbsp vegetable or peanut oil
2 cups sliced mushrooms
2 garlic cloves, chopped
    coarsely
2-inch/5-cm piece fresh
    galangal, sliced thinly
2 chicken breast portions
    (on the bone, skin on)
8 oz/225 g baby cremini
    or white mushrooms,
    quartered
juice of 1/2 lime
sprigs fresh flat-leaf parsley,
    to garnish

method

1 Place the dried mushrooms in a small bowl and pour over hot water to cover. Set aside to soak for 20–30 minutes. Drain the mushrooms, reserving the soaking liquid. Cut off and discard the stalks and chop the caps coarsely.

2 Pour the reserved soaking water into a pan with the measured water and bring to a boil. Reduce the heat to a simmer.

3 Meanwhile, heat the oil in a wok and stir-fry the soaked mushrooms, sliced fresh mushrooms, garlic, and galangal for 3–4 minutes. Add to the pan of hot water with the chicken breasts. Let simmer for 10–15 minutes, until the meat comes off the bones easily.

4 Remove the chicken from the pan. Peel off and set aside the skin. Remove the meat from the bones, slice, and set aside. Return the skin and bones to the stock and let simmer for an additional 30 minutes.

5 Remove the pan from the heat and strain the stock into a clean pan through a cheesecloth-lined strainer. Bring back to a boil and add the cremini or white mushrooms, sliced chicken, and lime juice. Reduce the heat and let simmer for 8–10 minutes. Ladle into warmed bowls, garnish with parsley sprigs, and serve immediately.

whole chicken soup

ingredients

SERVES 6–8

$3^1/_2$ oz/100 g Yunnan ham or
    ordinary ham, chopped

2 dried Chinese mushrooms,
    soaked in warm water for
    20 minutes

$3/_4$ cup fresh or canned
    bamboo shoots, rinsed
    (if using fresh shoots,
    boil in water first for
    30 minutes)

1 whole chicken

1 tbsp slivered scallion

8 slices fresh gingerroot

8 oz/225 g lean pork, chopped

2 tsp Shaoxing rice wine

12 cups water

2 tsp salt

$10^1/_2$ oz/300 g Chinese
    cabbage, cut into large
    chunks

sesame & scallion
    dipping sauce

2 tbsp light soy sauce

$1/_4$ tsp sesame oil

2 tsp finely chopped scallion

method

1 To make the dipping sauce, combine all the ingredients in a small bowl and set aside.

2 Blanch the Yunnan ham in boiling water for 30 seconds. Skim the surface, then remove the ham and set aside. Squeeze out any excess water from the mushrooms, then finely slice, discarding any tough stems. Chop the bamboo shoots into small cubes.

3 Stuff the chicken with the scallion and gingerroot. Put all the ingredients, except the cabbage and dipping sauce, in a casserole. Bring to a boil, then lower the heat and let simmer, covered, for 1 hour. Add the cabbage and simmer for an additional 3 minutes.

4 Remove the chicken skin before serving, then place a chunk of chicken meat in each individual bowl, adding pieces of vegetable and the other meats, and pour the soup on top. Serve with the dipping sauce.

chicken noodle soup

ingredients

SERVES 4–6

1 sheet dried egg noodles
    from a 9 oz/250 g package

1 tbsp corn oil

4 skinless, boneless chicken
    thighs, diced

1 bunch of scallions, sliced

2 garlic cloves, chopped

3/4-inch/2-cm piece fresh
    gingerroot, finely chopped

3 3/4 cups chicken stock

3/4 cup coconut milk

3 tsp Thai red curry paste

3 tbsp peanut butter

2 tbsp light soy sauce

salt and pepper

1 small red bell pepper,
    seeded and chopped

1/2 cup frozen peas

method

1 Place the noodles in a shallow heatproof dish and let soak in boiling water according to the package directions.

2 Meanwhile, heat the oil in a preheated wok. Add the chicken and stir-fry for 5 minutes, or until lightly browned. Add the white part of the scallions, the garlic, and gingerroot and stir-fry for 2 minutes.

3 Add the stock, coconut milk, curry paste, peanut butter, and soy sauce. Season to taste with salt and pepper. Bring to a boil, stirring constantly, then simmer for 8 minutes, stirring occasionally. Add the bell pepper, peas, and green scallion tops and cook for an additional 2 minutes.

4 Drain the noodles, then add them to the wok and heat through. Spoon into warmed serving bowls and serve immediately.

hot-&-sour soup

ingredients

SERVES 4–5

3 dried Chinese mushrooms,
    soaked in warm water for
    20 minutes
4 oz/115 g pork loin
$1/2$ cup fresh or canned
    bamboo shoots, rinsed
    (if using fresh shoots,
    boil in water first for
    30 minutes)
8 oz/225 g firm bean curd
$3^{3}/4$ cups chicken stock
1 tbsp Shaoxing rice wine
1 tbsp light soy sauce
$1^{1}/2$ tbsp white rice vinegar
1 tsp salt
1 tsp white pepper
1 egg, lightly beaten

method

1 Squeeze out any excess water from the mushrooms, then finely slice, discarding any tough stems. Finely slice the pork, bamboo shoots, and bean curd, all to a similar size.

2 Bring the stock to a boil. Add the pork and boil over high heat for 2 minutes. Add the mushrooms and bamboo shoots and boil for an additional 2 minutes. Next, add the Shaoxing, light soy sauce, rice vinegar, salt, and pepper. Bring back to a boil and let simmer, covered, for 5 minutes. Add the bean curd and boil, uncovered, for 2 minutes.

3 To serve, rapidly stir in the egg until it has formed fine shreds. Serve immediately.

wonton soup

ingredients

SERVES 6

30 square wonton skins

1 egg white, lightly beaten

2 tbsp finely chopped scallion,
    to serve

1 tbsp chopped cilantro
    leaves, to garnish

filling

6 oz/175 g ground pork,
    not too lean

8 oz/225 g shrimp, shelled,
    deveined, and chopped

$1/2$ tsp finely chopped fresh
    gingerroot

1 tbsp light soy sauce

1 tbsp Shaoxing rice wine

2 tsp finely chopped scallion

pinch of sugar

pinch of white pepper

dash of sesame oil

soup

8 cups chicken stock

2 tsp salt

$1/2$ tsp white pepper

method

1 Mix together the filling ingredients and stir well until the texture is thick and pasty. Set aside for at least 20 minutes.

2 To make the wontons, place a teaspoon of the filling in the center of a skin. Brush the edges with a little egg white. Bring the opposite points toward each other and press the edges together, creating a flowerlike shape. Repeat with the remaining skins and filling.

3 To make the soup, bring the stock to a boil and add the salt and pepper. Boil the wontons in the stock for about 5 minutes, or until the skins begin to wrinkle around the filling.

4 To serve, put the scallion in individual bowls, then spoon in the wontons and soup and top with the cilantro.

duck with scallion soup

ingredients

SERVES 4

2 duck breasts, skin on

2 tbsp Thai red curry paste

2 tbsp vegetable or peanut oil

bunch of scallions, chopped

2 garlic cloves, crushed

2-inch piece fresh gingerroot, grated

2 carrots, sliced thinly

1 red bell pepper, seeded and cut into strips

4 cups chicken stock

2 tbsp sweet chili sauce

3–4 tbsp Thai soy sauce

14 oz/400 g canned straw mushrooms, drained

method

1 Slash the skin of the duck 3 or 4 times with a sharp knife and rub in the curry paste. Cook the duck breasts, skin-side down, in a wok over high heat for 2–3 minutes. Turn over, reduce the heat, and cook for an additional 3–4 minutes, until cooked through. Lift out and slice thickly. Set aside and keep warm.

2 Meanwhile, heat the oil in a wok and stir-fry half the scallions, the garlic, gingerroot, carrots, and the red bell pepper for 2–3 minutes. Pour in the stock and add the chili sauce, soy sauce, and mushrooms. Bring to a boil, reduce the heat, and let simmer for 4–5 minutes.

3 Ladle the soup into warmed bowls, top with the duck slices, and garnish with the remaining scallions. Serve immediately.

thai-style seafood soup

ingredients

SERVES 4

5 cups fish stock

1 lemongrass stem, split
    lengthwise

pared rind of 1/2 lime or
    1 fresh kaffir lime leaf

1-inch/2.5-cm piece fresh
    gingerroot, sliced

1/4 tsp chili paste, or to taste

4–6 scallions

7 oz/200 g large or medium
    shrimp, shelled

salt

9 oz/250 g scallops (16–20)

2 tbsp cilantro leaves

finely chopped red bell pepper
    or fresh red chile rings,
    to garnish

method

1 Place the stock in a wok with the lemongrass, lime rind, gingerroot, and chili paste. Bring just to a boil, then reduce the heat and simmer, covered, for 10–15 minutes.

2 Cut the scallions in half lengthwise, then slice crosswise very thinly. Cut the shrimp almost in half lengthwise, keeping the tails intact. Devein if necessary.

3 Pour the stock through a strainer, then return to the wok and bring to a simmer, with bubbles rising at the edges and the surface trembling. Add the scallions and cook for 2–3 minutes. Taste and season with salt, if needed. Stir in a little more chili paste if wished.

4 Add the scallops and shrimp and poach for 1 minute, or until they turn opaque and the shrimp curl.

5 Drop in the cilantro leaves, then ladle the soup into warmed serving bowls, dividing the shellfish evenly, and garnish with bell pepper or chile rings.

spicy thai soup with shrimp

ingredients

SERVES 4

2 tbsp tamarind paste

4 fresh red Thai chiles,
   very finely chopped

2 garlic cloves, crushed

1-inch/2.5-cm piece fresh
   galangal, very finely
   chopped

4 tbsp Thai fish sauce

2 tbsp jaggery or superfine
   sugar

8 fresh kaffir lime leaves,
   coarsely torn

4 cups fish stock

1 cup very thinly sliced carrots

2 cups diced sweet potato

3 1/2 oz/100 g baby corn cobs,
   halved

3 tbsp cilantro, coarsely
   chopped

3 1/2 oz/100 g cherry tomatoes,
   halved

8 oz/225 g cooked fantail
   shrimp

method

1 Place the tamarind paste, chiles, garlic, galangal, fish sauce, sugar, lime leaves, and stock in a large, preheated wok. Bring to a boil, stirring constantly.

2 Reduce the heat and add the carrots, sweet potato, and baby corn cobs to the mixture in the wok.

3 Let the soup simmer for 10 minutes, or until the vegetables are just tender.

4 Stir the cilantro, cherry tomatoes, and shrimp into the soup and heat through for 5 minutes.

5 Transfer the soup to warmed serving bowls and serve hot.

crab & corn soup

ingredients

SERVES 4

4 oz/115 g fresh or frozen
  crabmeat
2$\frac{1}{2}$ cups water
15 oz/425 g canned
  cream-style corn, drained
$\frac{1}{2}$ tsp salt
pinch of pepper
2 tsp cornstarch, dissolved in
  2 tbsp water (optional)
1 egg, beaten

method

1 If using frozen crabmeat, blanch the flesh in boiling water for 30 seconds. Remove with a slotted spoon and set aside.

2 In a large pan, bring the water to a boil with the crab and corn and let simmer for 2 minutes. Season with the salt and pepper. Stir in the cornstarch, if using, and continue stirring until the soup has thickened. Rapidly stir in the egg and serve.

miso soup

ingredients

SERVES 4

1 quantity dashi stock

6 oz/175 g firm bean curd, cut
into 1/2-inch/1-cm cubes

4 shiitake or white
mushrooms, sliced

4 tbsp miso paste

2 scallions, finely sliced

2 tsp white sesame seeds,
toasted

method

1 Put the dashi stock into a pan and heat through. Add the cubed bean curd and sliced mushrooms, and let simmer gently for 3 minutes. Add the miso and stir until it has dissolved completely.

2 Turn off the heat, add the scallions, and divide the soup between 4 serving bowls. Scatter 1/2 tsp of the toasted sesame seeds over each serving.

thai shrimp & scallop soup

ingredients

SERVES 4

4 cups fish stock

juice of $1/2$ lime

2 tbsp rice wine or sherry

1 leek, sliced

2 shallots, finely chopped

1 tbsp grated fresh gingerroot

1 fresh red chile, seeded and
    finely chopped

8 oz/225 g shrimp, shelled
    and deveined

8 oz/225 g live scallops,
    shucked and cleaned

$1^1/2$ tbsp chopped fresh
    flat-leaf parsley, plus extra
    to garnish

salt and pepper

method

1 Put the stock, lime juice, rice wine, leek, shallots, gingerroot, and chile in a large pan. Bring to a boil over high heat, then reduce the heat, cover, and let simmer for 10 minutes.

2 Add the shrimp, scallops, and parsley, season with salt and pepper, and cook for 1–2 minutes.

3 Remove the pan from the heat and ladle the soup into warmed serving bowls. Garnish with chopped parsley and serve.

shrimp & papaya salad

ingredients

SERVES 4

1 papaya, peeled

12 oz/350 g large cooked
    shrimp, shelled

assorted baby salad greens

dressing

4 scallions, chopped finely

2 fresh red chiles, seeded and
    chopped finely

1 tsp fish sauce

1 tbsp vegetable or peanut oil

juice of 1 lime

1 tsp jaggery or soft light
    brown sugar

method

1 Scoop the seeds out of the papaya and slice thinly. Stir gently together with the shrimp.

2 Mix the scallions, chiles, fish sauce, oil, lime juice, and sugar together.

3 Arrange the salad greens in a bowl and top with the papaya and shrimp. Pour the dressing over and serve immediately.

crab & cilantro salad

ingredients

SERVES 4

12 oz/350 g canned white
    crabmeat, drained
4 scallions, finely chopped
handful of fresh cilantro,
    chopped
1 iceberg lettuce, shredded
3-inch/7.5-cm piece
    cucumber, chopped

dressing
1 garlic clove, crushed
1-inch/2.5-cm piece
    gingerroot, peeled and
    grated
2 lime leaves, torn into pieces
juice of 1 lime
1 tsp fish sauce

method

1 Put the crabmeat into a bowl and stir in the scallions and cilantro. Mix the ingredients for the dressing together.

2 Place the lettuce leaves on a serving platter and sprinkle with the cucumber.

3 Arrange the crab salad over the leaves and drizzle the dressing over the salad. Serve immediately.

tuna & tomato salad with gingerroot dressing

ingredients

SERVES 4

$^1/_2$ cup shredded Napa
   cabbage
3 tbsp rice wine or dry sherry
2 tbsp Thai fish sauce
1 tbsp finely shredded fresh
   gingerroot
1 garlic clove, finely chopped
$^1/_2$ small fresh red Thai chile,
   finely chopped
2 tsp brown sugar
2 tbsp lime juice
14 oz/400 g fresh tuna steak
corn oil, for brushing
$4^1/_2$ oz/125 g cherry tomatoes
fresh mint leaves and mint
   sprigs, coarsely chopped,
   to garnish

method

1 Place a small pile of shredded Napa cabbage on a large serving plate. Place the rice wine, fish sauce, gingerroot, garlic, chile, sugar, and 1 tablespoon of lime juice in a screw-top jar and shake well to combine.

2 Using a sharp knife, cut the tuna into strips of an even thickness. Sprinkle with the remaining lime juice.

3 Brush a wide skillet or ridged grill pan with oil and heat until very hot. Arrange the tuna strips in the skillet and cook until just firm and light golden, turning them over once. Remove the tuna strips from the skillet and reserve.

4 Add the tomatoes to the skillet and cook over high heat until lightly browned. Spoon the tuna and tomatoes over the Napa cabbage, then spoon over the dressing. Garnish with fresh mint and serve warm.

seaweed salad

ingredients

SERVES 4

³/₄ oz/20 g assorted dried
   seaweed, such as wakame,
   hijiki, and arame
1 English cucumber
2 scallions, shredded
1 package of mustard and
   cress, snipped

sesame dressing

2 tbsp rice vinegar
2 tsp Japanese soy sauce
1 tbsp mirin
2 tsp sesame oil
1 tsp white miso

method

1 Soak the different seaweeds in separate bowls of cold water—the wakame will need 10 minutes and the others 30 minutes. Drain.

2 Cook the wakame only in a pan of boiling water for 2 minutes, then drain and let cool. Put all the seaweeds in a serving bowl.

3 Halve the cucumber lengthwise. Reserve half for another recipe, scoop the seeds out of the remaining half, and finely slice the flesh. Add to the seaweeds with the chopped scallions and the snipped mustard and cress.

4 Place all the ingredients for the dressing in a small pitcher and stir to combine. Add to the bowl, and toss the salad before serving.

sea bass & mango salad

ingredients

SERVES 2

2 small sea bass, cleaned

1 tbsp red curry paste

small handful of fresh cilantro,
    chopped

2/3 cup coconut milk

2 tbsp sweet chili sauce

6–8 Thai basil leaves, chopped

1/2 tsp fish sauce

1 tsp rice wine vinegar

1 mango, pitted, peeled,
    and sliced

selection of mixed salad
    greens

method

1 Place the fish on a board. Mix the curry paste and cilantro together and stuff inside each fish cavity. Cover and let marinate for 1–2 hours.

2 Place the fish in a roasting pan. Mix the coconut milk, chili sauce, basil, fish sauce, and vinegar, and pour over the fish. Arrange the mango slices in the pan as well. Cover with foil and cook for 15 minutes.

3 Remove the foil and cook uncovered for an additional 10–15 minutes until cooked.

4 Place the fish on 2 warmed serving plates, drizzle with the cooking sauces, and serve with the mixed salad greens.

seared swordfish salad

ingredients

SERVES 4

3 oz/85 g daikon
   (long white radish)
1 medium carrot
$1/2$ English cucumber
9 oz/250 g fresh swordfish
   steak, skinned
2 tsp peanut oil
2 tsp white sesame seeds,
   toasted

sesame dressing
1 tbsp Japanese soy sauce
2 tbsp sesame oil
$1/2$ tsp wasabi paste
1 tsp rice vinegar

method

1 Place all the ingredients for the sesame dressing in a small bowl and stir to combine. Refrigerate until needed.

2 Shred the daikon and carrot using the finest setting on a mandolin. Alternatively, cut them into long thin slices and then cut each slice along its length as finely as possible. Rinse, drain, and then place in the refrigerator until needed. Shred the cucumber, discarding the seeded parts. Add to the daikon and carrot.

3 Trim the swordfish steak. Heat the oil in a skillet until very hot, then sear the swordfish for 30–60 seconds on both sides and the edges. Let cool.

4 Cut the seared swordfish into $1/3$-inch/8-mm thick pieces, using a wet, very sharp knife and slicing across the grain. Wipe your knife on a damp cloth between each cut.

5 Arrange the fish slices on 4 serving plates and place a mound of the shredded salad vegetables alongside. Drizzle the salad vegetables with the sesame dressing and sprinkle with the toasted sesame seeds.

chinese shrimp salad

ingredients

SERVES 4

9 oz/250 g dried thin Chinese egg noodles

3 tbsp sunflower oil

1 tbsp sesame oil

1 tbsp sesame seeds

generous 1 cup bean sprouts

1 mango, peeled, pitted, and sliced

6 scallions, sliced

2³/4 oz/75 g radishes, sliced

12 oz/350 g cooked shelled shrimp

2 tbsp light soy sauce

1 tbsp sherry

method

1 Put the noodles in a large, heatproof bowl and pour over enough boiling water to cover. Let stand for 10 minutes, then drain thoroughly and pat dry with paper towels.

2 Heat the sunflower oil in a large, preheated wok. Add the noodles and stir-fry for 5 minutes, tossing frequently.

3 Remove the wok from the heat and add the sesame oil, sesame seeds, and bean sprouts, tossing to mix well.

4 Mix the mango, scallions, radishes, shrimp, soy sauce, and sherry together in a separate bowl. Toss the shrimp mixture with the noodles. Alternatively, arrange the noodles around the edge of a serving plate and pile the shrimp mixture into the center. Serve at once.

shrimp & rice salad

ingredients

SERVES 4

generous $3/4$ cup mixed
    long-grain and wild rice
12 oz/350 g cooked shelled
    shrimp
1 mango, peeled, pitted,
    and diced
4 scallions, sliced
$1/4$ cup slivered almonds
1 tbsp finely chopped fresh
    mint
salt and pepper

dressing
1 tbsp extra virgin olive oil
2 tsp lime juice
1 garlic clove, crushed
1 tsp honey

method

1 Bring a large pan of lightly salted water to a boil. Add the rice, return to a boil, and cook for 35 minutes, or until tender. Drain, then transfer to a large bowl and stir in the shrimp.

2 To make the dressing, combine the olive oil, lime juice, garlic, and honey in a large pitcher, season to taste with salt and pepper, and whisk until well blended. Pour the dressing over the rice and shrimp mixture and let cool.

3 Add the mango, scallions, almonds, and mint to the salad and season to taste with pepper. Stir thoroughly, transfer to a large serving dish, and serve.

peppered beef salad

ingredients

SERVES 4

4 fillet steaks, 4 oz/115 g each

2 tbsp black peppercorns, crushed

1 tsp Chinese five spice powder

3/4 cup bean sprouts

1-inch/2.5-cm piece gingerroot, chopped finely

4 shallots, sliced finely

1 red bell pepper, seeded and sliced thinly

3 tbsp Thai soy sauce

2 fresh red chiles, seeded and sliced

1/2 lemongrass stalk, chopped finely

3 tbsp vegetable or peanut oil

1 tbsp sesame oil

method

1 Wash the steaks and pat dry on paper towels. Mix the peppercorns with the five spice and press onto all sides of the steaks. Cook on a grill pan or under a broiler for 2–3 minutes each side, or until cooked to your liking.

2 Meanwhile mix the bean sprouts, half the gingerroot, the shallots, and bell pepper together and divide between 4 plates. Mix the remaining gingerroot, soy sauce, chiles, lemongrass, and oils together.

3 Slice the beef and arrange on the vegetables. Drizzle with the dressing and serve immediately.

broiled beef salad

ingredients

SERVES 4

1³/₄ oz/50 g dried oyster
    mushrooms

1 lb 5 oz/600 g rump steak

1 red bell pepper, seeded and
    thinly sliced

scant ¹/₃ cup roasted
    cashew nuts

red and green lettuce leaves

fresh mint leaves, to garnish

dressing

2 tbsp sesame oil

2 tbsp Thai fish sauce

2 tbsp sweet sherry

2 tbsp oyster sauce

1 tbsp lime juice

1 fresh red chile, seeded and
    finely chopped

method

1 Put the mushrooms in a heatproof bowl, cover with boiling water, and let stand for 20 minutes. Drain, then cut into slices.

2 Preheat the broiler to medium or heat a ridged grill pan. To make the dressing, place all the ingredients in a bowl and whisk to combine.

3 Cook the steak under the preheated broiler or on the hot grill pan, turning once, for 5 minutes, or until browned on both sides but still rare in the center. Cook the steak longer if desired.

4 Slice the steak into thin strips and place in a bowl with the mushrooms, bell pepper, and nuts. Add the dressing and toss together.

5 Arrange the lettuce on a large serving platter and place the beef mixture on top. Garnish with mint leaves. Serve at room temperature.

red chicken salad

ingredients

SERVES 4

4 boneless chicken breasts

2 tbsp red curry paste

2 tbsp vegetable or peanut oil

1 head Napa cabbage,
    shredded

6 oz/175 g bok choy, torn into
    large pieces

1/2 savoy cabbage, shredded

2 shallots, chopped finely

2 garlic cloves, crushed

1 tbsp rice wine vinegar

2 tbsp sweet chili sauce

2 tbsp Thai soy sauce

method

1 Slash the flesh of the chicken several times and rub the curry paste into each cut. Cover and let chill overnight.

2 Cook the chicken in a heavy-bottom pan over medium heat or on a grill pan for 5–6 minutes, turning once or twice, until cooked through. Keep warm.

3 Heat 1 tablespoon of the oil in a wok or large skillet and stir-fry the Napa cabbage, bok choy, and savoy cabbage until just wilted. Add the remaining oil and the shallots and garlic, and stir-fry until just tender but not browned. Add the vinegar, chili sauce, and soy. Remove from the heat.

4 Arrange the leaves on 4 serving plates. Slice the chicken, arrange on the salad greens, and drizzle the hot dressing over. Serve immediately.

gingered chicken & vegetable salad

ingredients

SERVES 4

4 skinless, boneless chicken
    breasts
4 scallions, chopped
1-inch/2.5-cm piece
    gingerroot, chopped finely
4 garlic cloves, crushed
3 tbsp vegetable or peanut oil
1 onion, sliced
2 garlic cloves, chopped
4 oz/115 g baby corn, halved
4 oz/115 g snow peas, halved
    lengthwise
1 red bell pepper, seeded
    and sliced
3-inch/7.5-cm piece
    cucumber, peeled, seeded,
    and sliced
4 tbsp Thai soy sauce
1 tbsp jaggery or soft light
    brown sugar
few Thai basil leaves
6 oz/175 g fine egg noodles

method

1 Cut the chicken into large cubes, each about 1 inch/2.5 cm. Mix the scallions, gingerroot, garlic, and oil together in a shallow dish and add the chicken. Cover and let marinate for at least 3 hours. Lift the meat out of the marinade and set aside.

2 Heat the oil in a wok or large skillet and cook the onion for 1–2 minutes before adding the rest of the vegetables except the cucumber. Cook for 2–3 minutes, until just tender. Add the cucumber, half the soy sauce, the sugar, and the basil, and mix gently.

3 Soak the noodles for 2–3 minutes (check the package instructions) or until tender, and drain well. Sprinkle the remaining soy sauce over them and arrange on plates. Top with the cooked vegetables.

4 Add a little more oil to the wok if necessary and cook the chicken over fairly high heat until browned on all sides. Arrange the chicken cubes on top of the salad and serve hot or warm.

rice & turkey salad

ingredients

SERVES 4

4 cups chicken stock

scant 1 cup mixed long-grain
    and wild rice

2 tbsp corn oil

8 oz/225 g skinless, boneless
    turkey breast, trimmed of
    all visible fat and cut into
    thin strips

2 cups snow peas

4 oz/115 g oyster mushrooms,
    torn into pieces

1/4 cup shelled pistachio nuts,
    finely chopped

2 tbsp chopped fresh cilantro

1 tbsp snipped fresh garlic
    chives

salt and pepper

1 tbsp balsamic vinegar

fresh garlic chives, to garnish

method

1 Set aside 3 tablespoons of the chicken stock and bring the remainder to a boil in a large pan. Add the rice and cook for 30 minutes, or until tender. Drain and let cool slightly.

2 Meanwhile, heat 1 tablespoon of the oil in a preheated wok or skillet. Stir-fry the turkey over medium heat for 3–4 minutes, or until cooked through. Using a slotted spoon, transfer the turkey to a dish. Add the snow peas and mushrooms to the wok and stir-fry for 1 minute. Add the reserved stock, bring to a boil, then reduce the heat, cover, and let simmer for 3–4 minutes. Transfer the vegetables to the dish and let cool slightly.

3 Thoroughly mix the rice, turkey, snow peas, mushrooms, nuts, cilantro, and garlic chives together, then season to taste with salt and pepper. Drizzle with the remaining corn oil and the vinegar and garnish with fresh garlic chives. Serve warm.

duck salad

ingredients

SERVES 4

4 boneless duck breasts,
   skin on
1 lemongrass stalk, broken
   into three and each cut in
   half lengthwise
3 tbsp vegetable or peanut oil
2 tbsp sesame oil
1 tsp fish sauce
1 fresh green chile, seeded
   and chopped
2 tbsp red curry paste
1/2 fresh pineapple, peeled
   and sliced
3-inch/7.5-cm piece
   cucumber, peeled, seeded,
   and sliced
3 tomatoes, cut into wedges
1 onion, sliced thinly

dressing
juice of 1 lemon
2 garlic cloves, crushed
1 tsp jaggery or soft light
   brown sugar
2 tbsp vegetable or peanut oil

method

1 Unwrap the duck and let the skin dry out overnight in the refrigerator.

2 The following day, slash the skin side 5–6 times. Mix the lemongrass, 2 tablespoons of the vegetable oil, all the sesame oil, fish sauce, chile, and curry paste together in a shallow dish and place the duck breasts in the mixture. Turn to coat and to rub the marinade into the meat. Let chill for 2–3 hours.

3 Heat the remaining oil in a wok or large skillet and cook the duck, skin-side down, over medium heat for 3–4 minutes until the skin is browned and crisp and the meat cooked most of the way through.

4 Turn the breasts over and cook until browned and the meat is cooked to your liking.

5 Meanwhile, arrange the pineapple, cucumber, tomatoes, and onions on a platter. Mix the dressing ingredients together and pour over the top.

6 Lift the duck out of the wok and slice thickly. Arrange the duck slices on top of the salad and serve while still hot.

chinese tomato salad

ingredients

SERVES 4–6

2 large tomatoes

dressing
1 tbsp finely chopped scallions
1 tsp finely chopped garlic
$1/2$ tsp sesame oil
1 tbsp white rice vinegar
$1/2$ tsp salt
pinch of white pepper
pinch of sugar

method

1 Mix together all the ingredients for the dressing and set aside.

2 Thinly slice the tomatoes. Arrange on a plate and pour the dressing over the top. Serve immediately.

eggplant & onion salad

ingredients

SERVES 4

4 tbsp vegetable or peanut oil

1 onion, sliced

4 shallots, chopped finely

4 scallions, sliced

12 oz/350 g eggplants, cubed

2 tbsp Thai green curry paste

2 tbsp Thai soy sauce

1 tsp jaggery or soft light
    brown sugar

4 oz/115 g block creamed
    coconut, chopped

3 tbsp water

small handful of fresh cilantro,
    chopped

few Thai basil leaves, chopped

small handful of fresh parsley,
    chopped

2 1/2 cups arugula leaves

2 tbsp sweet chili sauce

method

1 Heat half the oil in a wok or large skillet and cook all the onions together for 1–2 minutes, until just softened but not browned. Lift out and set aside.

2 Add the eggplant cubes, in batches if necessary, adding more oil as needed, until they are crisp and golden brown.

3 Return the onions to the wok and add the curry paste, soy sauce, and sugar. Add the creamed coconut and water and cook until dissolved. Stir in most of the cilantro, the basil, and the parsley.

4 Toss the arugula in the chili sauce and serve with the eggplant and onion salad. Garnish with the remaining herbs.

daikon & cucumber salad

ingredients

SERVES 4

8-inch/20-cm piece of daikon
    (long white radish)
1 English cucumber
handful of baby spinach
    greens, chopped
3 red radishes, sliced into
    thin rounds
a few leaves of Chinese
    cabbage, cut into
    thin strips
1 tbsp sunflower seeds
2 tsp white sesame seeds,
    toasted

wasabi dressing
4 tbsp rice vinegar
2 tbsp grapeseed oil
1 tsp light soy sauce
1 tsp wasabi paste
1/2 tsp sugar
salt, to taste

method

1 Shred the daikon using the finest setting on a mandolin or a very sharp knife. If you are using a knife, then cut the daikon into long, thin slices and cut each slice along its length as finely as you can. Rinse under cold water, then drain well.

2 Halve the cucumber lengthwise, reserve half for another recipe, and use a teaspoon to scoop the seeds out of the remaining half. Peel and slice in the same way as the daikon.

3 Place the sliced daikon and cucumber in a salad bowl with the chopped spinach greens. Add the sliced radishes and Chinese cabbage.

4 Place the ingredients for the dressing in a small pitcher and stir to mix. Pour the dressing over the salad, toss gently to mix, and sprinkle with the sunflower seeds and the toasted sesame seeds.

julienne vegetable salad

ingredients

SERVES 4

4 tbsp vegetable or peanut oil

8 oz/225 g bean curd with
   herbs, cubed

1 red onion, sliced

4 scallions, cut into 2-inch
   lengths

1 garlic clove, chopped

2 carrots, cut into short,
   thin sticks

4 oz/115 g fine green beans,
   trimmed

1 yellow bell pepper, seeded
   and cut into strips

4 oz/115 g broccoli, cut into
   florets

1 large zucchini, cut into
   short, thin sticks

2 oz/55 g bean sprouts

2 tbsp Thai red curry paste

4 tbsp Thai soy sauce

1 tbsp rice wine vinegar

1 tsp jaggery or soft light
   brown sugar

few Thai basil leaves

12 oz/350 g rice vermicelli
   noodles

method

1 Heat the oil in a wok and cook the bean curd cubes for 3–4 minutes, until browned on all sides. Lift the cubes out of the oil and drain on paper towels.

2 Add the onions, scallions, garlic, and carrots to the hot oil and cook for 1–2 minutes before adding the rest of the vegetables, except for the bean sprouts. Stir-fry for 2–3 minutes. Add the bean sprouts, then stir in the curry paste, soy, vinegar, sugar, and basil leaves. Cook for 30 seconds.

3 Soak the noodles in boiling water or stock for 2–3 minutes (check the package instructions) or until tender, and drain well.

4 Pile the vegetables onto the noodles, and serve topped with the bean curd cubes. Garnish with extra basil if desired.

buckwheat noodle salad with smoked bean curd

ingredients

SERVES 2

7 oz/200 g buckwheat noodles

9 oz/250 g firm smoked bean curd, drained weight

2 1/4 cups finely shredded white cabbage

4 medium carrots, finely shredded

3 scallions, diagonally sliced

1 fresh red chile, seeded and finely sliced into circles

2 tbsp sesame seeds, lightly toasted

dressing

1 tsp grated fresh gingerroot

1 garlic clove, crushed

6 oz/175 g silken bean curd, drained weight

4 tsp tamari (wheat-free soy sauce)

2 tbsp sesame oil

4 tbsp hot water

salt

method

1 Cook the noodles in a large pan of lightly salted boiling water according to the package instructions. Drain and refresh under cold running water.

2 To make the dressing, blend the gingerroot, garlic, silken bean curd, tamari, oil, and water together in a small bowl until smooth and creamy. Season with salt.

3 Place the smoked bean curd in a steamer. Steam for 5 minutes, then cut into thin slices.

4 Meanwhile, put the cabbage, carrots, scallions, and chile into a bowl and toss to mix. To serve, arrange the noodles on serving plates and top with the carrot salad and slices of bean curd. Spoon over the dressing and sprinkle with sesame seeds.

hot-&-sour vegetable salad

ingredients

SERVES 4

2 tbsp vegetable or peanut oil

1 tbsp chili oil

1 onion, sliced

1-inch/2.5-cm piece
    gingerroot, grated

1 small head broccoli, cut into
    florets

2 carrots, cut into short thin
    sticks

1 red bell pepper, seeded and
    cut into squares

1 yellow bell pepper, seeded
    and cut into strips

2 oz/55 g snow peas, trimmed
    and halved

2 oz/55 g baby corn, halved

dressing

2 tbsp vegetable or peanut oil

1 tsp chili oil

1 tbsp rice wine vinegar

juice of 1 lime

1/2 tsp fish sauce

method

1 Heat the oils in a wok or large skillet and sauté the onion and gingerroot for 1–2 minutes until they start to soften. Add the vegetables and stir-fry for 2–3 minutes until they have softened slightly. Remove from the heat and set aside.

2 Mix the dressing ingredients together. Transfer the vegetables to a serving plate and drizzle the dressing over. Serve warm immediately, or let the flavors develop and serve cold.

curried egg salad

ingredients

SERVES 4

6 eggs

1 tbsp vegetable or peanut oil

1 onion, chopped

1 tbsp Thai yellow curry paste

4 tbsp plain yogurt

1/2 tsp salt

handful of fresh cilantro,
    chopped finely

bunch of watercress
    or arugula

2 zucchini, cut into short
    thin sticks

1 fresh green chile, seeded
    and chopped finely

1 tsp fish sauce

1 tsp rice wine vinegar

3 tbsp vegetable or peanut oil

method

1 Put the eggs in a pan, cover with cold water, and bring to a boil. Let simmer for 10 minutes, then drain and rinse in cold water. Shell and halve.

2 Meanwhile, heat the oil in a medium skillet and sauté the onion gently until softened but not browned. Remove from the heat and stir in the curry paste. Let cool slightly before stirring in the yogurt, salt, and half the cilantro. Set aside.

3 Arrange the watercress and zucchini is on a platter. Mix the chile, fish sauce, vinegar, and oil together and pour the dressing over the leaves.

4 Arrange the eggs on top and spoon the yogurt mixture over each one. Garnish with the remaining cilantro over the top and serve immediately.

classic stir-fried vegetables

ingredients

SERVES 4

3 tbsp sesame oil

6 scallions, chopped finely,
    plus 2 scallions, chopped
    finely, to garnish

1 garlic clove, crushed

1 tbsp grated fresh gingerroot

1 head of broccoli,
    cut into florets

1 orange or yellow bell pepper,
    chopped coarsely

1³/₄ cups shredded red
    cabbage

4¹/₂ oz/125 g baby corn

6 oz/175 g portobello or large
    cup mushrooms,
    sliced thinly

1¹/₃ cups fresh bean sprouts

9 oz/250 g canned water
    chestnuts, drained

4 tsp soy sauce, or to taste

cooked wild rice, to serve

method

1 Heat 2 tablespoons of the oil in a large skillet or wok over high heat. Stir-fry the 6 chopped scallions with the garlic and gingerroot for 30 seconds.

2 Add the broccoli, bell pepper, and red cabbage and stir-fry for 1–2 minutes. Mix in the baby corn and mushrooms and stir-fry for an additional 1–2 minutes.

3 Finally, add the bean sprouts and water chestnuts and cook for 2 minutes. Pour in the soy sauce and stir well.

4 Serve immediately over cooked wild rice, garnished with the remaining scallions.

cabbage & cucumber in a vinegar dressing

ingredients

SERVES 4–6

2^1/$_2$ cups finely shredded
  Chinese cabbage
1 tsp salt
1 cucumber, peeled, seeded,
  and finely chopped into
  short thin sticks
1 tsp sesame oil
2 tbsp white rice vinegar
1 tsp sugar

method

1 Sprinkle the cabbage with the salt and let stand for at least 10 minutes. Drain the cabbage if necessary, then mix with the cucumber pieces.

2 Whisk together the sesame oil, vinegar, and sugar and toss the vegetables in it. Serve immediately.

sweet-&-sour vegetables with cashew nuts

ingredients

SERVES 4

1 tbsp vegetable or peanut oil

1 tsp chili oil

2 onions, sliced

2 carrots, thinly sliced

2 zucchini, thinly sliced

1 small head broccoli, cut into
   florets

2 cups sliced white
   mushrooms

1 small bok choy, halved

2 tbsp jaggery or brown sugar

2 tbsp Thai soy sauce

1 tbsp rice vinegar

scant $1/2$ cup cashew nuts

method

1 Heat both the oils in a preheated wok or skillet, add the onions, and stir-fry for 1–2 minutes until beginning to soften.

2 Add the carrots, zucchini, and broccoli and stir-fry for 2–3 minutes. Add the mushrooms, bok choy, sugar, soy sauce, and vinegar and stir-fry for 1–2 minutes.

3 Meanwhile, heat a dry, heavy-bottom skillet over high heat, add the cashew nuts, and cook, shaking the skillet frequently, until lightly toasted. Sprinkle the cashew nuts over the stir-fry and serve immediately.

stir-fried green beans with red bell pepper

ingredients

SERVES 4–6

10 oz/280 g green beans, cut
    into 2$\frac{1}{2}$-inch/6-cm lengths
1 tbsp vegetable or peanut oil
1 red bell pepper, slivered
pinch of salt
pinch of sugar

method

1 Blanch the beans in a large pan of boiling water for 30 seconds. Drain and set aside.

2 In a preheated wok or deep pan, heat the oil and stir-fry the beans for 1 minute over high heat. Add the pepper and stir-fry for an additional 1 minute. Sprinkle the salt and sugar on top and serve.

spicy green beans

ingredients

SERVES 4

5$\frac{1}{2}$ oz/155 g green beans,
trimmed and cut diagonally
into 3–4 pieces

2 tbsp vegetable or peanut oil

4 dried chiles, cut into
2–3 pieces

$\frac{1}{2}$ tsp Sichuan peppers

1 garlic clove, finely sliced

6 thin slices of fresh gingerroot

2 scallions, white part only, cut
diagonally into thin pieces

pinch of sea salt

method

1 Blanch the beans in a large pan of boiling water for 30 seconds. Drain and set aside.

2 In a preheated wok or deep pan, heat 1 tablespoon of the oil. Over low heat, stir-fry the beans for about 5 minutes, or until they are beginning to wrinkle. Remove from the wok and set aside.

3 Add the remaining oil and stir-fry the chiles and peppers until they are fragrant. Add the garlic, gingerroot, and scallions and stir-fry until they begin to soften. Throw in the beans and toss, then add the sea salt and serve immediately.

green beans with sesame dressing

ingredients

SERVES 4

7 oz/200 g green beans
pinch of salt
1 tbsp sesame paste
1 tsp superfine sugar
1 tsp miso paste
2 tsp Japanese soy sauce

method

1 Cook the beans in a pan of simmering water for 4–5 minutes, until tender. Remove from the heat and drain.

2 Mix the remaining ingredients to a paste in a bowl that is large enough to take the beans. Toss the beans in the paste, then let cool before serving.

stir-fried broccoli

ingredients

SERVES 4

2 tbsp vegetable oil

2 medium heads of broccoli,
    cut into florets

2 tbsp soy sauce

1 tsp cornstarch

1 tbsp superfine sugar

1 tsp grated fresh gingerroot

1 garlic clove, crushed

pinch of hot chile flakes

1 tsp toasted sesame seeds,
    to garnish

method

1 In a large skillet or wok, heat the oil until almost smoking. Stir-fry the broccoli for 4–5 minutes.

2 In a small bowl, combine the soy sauce, cornstarch, sugar, gingerroot, garlic, and hot chile flakes. Add the mixture to the broccoli. Cook over gentle heat, stirring constantly, for 2–3 minutes until the sauce thickens slightly.

3 Transfer to a serving dish, garnish with the sesame seeds and serve immediately.

stir-fried chinese greens

ingredients

SERVES 4

1 tbsp vegetable or peanut oil

1 tsp finely chopped garlic

8 oz/225 g leafy Chinese
   greens, coarsely chopped

1/2 tsp salt

method

1 In a preheated wok or deep pan, heat the oil and stir-fry the garlic until fragrant.

2 Over high heat, toss in the Chinese greens and salt and stir-fry for 1 minute maximum. Serve immediately.

choi sum in oyster sauce

ingredients

SERVES 4–6

10^{1}/$_{2}$ oz/300 g choi sum

1 tbsp vegetable or peanut oil

1 tsp finely chopped garlic

1 tbsp oyster sauce

method

1 Blanch the choi sum in a large pan of boiling water for 30 seconds. Drain and set aside.

2 In a preheated wok or deep pan, heat the oil and stir-fry the garlic until fragrant. Add the choi sum and toss for 1 minute. Stir in the oyster sauce and serve.

hot-&-sour cabbage

ingredients

SERVES 4

1 lb/450 g firm white cabbage

1 tbsp vegetable or peanut oil

10 Sichuan peppers or more,
   to taste

3 dried chiles, coarsely
   chopped

$1/2$ tsp salt

1 tsp white rice vinegar

dash of sesame oil

pinch of sugar

method

1 To prepare the cabbage, discard the outer leaves and tough stems. Chop the cabbage into $1^{1}/4$-inch/3-cm squares, breaking up the chunks. Rinse thoroughly in cold water.

2 In a preheated wok or deep pan, heat the oil and cook the peppers until fragrant. Stir in the chiles. Throw in the cabbage, a little at a time, together with the salt, and stir-fry for 2 minutes.

3 Add the vinegar, sesame oil, and sugar and cook for an additional minute, or until the cabbage is tender. Serve immediately.

chunky potatoes with cilantro leaves

ingredients

SERVES 6–8

4 potatoes, peeled and cut into large chunks

vegetable or peanut oil, for frying

3½ oz/100 g pork, not too lean, finely chopped or ground

1 green bell pepper, finely chopped

1 tbsp finely chopped scallions, white part only

2 tsp salt

½ tsp white pepper

pinch of sugar

2–3 tbsp cooking water from the potatoes

2 tbsp chopped cilantro leaves

method

1 Boil the potatoes in a large pan of boiling water for 15–25 minutes, or until cooked. Drain, reserving some of the water.

2 In a wok or deep pan, heat plenty of the oil and cook the potatoes until golden. Drain and set aside.

3 In the clean preheated wok or pan, heat 1 tablespoon of the oil and stir-fry the pork, bell pepper, and scallions for 1 minute. Season with the salt, pepper, and sugar and stir-fry for an additional 1 minute.

4 Stir in the potato chunks and add the water. Cook for 2–3 minutes, or until the potatoes are warmed through. Turn off the heat, then stir in the cilantro and serve warm.

sichuan fried eggplant

ingredients

SERVES 4

vegetable or peanut oil,
    for frying
4 eggplants, halved lengthwise
    and cut diagonally into
    2-inch/5-cm pieces
1 tbsp chili bean sauce
2 tsp finely chopped fresh
    gingerroot
2 tsp finely chopped garlic
2–3 tbsp chicken stock
1 tsp sugar
1 tsp light soy sauce
3 scallions, finely chopped

method

1 In a preheated wok or deep pan, heat the oil and cook the eggplant pieces for 3–4 minutes, or until lightly browned. Drain on paper towels and set aside.

2 In the clean wok or deep pan, heat 2 tablespoons of the oil. Add the chili bean sauce and stir-fry rapidly, then add the gingerroot and garlic and stir until fragrant. Add the stock, sugar, and light soy sauce. Toss in the fried eggplant pieces and let simmer for 2 minutes. Stir in the scallions and serve.

eggplant with red bell pepper

ingredients

SERVES 4

3 tbsp vegetable or peanut oil

1 garlic clove, finely chopped

3 eggplants, halved lengthwise
and cut diagonally into
1-inch/2.5-cm pieces

1 tsp white rice vinegar

1 red bell pepper, finely sliced

2 tbsp light soy sauce

1 tsp sugar

1 tbsp finely chopped cilantro
leaves, to garnish

method

1 In a preheated wok or deep pan, heat the oil. When it begins to smoke, toss in the garlic and stir-fry until fragrant, then add the eggplant. Stir-fry for 30 seconds, then add the vinegar. Turn down the heat and cook, covered, for 5 minutes, stirring occasionally.

2 When the eggplant pieces are soft, add the bell pepper and stir. Add the light soy sauce and sugar and cook, uncovered, for 2 minutes.

3 Turn off the heat and rest for 2 minutes. Transfer to a dish, then garnish with cilantro and serve.

eggplant with miso

ingredients

SERVES 4

2 eggplants

oil, for stir-frying

1 fresh red chile, sliced

2 tbsp sake

4 tbsp mirin

2 tbsp shoyu (Japanese
    soy sauce)

3 tbsp hatcho miso

2 tbsp water

method

1 Cut the eggplants into wedges.

2 Preheat a wok over high heat. Add a little oil and heat until very hot. Stir-fry the eggplant, in batches, for 4 minutes, or until browned and cooked through.

3 Return all the eggplant to the wok together with the chile and stir together. Add the remaining ingredients and toss everything together. Cook, stirring, until the sauce thickens. Serve immediately.

braised straw mushrooms

ingredients

SERVES 4

1 tbsp vegetable or peanut oil

1 tsp finely chopped garlic

6 oz/175 g straw mushrooms,
    washed but left whole

2 tsp fermented black beans,
    rinsed and lightly mashed

1 tsp sugar

1 tbsp light soy sauce

1 tsp dark soy sauce

method

1 Heat the oil in a small claypot or pan. Cook the garlic until fragrant, then add the mushrooms and stir well to coat in the oil.

2 Add the beans, sugar, and soy sauces, then lower the heat and let simmer, covered, for about 10 minutes, or until the mushrooms are soft.

bamboo shoots with bean curd

ingredients

SERVES 4–6

3 dried Chinese mushrooms, soaked in warm water for 20 minutes

2 oz/55 g baby bok choy

vegetable or peanut oil, for deep-frying

1 lb/450 g firm bean curd, cut into 1-inch/2.5-cm squares

1/2 cup fresh or canned bamboo shoots, rinsed and finely sliced (if using fresh shoots, boil in water first for 30 minutes)

1 tsp oyster sauce

1 tsp light soy sauce

method

1 Squeeze out any excess water from the mushrooms and finely slice, discarding any tough stems. Blanch the bok choy in a large pan of boiling water for 30 seconds. Drain and set aside.

2 Heat enough oil for deep-frying in a wok, deep-fat fryer, or large heavy-bottom pan until it reaches 350–375°F/180–190°C, or until a cube of bread browns in 30 seconds. Cook the bean curd cubes until golden brown. Remove, then drain and set aside.

3 In a preheated wok or deep pan, heat 1 tablespoon of the oil, then toss in the mushrooms and bok choy and stir. Add the bean curd and bamboo shoots with the oyster and soy sauces. Heat through and serve.

stir-fried bean sprouts

ingredients

SERVES 4

1 tbsp vegetable or peanut oil

generous 1½ cups bean
    sprouts, trimmed

2 tbsp finely chopped scallions

½ tsp salt

pinch of sugar

method

1 In a preheated wok or deep pan, heat the oil and stir-fry the bean sprouts with the scallions for about 1 minute. Add the salt and sugar and stir.

2 Remove from the heat and serve immediately.

edamame

ingredients

SERVES 4

1 lb 2 oz/500 g frozen
    soybeans, in their pods
sea salt flakes

method

1 Bring a large pan of water to a boil. Add the beans and cook for 3 minutes, or until tender.

2 Drain well, sprinkle with salt flakes to taste, and toss together. Serve warm or cold.

mixed vegetables with quick-fried basil

ingredients

SERVES 4

2 tbsp vegetable or peanut oil

2 garlic cloves, chopped

1 onion, sliced

4 oz/115 g baby corn, cut in
    half diagonally

1/2 cucumber, peeled, halved,
    seeded, and sliced

8 oz/225 g canned water
    chestnuts, drained and
    rinsed

2 oz/55 g snow peas, trimmed

4 oz/115 g shiitake
    mushrooms, halved

1 red bell pepper, seeded and
    sliced thinly

1 tbsp jaggery or soft light
    brown sugar

2 tbsp Thai soy sauce

1 tbsp fish sauce

1 tbsp rice vinegar

vegetable or peanut oil,
    for cooking

8–12 sprigs fresh Thai basil

boiled rice, to serve

method

1 Heat the oil in a wok and stir-fry the garlic and onion for 1–2 minutes. Add the corn, cucumber, water chestnuts, snow peas, mushrooms, and red bell pepper, and stir-fry for 2–3 minutes, until starting to soften.

2 Add the sugar, soy sauce, fish sauce, and vinegar, and gradually bring to a boil. Let simmer for 1–2 minutes.

3 Meanwhile, heat the oil for the basil in a wok and, when hot, add the basil sprigs. Cook for 20–30 seconds, until crisp. Remove with a slotted spoon and drain on paper towels.

4 Garnish the vegetable stir-fry with the crispy basil and serve immediately, with the boiled rice.

cauliflower & beans with cashew nuts

ingredients

SERVES 4

1 tbsp vegetable or peanut oil

1 tbsp chili oil

1 onion, chopped

2 garlic cloves, chopped

2 tbsp Thai red curry paste

1 small cauliflower, cut into
   florets

6 oz/175 g yard-long beans,
   cut into 3-inch lengths

2/3 cup vegetable stock

2 tbsp Thai soy sauce

scant toasted cashews,
   to garnish

method

1 Heat both the oils in a wok and stir-fry the onion and garlic until softened. Add the curry paste and stir-fry for 1–2 minutes.

2 Add the cauliflower and beans and stir-fry for 3–4 minutes, until softened. Pour in the stock and soy sauce and let simmer for 1–2 minutes. Serve immediately, garnished with the cashews.

appetizers & accompaniments

In most Asian countries several dishes are served together at everyday meals rather than as separate courses so, strictly speaking, there are neither appetizers nor accompaniments except at banquets and formal occasions. However, all sorts of tasty snacks are served to guests, often with cups of tea, in the morning and afternoon and these also make an ideal first course.

Small parcels of meat, chicken, shellfish, or vegetables in a crisp coating, succulent bite-size dumplings, miniature skewers, spicy little meatballs or fishcakes, mini wraps and rolls, many of them served with individual bowls of dipping sauce, are a delight to the eye as well as the taste buds. Other enticing treats include pickles, fritters, toasts, and, of course, that Japanese picture on a plate, sushi. Asian cooks have perfected the art of tempting the appetite by appealing to all the senses with fragrant, colorful, utterly delicious miniature culinary masterpieces that surprise and please with their contrasting or melt-in-your-mouth textures.

Rice is an integral part of virtually every Asian meal, although we tend to think of it as an accompaniment. Perfectly cooked steamed rice goes with everything, but there are lots of different ways to cook rice to add extra flavor and interest. Asian cooks are expert at matching the type of grain to the

style of dish, from gently clinging sushi rice to sweetly fragrant jasmine rice.

Last but not least, there are recipes for dipping sauces. Whether sweet and sticky or warm and spicy, these add the final flourish and finishing touch to make any Asian meal special.

spring rolls

ingredients

MAKES 25

6 dried Chinese mushrooms, soaked in warm water for 20 minutes

1 tbsp vegetable or peanut oil

8 oz/225 g ground pork

1 tsp dark soy sauce

3½ oz/100 g fresh or canned bamboo shoots, rinsed and julienned (if using fresh shoots, boil in water first for 30 minutes)

pinch of salt

3½ oz/100 g shrimp, shelled, deveined, and chopped

8 oz/225 g bean sprouts, trimmed and coarsely chopped

1 tbsp finely chopped scallions

25 spring roll skins

1 egg white, lightly beaten

vegetable or peanut oil, for deep-frying

method

1 Squeeze out any excess water from the mushrooms and finely slice, discarding any tough stems.

2 In a preheated wok or deep pan, heat the tablespoon of oil and stir-fry the pork until it changes color. Add the dark soy sauce, bamboo shoots, mushrooms, and a little salt. Stir over high heat for 3 minutes.

3 Add the shrimp and cook for 2 minutes, then add the bean sprouts and cook for an additional minute. Remove from the heat and stir in the scallions. Let cool.

4 To assemble each roll, place a tablespoon of the mixture toward the bottom of a skin. Roll once to secure the filling, then fold in the sides to create a 4-inch/10-cm piece and continue to roll up. Seal with egg white.

5 Heat enough oil for deep-frying in a wok, deep-fat fryer or large heavy-bottom pan until it reaches 350–375°F/180–190°C, or until a cube of bread browns in 30 seconds. Without overcrowding the pan, fry the rolls for about 5 minutes until golden brown and crispy. Drain well on paper towels and serve at once.

vegetarian spring rolls

ingredients

MAKES 20

6 dried Chinese mushrooms, soaked in warm water for 20 minutes

2 oz/55 g cellophane noodles, soaked in warm water for 20 minutes

2 tbsp vegetable or peanut oil

1 tbsp finely chopped fresh gingerroot

2 medium carrots, julienned

scant 1 cup finely shredded cabbage

1 tbsp finely sliced scallions

1 tbsp light soy sauce

3 oz/85 g soft bean curd, cut into small cubes

1/2 tsp salt

pinch of white pepper

pinch of sugar

20 spring roll skins

1 egg white, lightly beaten

vegetable or peanut oil, for deep-frying

soy sauce, for dipping

method

1 Squeeze out any excess water from the mushrooms and finely chop, discarding any tough stems. Drain the cellophane noodles and coarsely chop.

2 In a preheated wok or deep pan, heat the oil, then toss in the gingerroot and cook until fragrant. Add the mushrooms and stir for about 2 minutes. Add the carrot, cabbage, and scallions and stir-fry for 1 minute. Add the cellophane noodles and light soy sauce and stir-fry for 1 minute. Add the bean curd and cook for an additional 1 minute. Season with the salt, pepper, and sugar and mix well. Continue cooking for 1–2 minutes, or until the carrot is soft. Remove from the heat and let the mixture cool.

3 To assemble each roll, place a tablespoon of the mixture toward the bottom of a skin. Roll once to secure the filling, then fold in the sides to create a 4-inch/10-cm piece and continue to roll up. Seal with egg white.

4 Heat enough oil for deep-frying in a wok, deep-fat fryer, or large heavy-bottom pan until it reaches 350–375°F/180–190°C, or until a cube of bread browns in 30 seconds. Without overcrowding the pan, cook the rolls in batches for about 5 minutes, or until golden brown and crispy. Serve with a good soy sauce for dipping.

soft-wrapped pork & shrimp rolls

ingredients

MAKES 20

4 oz/115 g firm bean curd

3 tbsp vegetable or peanut oil

1 tsp finely chopped garlic

2 oz/55 g lean pork, shredded

4 oz/115 g shrimp, shelled
   and deveined

1/2 small carrot, cut into short
   thin sticks

1/2 cup fresh or canned
   bamboo shoots, rinsed and
   shredded (if using fresh
   shoots, boil in water first for
   30 minutes)

11/4 cups finely sliced cabbage

2 oz/55 g snow peas,
   julienned

1-egg omelet, shredded

1 tsp salt

1 tsp light soy sauce

1 tsp Shaoxing rice wine

pinch of white pepper

20 soft spring roll skins

chili bean sauce, to serve

method

1 Slice the bean curd into thin slices horizontally and cook in 1 tablespoon of the oil until it turns golden brown. Cut into thin strips and set aside.

2 In a preheated wok or deep pan, heat the remaining oil and stir-fry the garlic until fragrant. Add the pork and stir for about 1 minute, then add the shrimp and stir for an additional minute. One by one, stirring well after each addition, add the carrot, bamboo shoots, cabbage, snow peas, bean curd, and, finally, the shredded omelet. Season with the salt, light soy sauce, Shaoxing rice wine, and pepper. Stir for one more minute, then turn into a serving dish.

3 To assemble each roll, smear a skin with a little chili bean sauce and place a heaped teaspoon of the filling toward the bottom of the circle. Roll up the bottom edge to secure the filling, turn in the sides, and continue to roll up gently. Serve accompanied by a bowl of chili sauce.

crispy egg rolls

ingredients

SERVES 4

2 tbsp vegetable or peanut oil

6 scallions, cut into 2-inch lengths

1 fresh green chile, seeded and chopped

1 carrot, cut into thin sticks

1 zucchini, cut into thin sticks

1/2 red bell pepper, seeded and thinly sliced

3/4 cup bean sprouts

4 oz/115 g canned bamboo shoots, drained and rinsed

3 tbsp Thai soy sauce

1–2 tbsp chili sauce

8 egg roll skins

vegetable or peanut oil, for deep-frying

method

1 Heat the oil in a wok and stir-fry the scallions and chile for 30 seconds. Add the carrot, zucchini, and red bell pepper and stir-fry for 1 minute more. Remove the wok from heat and stir in the bean sprouts, bamboo shoots, soy sauce, and chili sauce. Taste and add more soy sauce or chili sauce if necessary.

2 Place an egg roll skin on a counter and spoon some of the vegetable mixture diagonally across the center. Roll one corner over the filling and flip the sides of the skin over the top to enclose the filling. Continue to roll up to make an enclosed package. Repeat with the remaining skins and filling to make 8 egg rolls.

3 Heat the oil for deep-frying in a wok or large skillet. Deep-fry the egg rolls, 3–4 at a time, until crisp and golden brown. Remove with a slotted spoon, drain on paper towels while you cook the remainder, then serve immediately.

salmon & shrimp spring rolls with plum sauce

ingredients

SERVES 4

4 1/2 oz/125 g salmon fillet, skinned, boned and cut into 1/8-inch/3-mm cubes

2 1/4 oz/60 g bean sprouts

2/3 cup finely shredded Chinese cabbage

1/4 cup finely chopped scallion

1/2 medium red bell pepper, seeded and finely sliced into strips

1/4 tsp five-spice powder

2 1/4 oz/60 g cooked shelled shrimp

4 spring roll wrappers, halved widthwise

vegetable oil spray

1/4 tsp sesame seeds

plum sauce

scant 1/2 cup water

1/4 cup orange juice

1/2 tsp chopped red chile

1 tsp grated gingerroot

7 oz/200 g red plums, pitted weight

1 tsp chopped scallion

1 tsp chopped fresh cilantro

1/4 tsp sesame oil

method

1 To make the sauce, put the water, orange juice, chile, gingerroot, and plums into a pan and bring to a boil. Reduce the heat, cover, and let simmer for 10 minutes. Remove from the heat, blend with a hand-held electric mixer, or use a food processor, then stir in the scallion, cilantro, and sesame oil. Let cool.

2 Heat a nonstick wok over high heat, add the salmon, and stir-fry for 1 minute. Remove from the wok with a slotted spoon onto a plate. Using the cooking juices from the salmon, stir-fry the vegetables with the five-spice powder until just tender, drain in a colander, then stir in the cooked salmon and shrimp—the mixture should be quite dry to prevent the rolls from becoming soggy.

3 Divide the salmon and vegetable mixture into 8 portions. Spoon a portion along one short edge of each spring roll wrapper and roll up, tucking in the sides.

4 Lay the spring rolls on a nonstick cookie sheet and spray lightly with vegetable oil, sprinkle with sesame seeds, and bake in a preheated oven for 12–15 minutes, or until golden brown. Serve the spring rolls with the cold plum sauce separately.

omelet rolls

ingredients

SERVES 4

4 large eggs

2 tbsp water

1 tbsp Thai soy sauce

6 scallions, chopped finely

1 fresh red chile, seeded and
   chopped finely

1 tbsp vegetable or peanut oil

1 tbsp green curry paste

bunch of fresh cilantro,
   chopped

method

1 Put the eggs, water, and Thai soy sauce in a bowl. Set aside. Mix together the scallions and chopped chile to form a paste.

2 Heat half the oil in an 8-inch/20-cm skillet and pour in half the egg mixture. Tilt to coat the bottom of the skillet evenly and cook until set. Lift out and set aside. Heat the remaining oil and make a second omelet in the same way.

3 Spread the scallion, chili paste, and curry paste in a thin layer over each omelet and sprinkle the cilantro on top. Roll up tightly. Cut each one in half and then cut each piece on the diagonal in half again. Serve immediately, while still warm.

soba noodle rolls

ingredients

MAKES 24 PIECES

4 oz/115 g sashimi-grade tuna or piece of tuna fillet

1 tbsp vegetable oil (if using tuna fillet)

3$\frac{1}{2}$ oz/100 g soba noodles, broken into pieces

1 scallion, green part only, thinly sliced

1 tbsp light soy sauce

$\frac{1}{2}$ tbsp rice wine vinegar

wasabi paste

1 tbsp finely chopped pickled gingerroot, plus extra to serve

6 sheets of toasted nori

$\frac{1}{2}$ English cucumber, peeled and finely shredded, seeds removed

Japanese soy sauce, to serve

method

1 If using sashimi-grade tuna, cut into strips. If cooking the fish, heat the oil in a skillet. Sear the tuna for 30–60 seconds on all sides, so that the edges are sealed but the fish is rare in the middle. Let cool, then cut into strips.

2 Cook the soba noodles in a pan of boiling water until they are just cooked through, drain, and rinse under cold running water. Drain thoroughly. Gently mix the soba noodles with the scallion, soy sauce, rice wine vinegar, a pinch of wasabi, and the pickled gingerroot.

3 Put a sheet of nori smooth-side down on a rolling mat with one of the long ends in front of you. Spread a sixth of the noodle mixture over the bottom third of the nori. Lay a line of cucumber across the center of the noodles, then add a layer of tuna strips.

4 Pick up the nearest edge of the rolling mat. Slowly roll the mat away from you to wrap the nori around the filling. Use gentle, even pressure until you have finished the roll, and lift the mat out of the way as you go.

5 Transfer the roll to a chopping board, seam-side down. Cut it into 4 even-size pieces with a wet, very sharp knife. Repeat with the remaining ingredients. Serve with soy sauce, pickled gingerroot, and extra wasabi paste.

pork & gingerroot dumplings

ingredients

MAKES ABOUT 50

1 lb/450 g ground pork, not too lean

1 tbsp light soy sauce

1$\frac{1}{2}$ tsp salt

1 tsp Shaoxing rice wine

$\frac{1}{2}$ tsp sesame oil

generous 1 cup finely chopped cabbage

2 tsp minced fresh gingerroot

2 tsp finely chopped scallions

$\frac{1}{2}$ tsp white pepper

50 round wonton skins, about 2$\frac{3}{4}$ inches/7 cm in diameter

gingerroot & garlic dipping sauce

1 tbsp soy sauce

1 tbsp vinegar

$\frac{1}{2}$ tsp sugar

1 tsp chopped gingerroot

1 tsp chopped garlic

method

1 To make the dipping sauce, stir all the ingredients together and set aside.

2 For the filling, mix the pork with the light soy sauce and $\frac{1}{2}$ teaspoon salt. Stir carefully, always in the same direction, to create a thick paste. Add the Shaoxing and sesame oil and continue mixing in the same direction. Cover and let rest for at least 20 minutes.

3 Meanwhile, sprinkle the cabbage with the remaining salt to help draw out the water. Add the gingerroot, scallions, and white pepper and knead for at least 5 minutes into a thick paste. Combine with the filling.

4 To make the dumplings, place about 1 tablespoon of the filling in the center of each skin, holding the skin in the palm of one hand. Moisten the edges with water, then seal the edges with 2–3 pleats on each side and place on a lightly floured board.

5 To cook the dumplings, bring 4 cups water to a rolling boil in a large pan. Drop in about 20 dumplings at a time, stirring gently with a chopstick to prevent them sticking together. Cover, then bring back to a boil and cook for 2 minutes. Uncover and add about scant 1 cup cold water. Bring back to a boil, cover, and cook for an additional 2 minutes. Serve the dumplings with individual bowls of dipping sauce.

dumplings in a cold spicy sauce

ingredients

MAKES 20

20 square wheat skins

filling

1 tsp vegetable or peanut oil

7 oz/200 g ground pork,
    not too lean

1 tsp salt

1/2 tsp white pepper

sauce

scant 1/2 cup vegetable or
    peanut oil

1 tbsp dried chile flakes

1 tsp sesame oil

1 tsp sugar

1 tbsp light soy sauce

1/2 tsp white pepper

1 tsp salt

1 garlic clove, finely chopped

method

1 To prepare the filling, heat the oil in a small pan and stir-fry the pork with the salt and pepper for 3–4 minutes, stirring to break up any meat clumps and letting the juices begin to come out.

2 To prepare the sauce, heat the oil until smoking in a wok or deep pan and pour over the chile flakes. Let cool, then stir in all the other ingredients.

3 To make the dumplings, hold a skin in the palm of one hand and place a scant teaspoon of the filling in the center. Wet the edges and fold over to create a triangle, then, with the point facing toward you at the bottom of your index finger, cross the edges behind your finger, sealing with a little water. Take the point facing toward you and turn up to form a wonton.

4 Drop the dumplings into a large pan of boiling water and cook for 5 minutes.

5 To serve, assemble 4–5 pieces per serving on a small plate and pour over a generous amount of the sauce.

crispy pork dumplings

ingredients

SERVES 4

12 oz/350 g ground pork

2 tbsp finely chopped fresh cilantro

1 garlic clove, crushed

1 fresh green chile, deseeded and chopped

3 tbsp cornstarch

1 egg white

1/2 tsp salt

16 wonton skins

1 tbsp water

vegetable or peanut oil, for cooking

chili sauce, to serve

method

1 Put the pork in a bowl and beat in the cilantro, garlic, chile, 1 tablespoon of the cornstarch, the egg white, and salt. Beat together to a thick, smooth texture. With damp hands shape into 16 equal portions and roll into balls.

2 Put a pork ball in the center of each wonton skin. Make a paste by mixing the remaining cornstarch with 1 tablespoon of water. Brush the edges of the skins with the cornstarch paste and gather them up around the filling to make half into small, sacklike parcels, and the rest into triangular shapes.

3 Arrange the dumplings in a single layer (in batches if need be) in the top of a steamer and cook over boiling water for 10–15 minutes, until the meat is cooked through.

4 Heat the oil in a wok and carefully drop the parcels into it. Deep-fry for 2–3 minutes, until golden brown and crisp. Drain on kitchen paper.

5 Serve hot with chili sauce.

pork & crab meatballs

ingredients

SERVES 6

8 oz/225 g pork fillet, chopped
    finely

5³/₄ oz/65 g canned crabmeat,
    drained

3 scallions, chopped finely

1 garlic clove, chopped finely

1 tsp Thai red curry paste

1 tbsp cornstarch

1 egg white

vegetable or peanut oil,
    for deep-frying

boiled rice, to serve

s a u c e

1 tbsp vegetable or peanut oil

2 shallots, chopped

1 garlic clove, crushed

2 large fresh red chiles,
    seeded and chopped

4 scallions, chopped

3 tomatoes, chopped coarsely

method

1 Put the pork and crabmeat into a bowl and mix together. Add the scallions, garlic, curry paste, cornstarch, and egg white, and beat well to make a thick paste. With damp hands shape the mixture into walnut-size balls.

2 Heat the oil in a wok and deep-fry the balls, in batches, for 3–4 minutes, turning frequently, until golden brown and cooked. Drain on paper towels and keep warm.

3 To make the sauce, heat the oil in a wok and stir-fry the shallots and garlic for 1–2 minutes. Add the chiles and scallions and stir-fry for 1–2 minutes, then add the tomatoes. Stir together quickly, then spoon the sauce over the pork and crab balls. Serve immediately with rice.

beef satay with peanut sauce

ingredients

SERVES 4

1 lb 2 oz/500 g lean beef fillet

2 garlic cloves, crushed

$^3/_4$-inch/2-cm piece fresh
    gingerroot, finely grated

1 tbsp brown sugar

1 tbsp dark soy sauce

1 tbsp lime juice

2 tsp sesame oil

1 tsp ground coriander

1 tsp ground turmeric

$^1/_2$ tsp chili powder

chopped cucumber and red
    bell pepper pieces,
    to garnish

peanut sauce

1$^1/_4$ cups coconut milk

$^1/_2$ cup chunky peanut butter

$^1/_2$ small onion, grated

2 tsp brown sugar

$^1/_2$ tsp chili powder

1 tbsp dark soy sauce

method

1 Cut the beef into $^1/_2$-inch/1-cm cubes and place in a large bowl. Add the garlic, gingerroot, sugar, soy sauce, lime juice, sesame oil, coriander, turmeric, and chili powder. Mix well to coat the pieces of meat evenly. Cover and let marinate in the refrigerator for at least 2 hours or overnight.

2 Preheat the broiler to high. To make the peanut sauce, place all the ingredients in a small pan and stir over medium heat until boiling. Remove the pan from the heat and keep warm.

3 Thread the beef cubes onto presoaked bamboo skewers. Cook the skewers under the hot broiler for 3–5 minutes, turning frequently, until golden. Alternatively, grill over hot coals. Transfer to a large serving plate, then garnish with chopped cucumber and red bell pepper pieces and serve with the peanut sauce.

soy chicken wings

ingredients

SERVES 3–4

9 oz/250 g chicken wings,
    defrosted if frozen

1 cup water

1 tbsp sliced scallion

1-inch/2.5-cm piece of fresh
    gingerroot, cut into 4 slices

2 tbsp light soy sauce

1/2 tsp dark soy sauce

1 star anise

1 tsp sugar

method

1 Wash and dry the chicken wings. In a small pan, bring the water to a boil, then add the chicken, scallion, and gingerroot and bring back to a boil.

2 Add the remaining ingredients, then cover and let simmer for 30 minutes.

3 Remove the chicken wings from any remaining liquid and serve hot.

kara-age chicken

ingredients

SERVES 4

6 skinless, boneless chicken
thighs, about 3½ oz/
100 g each
4 tbsp shoyu (Japanese
soy sauce)
4 tbsp mirin
2 tsp finely grated fresh
gingerroot
2 garlic cloves, crushed
oil, for deep-frying
½ cup potato starch or
cornstarch
pinch of salt
lemon wedges, to serve

method

1 Cut the chicken into large cubes and put in a bowl. Add the soy sauce, mirin, gingerroot, and garlic and turn the chicken to coat well. Cover with plastic wrap and let marinate in a cool place for 20 minutes.

2 Preheat a wok, then fill one-third full with oil, or use a deep-fryer. Heat the oil to 350–375°F/180–190°C, or until a cube of bread browns in 30 seconds.

3 Meanwhile, mix the potato starch with the salt in a bowl. Lift the chicken out of the marinade and shake off any excess. Drop it into the potato starch and coat well, then shake off any excess.

4 Add the chicken to the oil, in batches, and cook for 6 minutes, or until crisp and brown. Remove, drain on paper towels, and keep hot while you cook the remaining chicken.

5 Serve with lemon wedges.

lemongrass chicken skewers

ingredients

SERVES 4

2 long or 4 short lemongrass
    stems
2 large skinless, boneless
    chicken breasts, about
    14 oz/400 g in total
1 small egg white
1 carrot, finely grated
1 small fresh red chile, seeded
    and chopped
2 tbsp snipped fresh garlic
    chives
2 tbsp chopped cilantro
salt and pepper
1 tbsp corn oil
cilantro sprigs and lime slices,
    to garnish
mixed salad greens, to serve

method

1 If the lemongrass stems are long, cut them in half across the center to make 4 short lengths. Cut each stem in half lengthwise, so that you have 8 sticks.

2 Coarsely chop the chicken breasts and place them in a food processor with the egg white. Process to a smooth paste, then add the carrot, chile, chives, cilantro, and salt and pepper to taste. Process for a few seconds to mix well. Transfer the mixture to a large bowl. Cover and chill in the refrigerator for 15 minutes.

3 Preheat the broiler to medium. Divide the mixture into 8 equal-size portions and use your hands to shape the mixture around the lemongrass "skewers."

4 Brush the skewers with oil and cook under the hot broiler for 4–6 minutes, turning them occasionally, until golden brown and thoroughly cooked. Alternatively, grill over medium–hot coals.

5 Transfer to serving plates. Garnish with cilantro sprigs and lime slices and serve hot with salad greens.

chicken satay

ingredients

SERVES 4

2 tbsp vegetable or peanut oil
1 tbsp sesame oil
juice of 1/2 lime
2 skinless, boneless chicken
    breasts, cut into small
    cubes

dip

2 tbsp vegetable or peanut oil
1 small onion, chopped finely
1 small fresh green chile,
    seeded and chopped
1 garlic clove, chopped finely
1/2 cup crunchy peanut butter
6–8 tbsp water
juice of 1/2 lime

method

1 Combine both the oils and the lime juice in a nonmetallic dish. Add the chicken cubes, cover with plastic wrap, and let chill for 1 hour.

2 To make the dip, heat the oil in a skillet and sauté the onion, chile, and garlic over low heat, stirring occasionally, for about 5 minutes, until just softened. Add the peanut butter, water, and lime juice and let simmer gently, stirring constantly, until the peanut butter has softened enough to make a dip—you may need to add extra water to make a thinner consistency.

3 Meanwhile, drain the chicken cubes and thread them onto 8–12 presoaked wooden skewers. Put under a hot broiler or on a barbecue, turning frequently, for about 10 minutes, until cooked and browned. Serve hot with the warm dip.

whitebait with green chile

ingredients

SERVES 4

6 oz/175 g whitebait

sauce

1 tbsp vegetable or peanut oil

1 large fresh green chile

2 drops of sesame oil

1 tbsp light soy sauce

pinch of salt

pinch of sugar

1 garlic clove, finely chopped

method

1 In a large pan of boiling water, cook the fish for 30 seconds–2 minutes, or until the flesh is turning soft but not breaking up. Drain, then set aside and let cool.

2 To prepare the sauce, first heat the oil in a small pan and, when smoking, cook the chile until the skin blisters. Remove the skin and finely chop the chile. When cool, mix with all the other ingredients.

3 To serve, pour the sauce over the fish and serve immediately.

shrimp toasts

ingredients

MAKES 16

3½ oz/100 g shrimp, shelled,
    and deveined
2 egg whites
2 tbsp cornstarch
½ tsp sugar
pinch of salt
2 tbsp finely chopped cilantro
    leaves
2 slices day-old white bread
vegetable or peanut oil,
    for deep-frying

method

1 Pound the shrimp to a pulp in a mortar and pestle or with the bottom of a cleaver.

2 Mix the shrimp with one of the egg whites and 1 tablespoon of the cornstarch. Add the sugar and salt and stir in the cilantro. Mix the remaining egg white with the remaining cornstarch.

3 Remove the crusts from the bread and cut each slice into 8 triangles. Brush the top of each piece with the egg white and cornstarch mixture, then add 1 teaspoon of the shrimp mixture. Smooth the top.

4 Heat enough oil for deep-frying in a wok, deep-fat fryer, or large heavy-bottom pan until it reaches 350–375°F/180–190°C, or until a cube of bread browns in 30 seconds. Without overcrowding the wok, cook the toasts shrimp-side up for about 2 minutes. Turn and cook for an additional 2 minutes, or until beginning to turn golden brown. Drain and serve warm.

crispy wrapped shrimp

ingredients

SERVES 4

16 large, unshelled cooked
    shrimp
juice of 1 lime
4 tbsp chili sauce
16 wonton skins
vegetable or peanut oil,
    for deep-frying
plum sauce, to serve

method

1 Remove the heads and shell the shrimp, but leave the tails intact. Place them in a nonmetallic bowl, add the lime juice, and toss lightly to coat. Set aside in a cool place for 30 minutes.

2 Spread a little chili sauce over a wonton skin. Place a shrimp diagonally across it, leaving the tail protruding. Fold the bottom corner of the skin over the shrimp, fold the next corner up over the head, and then roll the shrimp up in the skin so that the body is encased, but the tail is exposed. Repeat with the remaining skins, chili sauce, and shrimp.

3 Heat the oil in a wok or skillet and deep-fry the shrimp, in batches, until crisp and browned. Serve hot with plum sauce for dipping.

crisp sesame shrimp

ingredients

SERVES 4

generous ¾ cup self-rising
   flour

3 tbsp sesame seeds, toasted
   or dry-fried

1 tsp Thai red curry paste

1 tbsp fish sauce

5 fl oz/150 ml water

vegetable or peanut oil,
   for deep-frying

20 large, shrimp, shelled with
   tails intact

chili sauce, for dipping

method

1 Combine the flour and sesame seeds in a bowl. Stir the curry paste, fish sauce, and water together in a pitcher until mixed. Gradually pour the liquid into the flour, stirring constantly, to make a thick batter.

2 Heat the oil for deep-frying in a wok. Holding the shrimp by their tails, dip them into the batter, one at a time, then carefully drop into the hot oil. Cook for 2–3 minutes, until crisp and brown. Drain on paper towels.

3 Serve immediately with chili sauce.

crab parcels

ingredients

SERVES 4

12 oz/350 g canned white
   crabmeat, drained

1 fresh red chile, seeded and
   chopped

4 scallions, sliced finely

1 tbsp Thai red curry paste

juice of 1/2 lime

1/2 tsp salt

20 wonton skins

oil for cooking

d i p

1/4 cup superfine sugar

2 tbsp water

2 tbsp rice wine vinegar

3 pieces preserved gingerroot,
   sliced

1 tbsp gingerroot syrup from
   the jar

method

1 Put the crabmeat into a bowl and add the chile, scallions, and curry paste. Stir together with the lime juice and salt.

2 Put the skins in a pile and put 1 portion of the crabmeat in the center of the top skin. Brush the edges with a little water and roll up the edges to make a small cigar-shaped package. Continue to make packages with the skins— you need at least 20.

3 Heat the oil in a wok and cook the packages, a few at a time, until golden brown. Drain on paper towels.

4 Put all the ingredients for the dip in a small pan and heat gently until the sugar has melted. Serve warm with the crab packages.

fish cakes

ingredients

SERVES 4

1 lb/ 450 g white fish fillets, skinned and cut into cubes

1 egg white

2 kaffir lime leaves, torn coarsely

1 tbsp Thai green curry paste

2 oz/55 g green beans, chopped finely

1 fresh red chile, seeded and chopped finely

bunch of fresh cilantro, chopped

vegetable or peanut oil for cooking

1 fresh green chile, seeded and sliced, to serve

dipping sauce

generous 1/2 cup superfine sugar

1/4 cup white wine vinegar

1 small carrot, cut into thin sticks

2-inch/5-cm piece cucumber, peeled, seeded, and cut into thin sticks

method

1 Put the fish into a food processor with the egg white, lime leaves, and curry paste, and process until smooth. Scrape the mixture into a bowl and stir in the green beans, red chile, and cilantro. With dampened hands, shape the mixture into small patties, about 2 inches/5 cm across. Place them on a large plate in a single layer and let chill for 30 minutes.

2 Meanwhile, make the dipping sauce. Put the sugar in a pan with 1 1/2 tablespoons water and the vinegar and heat gently, stirring until the sugar has dissolved. Add the carrot and cucumber, then remove from the heat and let cool.

3 Heat the oil in a skillet and cook the fish cakes, in batches, until golden brown on both sides. Drain on paper towels and keep warm while you cook the remaining batches. If desired, reheat the dipping sauce. Serve the fish cakes immediately with warm or cold dipping sauce, topped with chile slices.

wontons

ingredients

SERVES 4

filling

2 tbsp vegetable or peanut oil

6 scallions, chopped

generous 2 cups chopped
    mushrooms

2 oz/55 g fine green beans,
    chopped

2 oz/55 g corn kernels,
    drained if canned

1 egg, beaten

3 tbsp Thai soy sauce

1 tbsp jaggery or soft light
    brown sugar

1/2 tsp salt

wontons

24 wonton skins

1 egg, beaten

vegetable or peanut oil,
    for deep-frying

plum or chili sauce, to serve

method

1 To make the filling, heat the oil in a preheated wok and stir-fry the scallions, mushrooms, and beans for 1–2 minutes, until softened. Add the corn, stir well to mix, and then push the vegetables to the side. Pour in the egg. Stir until lightly set before incorporating the vegetables and adding the soy sauce, sugar, and salt. Remove the wok from the heat.

2 Place the wonton skins in a pile on a counter. Put a teaspoonful of the filling in the center of the top skin. Brush the edges with beaten egg and fold in half diagonally to make a small triangular package. Repeat with the remaining skins and filling.

3 Heat the oil for deep-frying in a wok or large skillet. Add the packages, in batches, and deep-fry for 3–4 minutes, until golden brown. Remove from the wok with a slotted spoon and drain on paper towels. Keep warm while you cook the remaining wontons. Serve hot with plum or chili sauce.

crispy crab wontons

ingredients

MAKES 24

6 oz/175 g white crabmeat, drained if canned and thawed if frozen, flaked

1^3/$_4$ oz/50 g canned water chestnuts, drained, rinsed and chopped

1 small fresh red chile, chopped

1 scallion, chopped

1 tbsp cornstarch

1 tsp dry sherry

1 tsp light soy sauce

^{1}/$_2$ tsp lime juice

24 wonton skins

vegetable oil, for deep-frying

lime slices, to garnish

method

1 To make the filling, mix the crabmeat, water chestnuts, chile, scallion, cornstarch, sherry, soy sauce, and lime juice together in a bowl.

2 Spread the wonton skins out on a counter and spoon an equal portion of the filling into the center of each wonton skin.

3 Dampen the edges of the wonton skins with a little water and fold them in half to form triangles. Fold the 2 pointed ends in toward the center, moisten with a little water to secure, then pinch together to seal.

4 Heat the oil in a deep-fat fryer, large, heavy-bottom pan, or wok to 350–375°F/ 180–190°C, or until a cube of bread browns in 30 seconds. Deep-fry the wontons in batches for 2–3 minutes until golden brown and crisp (if you deep-fry too many at one time, the oil temperature will drop and they will be soggy).

5 Remove the wontons with a slotted spoon, drain on paper towels, and serve hot, garnished with lime slices.

onion pancakes

ingredients

MAKES ABOUT 16

4 tbsp oil

4 tbsp finely sliced scallions

2 eggs, plus 2 egg yolks

1$\frac{1}{3}$ cups all-purpose flour

1 tsp salt

1$\frac{3}{4}$ cups milk

1 cup water

method

1 Heat 1 tablespoon of the oil in a skillet and lightly cook the scallions until beginning to soften. Remove and set aside.

2 Lightly beat the eggs, together with the egg yolks, and set aside. Sift the flour and salt into a large bowl and lightly mix in the eggs.

3 Slowly add the milk and water, beating by hand, until the batter is creamy. Stir in the remaining oil and continue to beat for a few more minutes. Finally, stir in the scallions.

4 In a nonstick skillet, pour in 1 tablespoon of the batter and cook until set, but not brown. To serve, loosely roll the pancakes and cut each one into 3 pieces.

tea-scented eggs

ingredients

SERVES 6

6 eggs

about 2$^1/_4$ cups water

2 tbsp black tea leaves

method

1 Bring to a boil a pan of water deep enough to cover the eggs. Lower the eggs into the pan and cook for 10 minutes. Remove the eggs from the pan and lightly crack the shells with the back of a spoon.

2 Bring the water back to a boil and simmer the tea leaves for 5 minutes. Turn off the heat. Place the eggs in the tea and let stand until the tea has cooled.

3 Serve the eggs whole for breakfast or as part of a meal, shelled or, more traditionally, unshelled.

lettuce wraps

ingredients

MAKES 12

3¹/₂ oz/100 g dried cellophane noodles

3 tbsp crunchy peanut butter

2 tbsp rice vinegar

1 tbsp oyster sauce

peanut or corn oil (optional)

soy sauce, to taste

4 red radishes, grated

2 carrots, peeled and coarsely grated

1 zucchini, coarsely grated

4 oz/115 g canned corn kernels, drained

12 large lettuce leaves, such as iceberg, rinsed and dried

dipping sauce

10 tbsp rice vinegar

4 tbsp clear honey

2 tbsp toasted sesame oil

1 tsp bottled chili sauce

1-inch/2.5-cm piece fresh gingerroot, peeled and very finely chopped

method

1 Put the noodles in a bowl, pour over enough lukewarm water to cover, and let soak for 20 minutes, until soft. Alternatively, follow the package instructions. Drain and rinse, then cut into 3-inch/7.5-cm lengths.

2 Beat the peanut butter, vinegar, and oyster sauce together in a large bowl, adding a little oil to lighten the mixture, if necessary. Toss with the noodles in the bowl to coat, then add soy sauce to taste. Cover and let chill until 15 minutes before you plan to serve.

3 Meanwhile, mix together the dipping sauce ingredients in a small bowl.

4 When you are ready to serve, stir the radishes, carrots, zucchini, and corn into the noodles and transfer to a serving dish. To assemble the lettuce wraps, place some noodles in a lettuce leaf and roll up the leaf to enclose the filling.

pickled baby cucumbers

ingredients

SERVES 4

1 tbsp vegetable or peanut oil,
    for frying
14 oz/400 g baby cucumbers
2¼ cups white rice vinegar
1 tbsp salt
3 tbsp sugar
3 red Thai chiles, seeded and
    finely chopped

method

1 In a wok or deep pan, heat the oil and cook the cucumbers for 3–5 minutes, or until they are bright green. Drain and set aside. When cool, score the skin many times on all sides. Place in a large dish.

2 Combine the vinegar, salt, sugar, and chile and pour over the cucumbers, immersing them in the liquid. Let marinate for 24 hours, then serve cold in chunks.

pickled cucumber

ingredients

SERVES 4

1/2 English cucumber

1 1/8 tsp salt

1 tbsp rice vinegar

1 tsp sugar

method

1 Slice the cucumber into thin rounds. Place the slices in a shallow bowl and sprinkle with 1 tsp of the salt. Leave to stand for 5 minutes.

2 Rinse the cucumber slices under running water, then drain well.

3 Place the remaining 1/8 tsp salt, rice vinegar, and sugar in a bowl that is large enough to take the cucumber, and stir to mix. Add the cucumber slices and toss to coat. Refrigerate for 8 hours or overnight.

corn fritters

ingredients

SERVES 4

fritters

3 scallions, chopped finely

11 1/2 oz/325 g canned corn kernels, drained

1 red bell pepper, seeded and finely chopped

small handful of fresh cilantro, chopped

2 garlic cloves, crushed

2 eggs

2 tsp superfine sugar

1 tbsp fish sauce

2 tbsp rice flour or cornstarch

vegetable or peanut oil, for pan-frying

dip

2 red bell peppers, seeded and halved

2 tomatoes, peeled, seeded, and chopped coarsely

1 tbsp vegetable or peanut oil, for pan-frying

1 onion, chopped

1 tbsp Thai red curry paste

3–4 sprigs fresh cilantro, chopped

method

1 Combine all the ingredients for the fritters in a bowl. Heat the oil in a skillet and cook spoonfuls of the mixture, in batches, until golden brown on the underside. Flip over with a spatula to cook the second side. Remove from the skillet, drain on paper towels, and keep warm.

2 To make the dip, put the red bell peppers on a baking sheet and place, skin-side up, under a hot broiler, until blackened. Using tongs, transfer to a plastic bag, tie the top, and let cool slightly.

3 When the bell peppers are cool enough to handle, peel off the skins and chop the flesh. Put into a blender or food processor with the tomatoes and process until smooth.

4 Heat the oil in a heavy-bottom pan and cook the onion and curry paste for 3–4 minutes, until softened. Add the bell pepper and tomato puree and cook gently until tender and hot. Stir in the chopped cilantro, cook for 1 minute, and serve hot with the fritters.

thai bean curd cakes with chili dip

ingredients

SERVES 8

10¹/₂ oz/300 g firm bean curd, drained weight, coarsely grated

1 lemongrass stalk, outer layer discarded, finely chopped

2 garlic cloves, chopped

1-inch/2.5-cm piece fresh gingerroot, grated

2 kaffir lime leaves, finely chopped (optional)

2 shallots, finely chopped

2 fresh red chiles, seeded and finely chopped

4 tbsp chopped fresh cilantro

²/₃ cup gluten-free all-purpose flour, plus extra for flouring

¹/₂ tsp salt

corn oil, for cooking

chili dip

3 tbsp white distilled vinegar or rice wine vinegar

2 scallions, finely sliced

1 tbsp superfine sugar

2 fresh chiles, finely chopped

2 tbsp chopped fresh cilantro

pinch of salt

method

1 To make the chili dip, mix all the ingredients together in a small serving bowl and set aside.

2 Mix the bean curd with the lemongrass, garlic, gingerroot, lime leaves, if using, shallots, chiles, and cilantro in a mixing bowl. Stir in the flour and salt to make a coarse, sticky paste. Cover and let chill in the refrigerator for 1 hour to let the mixture firm up slightly.

3 Form the mixture into 8 large walnut-size balls and, using floured hands, flatten into circles. Heat enough oil to cover the bottom of a large, heavy-bottom skillet over medium heat. Cook the cakes in 2 batches, turning halfway through, for 4–6 minutes, or until golden brown. Drain on paper towels and serve warm with the chili dip.

pickled daikon & carrot

ingredients

SERVES 4

4-inch/10-cm daikon (long
   white radish), peeled

1 carrot, peeled

1/2 tsp salt

1 tbsp sugar

2 tbsp rice vinegar

1 tsp white sesame seeds,
   toasted

method

1 Use a mandolin or vegetable peeler to slice the daikon and carrot into long thin slivers. Sprinkle the slices with the salt, cover, and let stand for 30 minutes. Place in a strainer and gently press to extract the water.

2 Put the sugar and rice vinegar into a bowl that is large enough to take the daikon and carrot. Stir until the sugar has dissolved.

3 Add the daikon and carrot, and toss to coat. Refrigerate for 8 hours or overnight. Sprinkle with the toasted sesame seeds before serving.

homemade pickled gingerroot

ingredients

MAKES 115 G/1 CUP

4½-inch/11.5-cm piece fresh
    gingerroot
1 tsp salt
½ cup rice vinegar
2 tbsp superfine sugar
4 tbsp water

method

1 Peel the gingerroot. Use a mandolin or vegetable peeler to slice it into long thin slivers, cutting along the grain. Sprinkle the slices with the salt, cover, and let stand for 30 minutes.

2 Place the salted gingerroot in boiling water for 30 seconds to blanch. Drain well.

3 Put the rice vinegar, sugar, and water into a small bowl. Stir to dissolve the sugar.

4 Place the gingerroot slices in a bowl, pour over the rice vinegar mixture, and turn to coat. Cover and let marinate for at least 24 hours in the refrigerator (it will turn slightly pink). Pickled gingerroot will keep for several weeks if stored in a sterile airtight container in the refrigerator.

vegetable parcels

ingredients

SERVES 4

2 tbsp vegetable or peanut oil

8 oz/225 g potatoes, diced
   and boiled for 5 minutes

2 garlic cloves, crushed

1 onion, chopped

2 tbsp Thai green curry paste

1/2 cup frozen peas, thawed

juice of 1 lime

1/2 tsp salt

16 egg roll skins,
   4-inch/10-cm square

1 egg, beaten

vegetable or peanut oil,
   for deep-frying

sweet chili sauce or Thai soy
   sauce, to serve

method

1 Heat the oil in a wok and stir-fry the potatoes, garlic, onion, and curry paste until lightly browned. Stir in the peas, lime juice, and salt, and stir-fry for 1–2 minutes. Remove from the heat.

2 Brush 1 egg roll skin with egg. Put a small spoonful of the potato mixture in the center and fold up the edges to enclose the filling and make a purse-shaped package. Press the skin tightly together to seal the package. Repeat with the remaining skins and filling to make 16 small packages.

3 Heat the oil for deep-frying in a wok. Add the vegetable packages, in batches, and deep-fry for 3–4 minutes, until golden brown. Drain on paper towels and keep warm while you cook the remaining packages.

4 Serve hot with a bowl of chili sauce or soy sauce for dipping.

crispy seaweed

ingredients

SERVES 4

2 lb 4 oz/ 1 kg bok choy

3¼ cups peanut oil

1 tsp salt

1 tbsp superfine sugar

⅔ cup toasted pine nuts

method

1 Rinse the bok choy leaves under cold running water, then pat dry thoroughly with paper towels.

2 Discarding any tough outer leaves, roll each bok choy leaf up, then slice thinly so that the leaves are finely shredded. Alternatively, use a food processor to shred the bok choy.

3 Heat the peanut oil in a large preheated wok. Carefully add the shredded bok choy and cook for 30 seconds, or until it shrivels up and becomes crispy. (You will probably need to do this in several batches.) Remove from the wok with a strainer and drain on paper towels.

4 Transfer to a large bowl, toss with the salt, sugar, and toasted pine nuts, and serve.

tempura

ingredients

SERVES 4

5^1/$_2$ oz/150 g package
tempura mix

4 shiitake mushrooms

4 fresh asparagus spears

4 slices sweet potato

1 red bell pepper, seeded and
cut into strips

4 onion slices, cut widthwise
into rings

oil, for deep-frying

dipping sauce

2 tsp mirin

1 tbsp shoyu (Japanese
soy sauce)

pinch of dashi granules,
dissolved in 2 tbsp boiling
water

method

1 To make the dipping sauce, mix the ingredients together in a small dipping dish.

2 Mix the tempura with water according to the package instructions. Don't try to make the batter smooth—it should be a little lumpy. Drop the vegetables into the batter.

3 Preheat a wok, then fill two-thirds full with oil, or use a deep-fryer. Heat the oil to 350–375°F/180–190°C, or until a cube of bread browns in 30 seconds.

4 Lift 2–3 pieces of tempura out of the batter, add to the oil, and cook for 2–3 minutes, or until the batter is a light golden color. Remove, drain on paper towels, and keep hot while you cook the remaining tempura pieces.

5 Serve with the dipping sauce.

vegetable & bean curd tempura

ingredients

SERVES 4

5 1/2 oz/150 g package tempura mix

1 potato, peeled and cut into 1/2-inch/1-cm thick pieces

1/4 butternut squash, peeled and cut into 1/2-inch/1-cm thick pieces

1 small sweet potato, peeled and cut into 1/2-inch/1-cm thick pieces

1 small eggplant, cut into 1/2-inch/1-cm thick pieces

6 green beans, trimmed

1 red bell pepper, seeded and cut into thick strips

6 whole shiitake or white mushrooms, stalks removed

1 stalk broccoli, broken into florets

12 oz/350 g firm bean curd, cubed

vegetable oil, for deep-frying

sweet chili sauce or tempura dipping sauce, to serve

method

1 Blend the tempura mix with the amount of water described on the package instructions until you have a lumpy batter full of air bubbles. Do not try to make the batter smooth or it will be too heavy.

2 Coat all the prepared vegetables and cubed bean curd in the batter.

3 Add the oil to a deep-fryer and heat to 350–375°F/180–190°C, or until a cube of bread browns in 30 seconds.

4 Put the battered vegetables into the oil 3 at a time. If you add too many pieces at one time the oil temperature will drop and the batter will be soggy. Cook for 2–3 minutes, until the batter turns a light golden color. Remove and drain on paper towels to blot up the excess oil.

5 Serve hot, with the sweet chili sauce or tempura dipping sauce on the side.

seafood tempura

ingredients

SERVES 4

8 large shrimp, shelled and deveined

8 squid rings

5^1/$_2$ oz/150 g package tempura mix

4 scallops, without corals, cleaned

7 oz/200 g firm white fish fillets, cut into strips

vegetable oil, for deep-frying

Japanese soy sauce or tempura dipping sauce, to serve

method

1 Make little cuts on the underside of the shrimp to keep them straight while they cook. Pull any membranes off the squid rings.

2 Blend the tempura mix with the amount of water described on the package instructions until you have a lumpy batter full of air bubbles. Do not try to make the batter smooth or it will be too heavy.

3 Coat all the prepared seafood in the batter.

4 Add the oil to a deep-fryer and heat to 350–375°F/180–190°C, or until a cube of bread browns in 30 seconds.

5 Add the battered seafood pieces 3 at a time. If you add too many pieces at one time the oil temperature will drop and the batter will be soggy. Cook for 2–3 minutes, until the batter turns a light golden color. Remove and drain on paper towels to blot up the excess oil.

6 Serve hot, with the soy sauce or tempura dipping sauce on the side.

classic tuna nori rolls

ingredients

MAKES 24 PIECES

2 sheets of toasted nori

$1/2$ quantity freshly cooked
   sushi rice

wasabi paste

2 oz/55 g sashimi-grade tuna,
   cut into strips $1/4$ inch/
   5 mm square

Japanese soy sauce and
   pickled gingerroot, to serve

method

1 Fold a nori sheet in half lengthwise, press all along the fold, and tear it into 2 equal pieces. Place a half-sheet smooth-side down on a sushi rolling mat so that one of the long edges is directly in front of you.

2 Divide the rice into 4 equal portions. Wet your hands, then spread 1 portion of rice evenly over the nori, leaving a $1/2$-inch/1-cm clear border along the furthest edge.

3 Dab a thin line of wasabi paste across the rice at the end nearest you. Cover with a quarter of the tuna strips, arranged in a continuous line.

4 Pick up the nearest edge of the rolling mat. Slowly roll the mat away from you to wrap the nori around the filling. Use gentle, even pressure and lift the mat out of the way as you go. Press the roll onto the uncovered border of the nori to seal it.

5 Transfer the roll to a chopping board, seam-side down. Cut it in half and then cut each half into 3 equal pieces using a wet, very sharp knife. Wipe your knife between each cut. Repeat to make 3 more rolls. Serve with soy sauce, pickled gingerroot, and extra wasabi.

tuna sesame blocks

ingredients

MAKES 12 PIECES

3$^1/_4$ x 2$^1/_2$-inch/8 x 6-cm piece
of tuna fillet, about
$^3/_4$ inch/2 cm thick

2 tsp sesame oil

2 tbsp white sesame seeds,
toasted

3 sheets of toasted nori, each
cut into 4 strips lengthwise

2 tbsp vegetable oil

method

1 Cut the tuna into 12 cubes and roll the cubes first in the sesame oil and then in the toasted sesame seeds.

2 Roll each sesame-covered cube in a strip of nori, trimming off any excess so that the nori goes round the tuna once with little overlap.

3 Heat the vegetable oil in a skillet and put the cubes into the pan, standing them up on one nori-free end. Cook for 2 minutes, then turn over to cook the other nori-free end. The sesame seeds should be a dark brown, but not burned, and the tuna should have cooked most of the way through, leaving a rare patch in the center. If you prefer your tuna fully cooked, cook each end for a little longer.

salmon & arugula rolls with pesto

ingredients

MAKES 24 PIECES

2 sheets of toasted nori

$1/2$ quantity freshly cooked
   sushi rice

pesto

2 oz/55 g skinless sashimi-
   grade fillet of salmon,
   cut into strips $1/2$ inch/
   1 cm square

$1^1/2$ oz/40 g arugula, stalks
   removed

Japanese soy sauce, pickled
   gingerroot, and wasabi
   paste, to serve

method

1 Fold a nori sheet in half lengthwise, press all along the fold, and tear it into 2 equal pieces. Place a half-sheet smooth-side down on a sushi rolling mat so that one of the long edges is directly in front of you.

2 Divide the rice into 4 equal portions. Using wet hands, spread 1 portion of the rice evenly over the nori, leaving a $1/2$-inch/1-cm clear border along the furthest edge.

3 Dab a thin line of pesto across the rice at the end nearest you. Cover with a quarter of the salmon strips, arranging them in a continuous line, and top with arugula.

4 Pick up the nearest edge of the rolling mat. Slowly roll the mat away from you to wrap the nori around the filling. Use gentle, even pressure and lift the mat out of the way as you go. Press the roll onto the uncovered border of the nori to seal it.

5 Transfer the roll to a chopping board, seam-side down. Cut it in half and then cut each half into 3 equal pieces using a wet, very sharp knife. Repeat to make 3 more rolls. Arrange on a plate, and serve with soy sauce, pickled gingerroot, and wasabi paste.

smoked salmon sushi balls

ingredients

MAKES 10 PIECES

1–2 slices of smoked salmon
juice of $1/4$ lemon
$1/4$ quantity freshly cooked
    sushi rice
wasabi paste
lemon zest, to garnish
Japanese soy sauce, pickled
    gingerroot, and wasabi
    paste, to serve

method

1 Cut the salmon into 10 small pieces about 1 inch/2.5 cm square, then squeeze the lemon juice over the top.

2 Cut a square of plastic wrap measuring 4 inch x 4 inch/10 cm x 10 cm. Place 1 piece of smoked salmon in the center of the wrap.

3 Take $1^1/2$ tsp sushi rice and gently roll it into a ball. Lay it on top of the salmon.

4 Wrap the plastic wrap around the rice and salmon, twisting the 4 corners together to form a tight package so that the rice inside makes a smooth ball. Repeat to make 10 balls in total.

5 Unwrap the balls just before serving. Put a dab of wasabi and a tiny strip of lemon zest on top of each ball to garnish. Serve with soy sauce, pickled gingerroot, and wasabi paste.

salmon, spinach & wasabi mash rolls

ingredients

MAKES 24 PIECES

2 large starchy potatoes, peeled and cut into quarters

salt

1 scallion, finely chopped

wasabi paste

4 oz/115 g sashimi-grade salmon, or piece of salmon fillet, skin removed

1 tbsp vegetable oil (if using salmon fillet)

6 sheets of toasted nori

handful of baby spinach greens, stalks removed

method

1 Cook the potatoes in a pan of boiling salted water for 20–30 minutes, until tender. Mash, then mix with the scallion and wasabi to taste. Season with salt. Let cool, then refrigerate for 30 minutes or until very firm.

2 If using sashimi-grade salmon, cut into strips. If cooking the fish, remove any bones. Heat the oil in a skillet, then cook the salmon over medium heat for 4 minutes on each side, until cooked through. Let cool. Cut into strips.

3 Place a sheet of nori smooth-side down on a rolling mat with one of the long ends in front of you. Spread a sixth of the mashed potatoes over the bottom third of the nori. Lay a sixth of the spinach greens on top, then add a layer of salmon strips.

4 Pick up the nearest edge of the rolling mat. Slowly roll the mat away from you to wrap the nori around the filling, using gentle, even pressure. Press the roll onto the uncovered border of the nori to seal it.

5 Transfer the roll to a chopping board, seam-side down. Cut into 4 even-size pieces with a wet, very sharp knife. Repeat with the remaining ingredients.

seven-spiced salmon rolls

ingredients

MAKES 24 PIECES

5¹/₂-oz/150-g piece of salmon
    fillet, skin removed
sichimi togarashi (seven-spice
    powder)
red pepper flakes
1 tbsp vegetable oil
1 quantity freshly cooked
    sushi rice
6 sheets of toasted nori
2 tbsp Japanese mayonnaise
Japanese soy sauce, wasabi
    paste, and pickled
    gingerroot, to serve

method

1 Remove any bones from the salmon fillet. Dust the surface heavily with sichimi togarashi and sprinkle over a few red pepper flakes. Heat the oil in a skillet and cook the salmon over medium heat for 4 minutes on each side, or until cooked through. Let cool, then flake into large pieces.

2 Divide the rice into 6 equal portions. Put a sheet of nori smooth-side down on a rolling mat with one of the long ends toward you. With wet hands, spread 1 portion of the rice evenly over the nori, leaving a ¹/₂-inch/1-cm clear border along the furthest edge.

3 Spread 1 tsp of the mayonnaise across the the rice at the end nearest you. Lay a sixth of the flaked salmon on top of the mayonnaise.

4 Pick up the nearest edge of the rolling mat. Slowly roll the mat away from you to wrap the nori around the filling. Use gentle, even pressure and lift the mat out of the way as you go. Press the roll onto the uncovered border of the nori to seal it.

5 Transfer the roll to a chopping board, seam-side down. Cut it into 4 equal pieces with a wet, very sharp knife. Repeat with the remaining ingredients. Serve with soy sauce, wasabi, and pickled gingerroot.

salmon, asparagus & mayonnaise rolls

ingredients

MAKES 24 PIECES

6 thin asparagus spears

5$1/2$ oz/150 g sashimi-grade salmon, or piece of salmon fillet, skin and any bones removed

1 tbsp vegetable oil (if using salmon fillet)

6 sheets of toasted nori

1 quantity freshly cooked sushi rice

wasabi paste

1 tbsp Japanese mayonnaise

1 tbsp white sesame seeds, toasted

Japanese soy sauce and pickled gingerroot, to serve

method

1 Lay the asparagus spears flat in a skillet filled with simmering water and cook for 3–4 minutes or until tender. Cut into 3$1/2$-inch/9-cm lengths and let cool.

2 If using raw salmon, cut it into thin strips. If cooking the fish, heat the oil in a skillet and cook over medium heat for 4 minutes on each side, or until cooked. Let cool, then flake.

3 Put a sheet of nori smooth-side down on a rolling mat so that one of the long ends is in front of you. With wet hands, spread a sixth of the rice over the nori, leaving a $1/2$-inch/1-cm clear border along the furthest edge.

4 Dab a line of wasabi across the rice at the end nearest you. Cover with $1/2$ tsp of mayonnaise. Lay a cooked asparagus spear over the top and place a sixth of the salmon alongside. Sprinkle the filling with $1/2$ tsp of the sesame seeds.

5 Pick up the nearest edge of the mat. Roll it away from you to wrap the nori around the filling, using even pressure. Press the roll onto the clear border of nori to seal it, then transfer to a chopping board. Cut it into 4 even-size pieces using a wet, very sharp knife. Repeat with the rest of the ingredients. Serve with soy sauce, pickled gingerroot, and more wasabi.

steamed shrimp rolls with lime dipping sauce

ingredients

MAKES 24 PIECES

2¼ cups shelled raw shrimp, deveined

2 tbsp chopped fresh cilantro

1 large kaffir lime leaf, finely shredded

1 tbsp freshly squeezed lime juice

2 tsp sweet chili sauce

1½ tbsp fish sauce

2 tsp mirin

1 egg white

4 sheets of toasted nori

lime slices, to garnish

lime dipping sauce

4 tbsp sake

4 tbsp Japanese soy sauce

2 tsp mirin

1 tbsp freshly squeezed lime juice

method

1 Put the ingredients for the dipping sauce into a small bowl and stir to mix.

2 Place the shrimp in a blender or food processor with the chopped cilantro, shredded lime leaf, lime juice, sweet chili sauce, fish sauce, and mirin. Blend until smooth, then add the egg white and blend briefly to mix.

3 Lay a nori sheet smooth-side down on a rolling mat so that one of the short sides is in front of you. Spread a quarter of the shrimp mixture over the nori, leaving a ½-inch/1-cm clear border along the furthest edge.

4 Pick up the nearest edge of the mat. Roll the mat away from you to wrap the nori tightly around the filling, creating a pinwheel effect. Use gentle, even pressure, lifting the mat out of the way as you go. Press the roll onto the clear border to seal it. Repeat to make 3 more rolls. Place them in the refrigerator for 1 hour.

5 Transfer each roll to a chopping board, seam-side down. Cut it in half and then cut each half into 3 equal pieces using a wet, very sharp knife. Place in a steamer and cook over boiling water for 5 minutes or until the shrimp mixture is cooked. Arrange on serving plates, garnished with lime slices, with the lime dipping sauce alongside.

bell pepper-wrapped shrimp rolls

ingredients

MAKES 12 PIECES

2 red bell peppers

1 small ripe avocado, pitted, peeled, and cut into slices

8 large cooked shelled shrimp

salt and black pepper

method

1 Preheat the oven to 400°F/200°C. Put the bell peppers in a roasting pan and cook them for 30 minutes, or until the skins have browned and started to puff away from the flesh. Let cool, then pull off the skins. Cut each bell pepper in half and discard the stalk, seeds, and membrane.

2 Lay out each bell-pepper half on a chopping board and place a pile of avocado slices on one side. Top with 2 shrimp and season well with salt and pepper. Roll up the bell peppers tightly, wrap each roll in plastic wrap, and let chill for 30 minutes.

3 Carefully unwrap the plastic wrap from the bell peppers and trim each end to make it straight. Cut each roll into 3 pieces with a wet, very sharp knife. Turn the pieces on their ends and arrange them on a plate.

crab, asparagus & shiitake rolls

ingredients

MAKES 24 PIECES

6 thin asparagus spears

1 tbsp vegetable oil

6 fresh shiitake mushrooms, stalks discarded, then thinly sliced

6 sheets of toasted nori

1 quantity freshly cooked sushi rice

wasabi paste

6 crab sticks, split in half lengthwise

ponzu dipping sauce, to serve

method

1 Lay the asparagus spears flat in a skillet filled with simmering water and cook for 3 minutes or until tender. Cut the spears into 3¹/₂-inch/9-cm lengths and let cool.

2 Heat the oil in a skillet, add the mushrooms, and cook over medium heat for 5 minutes, or until softened.

3 Place a sheet of nori smooth-side down on a rolling mat so that one of the long ends is toward you. With wet hands, spread a sixth of the rice over the nori, leaving a ¹/₂-inch/1-cm clear border along the furthest edge.

4 Dab a line of wasabi across the rice at the end nearest to you. Lay some of the cooked asparagus lengths on top of the wasabi, then put 2 pieces of crab stick next to it. Add a line of sliced mushrooms.

5 Pick up the nearest edge of the rolling mat. Roll the mat away from you to wrap the nori around the filling, using gentle, even pressure. Press the roll onto the clear border of nori to seal it. Remove the roll from the mat and cut it into 4 even-size pieces with a wet, very sharp knife. Repeat with the remaining ingredients. Serve with the ponzu dipping sauce.

scallop, potato & sesame rolls

ingredients

MAKES 12 PIECES

2 large starchy potatoes, peeled and cut into quarters

2 tbsp butter

salt and black pepper

1 tbsp olive oil

8 large scallops, without corals, cleaned

6 sheets of toasted nori

2 tbsp Japanese mayonnaise

2 tbsp white sesame seeds, toasted

method

1 Cook the potatoes in a pan of boiling salted water for 20–30 minutes, until tender. Mash with the butter and season with salt and pepper. Refrigerate for 30 minutes, until the mashed potatoes are very firm.

2 Heat the oil in a skillet and sauté the scallops for 2–3 minutes on each side, until cooked through. Slice them thinly into 3 coin-shaped pieces and season with salt to taste.

3 Place a sheet of nori smooth-side down on a rolling mat so that one of the long ends is toward you. Spread the mashed potatoes over the bottom third of the nori. Spread 1 tsp of mayonnaise over the top, then sprinkle on 1 tsp of the toasted sesame seeds. Add a sixth of the scallop slices.

4 Pick up the nearest edge of the rolling mat. Slowly roll the mat away from you to wrap the nori around the filling. Use gentle, even pressure until you have finished the roll, and lift the mat out of the way as you go.

5 Transfer the roll seam-side down to a chopping board and cut it into 4 even-size pieces using a wet, very sharp knife. Repeat with the remaining ingredients.

shrimp & avocado skewers

ingredients

MAKES 6 SKEWERS

1 quantity freshly cooked
    sushi rice

6 sheets of toasted nori

1 tbsp Japanese mayonnaise

1 tsp lemon zest

12 cooked jumbo shrimp,
    shelled and deveined

2 ripe avocados, pitted,
    peeled, and cut into strips

2-inch/5-cm piece of
    cucumber, peeled and cut
    into thin sticks

pickled gingerroot and wasabi
    paste, to serve

method

1 Divide the rice into 6 equal portions. Put a sheet of nori smooth-side down on a rolling mat with one of the long ends toward you. Wet your hands, then spread 1 portion of the rice evenly over the nori, leaving a 1/2-inch/1-cm clear border along the furthest edge.

2 Mix the mayonnaise with the lemon zest and spread about 1/2 tsp in a line across the rice at the end nearest to you. Lay 2 shrimp end to end on top of the mayonnaise. Place a line of avocado next to the shrimp and then add a line of cucumber sticks.

3 Pick up the nearest edge of the rolling mat. Slowly roll the mat away from you to wrap the nori around the filling. Use gentle, even pressure and lift the mat out of the way as you go. Press the roll onto the uncovered border of the nori to seal it.

4 Transfer the roll to a chopping board, seam-side down. Cut into 4 even-size pieces with a wet, very sharp knife. Lay the pieces on their side and push a bamboo skewer through them. Repeat with the remaining ingredients to make 6 skewers in total. Serve with pickled gingerroot and wasabi paste.

chicken teriyaki rolls

ingredients

MAKES 24 PIECES

1 skinless, boneless chicken breast, weighing about 5 oz/150 g, cut into strips

2 tbsp teriyaki sauce

1 tbsp vegetable oil

1 quantity freshly cooked sushi rice

6 sheets of toasted nori

2-inch/5-cm piece of English cucumber, peeled and cut into thin sticks

Japanese soy sauce, wasabi paste, and pickled gingerroot, to serve

method

1 Preheat the broiler to its highest setting. Toss the chicken in the teriyaki sauce, then the oil, and lay out on a foil-lined broiler pan. Broil the chicken strips for 4 minutes on each side, put into a bowl with any cooking juices, and let cool.

2 Divide the rice into 6 equal portions. Place a sheet of nori smooth-side down on a rolling mat so that one of the longest ends is directly in front of you. Wet your hands, then spread 1 portion of the rice evenly over the nori, leaving a 1/2-inch/1-cm clear border along the furthest edge.

3 Lay some of the chicken strips across the rice at the end nearest to you. Place a line of thin cucumber sticks alongside.

4 Pick up the nearest edge of the rolling mat. Slowly roll the mat away from you to wrap the nori around the filling. Use gentle, even pressure and lift the mat out of the way as you go. Press the roll onto the uncovered border of the nori to seal it.

5 Transfer the roll to a chopping board and cut it into 4 even-size pieces with a wet, very sharp knife. Repeat with the remaining ingredients. Serve with soy sauce, wasabi, and pickled gingerroot.

california rolls

ingredients

MAKES 24 PIECES

1 quantity freshly cooked
    sushi rice
6 sheets of toasted nori
wasabi paste
$1/2$ ripe avocado, pitted,
    peeled, and cut into thin
    strips
6 crab sticks, split in half
    lengthwise
2-inch/5-cm piece of English
    cucumber, peeled and cut
    into thin sticks
Japanese soy sauce and
    pickled gingerroot, to serve

method

1 Divide the rice into 6 equal portions. Place a sheet of nori smooth-side down on a rolling mat so that one of the longest ends is directly in front of you. Wet your hands and then spread 1 portion of the rice evenly over the nori, leaving a $1/2$-inch/1-cm clear border along the furthest edge.

2 Dab a small amount of wasabi across the rice at the end nearest you. Lay a line of avocado strips on top of the wasabi, then put 2 pieces of crab stick next to them. Add a line of cucumber sticks.

3 Pick up the nearest edge of the rolling mat. Slowly roll the mat away from you to wrap the nori around the filling. Use gentle, even pressure and lift the mat out of the way as you go. Press the roll onto the uncovered border of the nori to seal it.

4 Transfer the roll to a chopping board, seam-side down. Cut it into 4 even-size pieces using a wet, very sharp knife. Repeat with the remaining ingredients. Serve with soy sauce, pickled gingerroot, and more wasabi.

pork tonkatsu rolls

ingredients

MAKES 24 PIECES

2 tbsp flour

1 egg, lightly beaten

4 tbsp tonkatsu crumbs or
dried white breadcrumbs

7 oz/200 g pork tenderloin,
cut into 1/4-inch/5-mm
thick slices

4 tbsp vegetable oil

1 quantity freshly cooked
sushi rice

6 sheets of toasted nori

2 tbsp Japanese mayonnaise

Japanese soy sauce, pickled
gingerroot, and wasabi
paste, to serve

method

1 Put the flour, egg, and crumbs in separate bowls. One by one, dust each piece of pork in the flour, dip it in the egg, then finally press it into the crumbs. Lay the breaded pork on a plate and refrigerate for 20 minutes.

2 Heat the oil in a skillet. Add the pork and cook over medium heat for 3 minutes on each side, or until the crumbs are golden brown and the pork is cooked through. Cut the cooked slices into thin strips.

3 Divide the rice into 6 equal portions. Put a sheet of nori smooth-side down on a rolling mat so that one of the long ends is toward you. With wet hands, spread 1 portion of the rice evenly over the nori, leaving a 1/2-inch/1-cm clear border along the furthest edge.

4 Spread 1 tsp of the mayonnaise across the rice at the end nearest to you. Lay a sixth of the pork strips on top.

5 Pick up the nearest edge of the rolling mat. Roll the mat away from you to wrap the nori around the filling. Use gentle, even pressure and lift the mat out of the way as you go. Press the roll onto the clear border to seal it.

6 Transfer the roll to a chopping board and cut it into 4 equal pieces with a wet, very sharp knife. Repeat with the remaining ingredients. Serve with soy sauce, pickled gingerroot, and wasabi paste on the side.

inside-out rolls with beef teriyaki

ingredients

MAKES 24 PIECES

5¹/₂ oz/150 g tenderloin steak,
    trimmed

2 tbsp teriyaki sauce

1 tbsp vegetable oil

6 sheets of toasted nori

1 quantity freshly cooked
    sushi rice

2 scallions, shredded

3 tbsp white sesame seeds,
    toasted

Japanese soy sauce, pickled
    gingerroot, and wasabi
    paste, to serve

method

1 Beat the steak out flat using a meat mallet or rolling pin. Coat the steak in the teriyaki sauce and let marinate for 1 hour. Heat the oil in a skillet and cook the steak for 3 minutes on each side. Cut the cooked steak into strips.

2 Place a sheet of nori smooth-side down on the mat with one of the long ends toward you. With wet hands, spread a sixth of the rice evenly over the nori. Lay a sheet of plastic wrap on top and turn the whole thing over so that the plastic wrap is under the rice and the nori side faces upward.

3 Arrange a sixth of the beef teriyaki across the nori at the end nearest to you. Top with shredded scallion, and sprinkle with ¹/₂ tsp of the sesame seeds.

4 Pick up the nearest edge of the rolling mat and slowly roll the mat away from you to wrap the rice-covered nori around the filling. Lift the mat and plastic wrap out of the way as you go. Spread 2 tbsp of the sesame seeds on a plate and roll the sushi in it to coat the rice.

5 Transfer the roll to a chopping board, seam-side down. Cut it into 4 even-size pieces with a wet, very sharp knife. Repeat with the remaining ingredients. Serve with soy sauce, pickled gingerroot, and wasabi paste.

steamed white rice

ingredients

SERVES 3–4

8 oz/225 g rice

cold water

method

1 Wash the rice. Place in a pan with the same volume of water plus a little extra (the water should just cover the rice). Bring to a boil, then cover and let simmer for about 15 minutes.

2 Turn off the heat and let the rice continue to cook in its own steam for about 5 minutes. At this point, the grains should be cooked through but not sticking together.

egg-fried rice

ingredients

SERVES 4

2 tbsp vegetable or peanut oil

2^1/$_2$ cups cooked rice, chilled

1 egg, well beaten

method

1 Heat the oil in a preheated wok or deep pan and stir-fry the rice for 1 minute, breaking it down as much as possible into individual grains.

2 Quickly add the egg, stirring, so as to coat each piece of rice. Stir until the egg is cooked and the rice, as far as possible, is in single grains. Serve immediately.

perfect sushi rice

ingredients

MAKES ABOUT 3 CUPS

10 oz/300 g sushi rice

1 1/2 cups water

2-inch/5-cm square piece of kombu (sun-dried kelp, optional)

2 tbsp sushi rice seasoning (or 2 tbsp rice vinegar, 1 tbsp sugar, and 1/4 tsp salt combined)

method

1 Place the rice in a strainer and rinse under cold water until the water runs completely clear. Drain the rice, then place in a pan with the water.

2 Cut a few slits in the kombu, if using, to help release the flavor, then add to the rice. Cover the pan with a tight-fitting lid and bring to a boil. Remove the kombu and quickly replace the lid. Reduce the heat and let simmer for 10 minutes. Remove from the heat and let stand for 15 minutes. Do not lift the lid to take a look once you have removed the kombu.

3 Turn the cooked rice into a large, flat-bottomed, nonmetallic bowl. Pour the rice seasoning evenly over the surface of the rice, then use quick cutting strokes to mix it in with a spatula. Do not stir or you will break the rice grains. As you work, fan the rice with either a hand-held fan or an electric one set to the lowest setting.

4 Keep slicing and fanning until the rice has reached room temperature and looks shiny. Cover with a damp cloth and use the same day; do not refrigerate.

chinese fried rice

ingredients

SERVES 4

3 cups water

$1/2$ tsp salt

$10 1/2$ oz/300 g long-grain rice

2 eggs

salt and pepper

4 tsp cold water

3 tbsp sunflower oil

4 scallions, sliced diagonally

1 red, green, or yellow bell
   pepper, cored, seeded,
   and thinly sliced

3–4 lean bacon slices, rinded
   and cut into strips

generous 1 cup fresh bean
   sprouts

$1 1/8$ cups frozen peas, thawed

2 tbsp soy sauce (optional)

method

1 Pour the water into the wok with the salt and bring to a boil. Rinse the rice in a strainer under cold running water until the water runs clear, drain thoroughly, and add to the boiling water. Stir well, then cover the wok tightly with the lid, and let simmer gently for 12–13 minutes. (Do not remove the lid during cooking or the steam will escape and the rice will not be cooked.)

2 Remove the lid, give the rice a good stir, and spread out on a large plate or baking sheet to cool and dry.

3 Meanwhile, beat each egg separately with salt and pepper and 2 teaspoons of cold water. Heat 1 tablespoon of oil in a preheated wok, pour in the first egg, swirl it around, and let cook undisturbed until set. Transfer to a cutting board and cook the second egg. Cut the omelets into thin slices.

4 Add the remaining oil to the wok and when really hot stir-fry the scallions and bell pepper for 1–2 minutes. Add the bacon and continue to stir-fry for an additional 2 minutes. Add the bean sprouts and peas and toss together thoroughly. Stir in the soy sauce, if using.

5 Add the rice and salt and pepper to taste and stir-fry for 1 minute, then add the strips of omelet and continue to stir-fry for 2 minutes, or until the rice is piping hot. Serve immediately.

golden rice

ingredients

SERVES 4

1 tsp saffron threads

2 tbsp hot water

2 tbsp ghee or vegetable oil

3 onions, chopped

3 tbsp butter

1 tsp ground cumin

1 tsp ground cinnamon

1 tsp salt

$\frac{1}{2}$ tsp pepper

$\frac{1}{2}$ tsp paprika

3 bay leaves

2 cups long-grain rice, rinsed
and drained

3$\frac{1}{4}$ cups vegetable stock or
water

$\frac{2}{3}$ cup cashew halves, toasted

method

1 Put the saffron threads and hot water into a small bowl and set aside to soak.

2 Meanwhile, heat the ghee in a large pan over low heat, add the onions, and cook, stirring frequently, for 5 minutes. Add the butter, cumin, cinnamon, salt, pepper, paprika, and bay leaves and cook, stirring, for 2 minutes, then add the rice and cook, stirring, for 3 minutes. Add the saffron and its soaking liquid and pour in the stock.

3 Bring to a boil, then reduce the heat, cover, and let simmer for 20–25 minutes until all the liquid has been absorbed. If the rice grains have not cooked through, add a little more stock and cook until tender and all the liquid has been absorbed.

4 Remove from the heat and remove and discard the bay leaves. Taste and adjust the seasoning, if necessary. Add the cashews and stir well. Serve hot.

crab fried rice

ingredients

SERVES 4

5$\frac{1}{2}$ oz/150 g long-grain rice

salt

2 tbsp peanut oil

125 g/4$\frac{1}{2}$ oz canned white
    crabmeat, drained

1 leek, sliced

150 g/5$\frac{1}{2}$ oz bean sprouts

2 eggs, beaten

1 tbsp light soy sauce

2 tsp lime juice

1 tsp sesame oil

sliced lime, to garnish

method

1 Cook the rice in a pan of lightly salted boiling water for 15 minutes. Drain, rinse under cold running water, and drain again.

2 Heat the oil in a preheated wok or large, heavy-bottom skillet until it is really hot. Add the crabmeat, leek, and bean sprouts to the wok or skillet and stir-fry for 2–3 minutes. Remove the mixture with a slotted spoon and set aside.

3 Add the eggs to the wok and cook, stirring occasionally, for 2–3 minutes, until they begin to set. Stir the rice and crabmeat mixture into the eggs in the wok.

4 Add the soy sauce and lime juice to the mixture in the wok. Cook for 1 minute, stirring to combine. Sprinkle with the sesame oil and toss lightly to mix. Garnish with sliced lime and serve.

tuna rice

ingredients

SERVES 4

3 tbsp peanut or corn oil

4 scallions, chopped

2 garlic cloves, finely chopped

7 oz/200 g canned tuna in oil,
    drained and flaked

6 oz/175 g frozen or canned
    corn kernels and bell
    peppers

5 cups cold boiled rice

2 tbsp Thai fish sauce

1 tbsp light soy sauce

salt and pepper

2 tbsp chopped fresh cilantro,
    to garnish

method

1 Heat the peanut oil in a preheated wok or large, heavy-bottomed skillet. Add the scallions and stir-fry for 2 minutes, then add the garlic and stir-fry for an additional 1 minute.

2 Add the tuna and the corn and bell peppers, and stir-fry for 2 minutes.

3 Add the rice, fish sauce, and soy sauce and stir-fry for 2 minutes. Season to taste with salt and pepper and serve immediately, garnished with chopped cilantro.

asian coconut rice

ingredients

SERVES 4

2 tbsp vegetable oil

1 onion, chopped

2 cups long-grain rice, rinsed
   and drained

1 tbsp freshly chopped
   lemongrass

2$\frac{1}{4}$ cups coconut milk

1$\frac{3}{4}$ cups water

6 tbsp flaked coconut, toasted

method

1 Heat the oil in a large pan over low heat, add the onion, and cook, stirring frequently, for 3 minutes. Add the rice and lemongrass and cook, stirring, for an additional 2 minutes.

2 Stir in the coconut milk and water and bring to a boil. Reduce the heat, cover, and let simmer for 20–25 minutes until all the liquid has been absorbed. If the rice grains have not cooked through, add a little more water and cook until tender and all the liquid has been absorbed.

3 Remove from the heat and add half the flaked coconut. Stir gently. Sprinkle over the remaining coconut flakes and serve.

jasmine rice with lemon & basil

ingredients

SERVES 4

14 oz/400 g jasmine rice

3 cups water

finely grated rind of $1/2$ lemon

2 tbsp shredded fresh basil,
  to serve

method

1 Wash the rice in several changes of cold water until the water runs clear. Bring the measured water to a boil in a large pan, then add the rice.

2 Return to a rolling boil. Turn the heat to a low simmer, then cover the pan and simmer for an additional 12 minutes. Remove the pan from the heat and let stand, covered, for 10 minutes.

3 Fluff up the rice with a fork, then stir in the lemon rind. Serve sprinkled with shredded basil.

gingerroot & sesame dipping sauce

ingredients

MAKES. 1/2 CUP

1 1/2-inch/4-cm piece very
    fresh gingerroot

4 tbsp Japanese soy sauce

2 tbsp mirin

2 tbsp sake

1/4 tsp sesame oil

1 tsp rice vinegar

method

1 Shred the gingerroot into a small bowl and then press the flesh with the back of a teaspoon. Pour off 1 tsp fresh gingerroot juice and discard the pulp.

2 Place the gingerroot juice in a small bowl, add the soy sauce, mirin, sake, sesame oil, and rice vinegar, and stir to combine. Serve straight away or keep in a sealed container in the refrigerator for up to a week.

ponzu dipping sauce

ingredients

MAKES ½ CUP

2 tbsp mirin

1½ tbsp rice vinegar

2 tsp light soy sauce

1½ tbsp bonito flakes

3 tbsp fresh lemon juice

method

1 Place all the ingredients in a small pan and bring to a boil. Remove from the heat and let cool before serving as a dipping sauce.

teriyaki dipping sauce

ingredients

MAKES ½ CUP

4 tbsp Japanese soy sauce

2 tbsp mirin

2 tbsp sake

2 tsp superfine sugar

1 tsp shredded gingerroot
   (optional)

1 garlic clove, crushed
   (optional)

method

1 Place the soy sauce, mirin, sake, and sugar in a small pan with the shredded gingerroot and crushed garlic, if using.

2 Set over low heat and stir until the sugar has dissolved. Heat for 15 minutes or until the sauce has thickened. Let cool before serving.

meat & poultry

Nowhere is the diversity of Asian cooking more apparent than in meat dishes. This is partly because of topography and partly a cultural difference. In some countries, such as China, pork is a favorite meat not least because hogs are economical to rear and cooks can use just about every part of them. However, in places where there is a large Muslim population, such as Indonesia, lamb or beef is preferred. Chicken dishes are found throughout Asia, simply because it is such a versatile meat, while the Chinese have made a specialty of preparing and cooking duck.

Southeast Asia is the natural habitat for many spices such as gingerroot and lemongrass, though, perhaps surprisingly, not chiles. Consequently, meat and poultry dishes are traditionally highly spiced—Thai curries and Indonesian satays are typical of the region. On the other hand, the Japanese, who were latecomers to cooking meat because of religious principles, have become masters of the subtle, aromatic marinade for pork, chicken, and beef. Frying is the keynote, although braising in flavored stock is also a favorite technique. Chinese meat and poultry dishes usually incorporate a wide range of other ingredients, including vegetables, shellfish, noodles, and flavorings such as hoisin and oyster sauce. Stir-frying is still the most

popular everyday cooking method with roasted and braised dishes reserved for special occasions. In short, you are sure to find dishes to suit all tastes and budgets in Asia's imaginative, varied, and delicious ways of preparing and cooking meat and poultry.

roast beef wraps with wasabi mayonnaise

ingredients

MAKES 6 PIECES

2 oz/55 g fresh daikon (long white radish), peeled

3 sheets of toasted nori

1/4 quantity freshly cooked sushi rice

2 oz/55 g mizuna greens

6 thin slices rare roast beef

wasabi mayonnaise

2 tbsp mayonnaise

1 tsp wasabi paste, or to taste

method

1 Shred the daikon using the finest setting on a mandolin. Alternatively, cut it into long thin slices and then cut each slice along its length as finely as possible. Rinse, drain, and then place in the refrigerator until needed.

2 Make the wasabi mayonnaise by combining the mayonnaise and wasabi paste in a bowl.

3 Fold a nori sheet in half lengthwise, press along the fold, and then tear it into 2 pieces.

4 Lay a half-sheet of nori smooth-side down on a work surface and place a heaping tbsp of rice on the left-hand side. Spread 1 tsp wasabi mayonnaise over the rice, then add a few mizuna greens and a sixth of the chilled shredded daikon. Roll up 1 slice of beef into a cone shape and place it on top.

5 Fold the bottom left-hand corner of the nori over the rice and filling, so that the folded edge forms a right angle with the bottom edge. Continue folding along that line to make a cone with a sharp point at the bottom. Place a drop of vinegared water on the underside of the join to seal it. Repeat with the rest of the ingredients to make 6 cones in total.

marinated beef with vegetables

ingredients

SERVES 4

1 lb 2 oz/500 g rump steak,
   cut into thin strips

3 tbsp sesame oil

1/2 tbsp cornstarch

1/2 tbsp soy sauce

1 head of broccoli,
   cut into florets

2 carrots, cut into thin strips

4 oz/125 g snow peas

1/2 cup beef stock

9 oz/250 g baby spinach,
   shredded

freshly cooked rice or noodles,
   to serve

marinade

1 tbsp dry sherry

1/2 tbsp soy sauce

1/2 tbsp cornstarch

1/2 tsp superfine sugar

2 garlic cloves, chopped finely

1 tbsp sesame oil

method

1 To make the marinade, mix the sherry, soy sauce, cornstarch, sugar, garlic, and sesame oil in a bowl. Add the beef to the mixture and cover with plastic wrap. Set aside to marinate for 30 minutes, then remove the beef and discard the marinade.

2 Heat 1 tablespoon of the sesame oil in a skillet or wok. Stir-fry the beef for 2 minutes until medium-rare. Remove from the skillet and set aside.

3 Combine the cornstarch and soy sauce in a bowl and set aside. Heat the remaining 2 tablespoons of sesame oil into the skillet, add the broccoli, carrots, and snow peas and stir-fry for 2 minutes.

4 Add the stock, cover the skillet, and steam for one minute. Stir in the spinach, beef, and the cornstarch mixture. Cook until the juices boil and thicken. Serve on a bed of freshly cooked rice or noodles.

beef chop suey

ingredients

SERVES 4

1 lb/450 g ribeye or sirloin
   steak, finely sliced
1 head of broccoli, cut into
   small florets
2 tbsp vegetable or peanut oil
1 onion, finely sliced
2 celery stalks, finely sliced
   diagonally
2 cups snow peas, sliced in
   half lengthwise
2 oz/55 g fresh or canned
   bamboo shoots, rinsed and
   julienned (if using fresh
   shoots, boil in water first for
   30 minutes)
8 water chestnuts, finely sliced
4 cups finely sliced
   mushrooms
1 tbsp oyster sauce
1 tsp salt

marinade
1 tbsp Shaoxing rice wine
pinch of white pepper
pinch of salt
1 tbsp light soy sauce
1/2 tsp sesame oil

method

1 Combine all the marinade ingredients in a bowl and marinate the beef for at least 20 minutes. Blanch the broccoli florets in a large pan of boiling water for 30 seconds. Drain and set aside.

2 In a preheated wok or deep pan, heat 1 tablespoon of the oil and stir-fry the beef until the color has changed. Remove and set aside.

3 In the clean wok or deep pan, heat the remaining oil and stir-fry the onion for 1 minute. Add the celery and broccoli and cook for 2 minutes. Add the snow peas, bamboo shoots, chestnuts, and mushrooms and cook for 1 minute. Add the beef, then season with the oyster sauce and salt and serve immediately.

hot sesame beef

ingredients

SERVES 4

1 lb 2 oz/500 g beef fillet,
    cut into thin strips

1¹/₂ tbsp sesame seeds

¹/₂ cup beef stock

2 tbsp soy sauce

2 tbsp grated fresh gingerroot

2 garlic cloves, chopped finely

1 tsp cornstarch

¹/₂ tsp chile flakes

3 tbsp sesame oil

1 large head of broccoli,
    cut into florets

1 orange bell pepper, sliced
    thinly

1 red chile, seeded and sliced
    finely

1 tbsp chili oil, to taste

1 tbsp chopped fresh cilantro,
    to garnish

method

1 Mix the beef strips with 1 tablespoon of the sesame seeds in a small bowl. In a separate bowl, whisk together the beef stock, soy sauce, gingerroot, garlic, cornstarch, and chile flakes.

2 Heat 1 tablespoon of the sesame oil in a large skillet or wok. Stir-fry the beef strips for 2–3 minutes. Remove and set aside.

3 Discard any oil left in the pan, then wipe with paper towels to remove any stray sesame seeds. Heat the remaining oil, add the broccoli, orange bell pepper, chile, and chili oil, if using, and stir-fry for 2–3 minutes. Stir in the beef stock mixture, cover, and let simmer for 2 minutes.

4 Return the beef to the skillet and let simmer until the juices thicken, stirring occasionally. Cook for another 1–2 minutes.

5 Sprinkle with the remaining sesame seeds. Serve garnished with chopped cilantro.

beef stir-fry

ingredients

SERVES 4

2 tbsp vegetable or peanut oil

2 medium red onions, sliced
    thinly

2 garlic cloves, chopped

1-inch/2.5-cm piece
    gingerroot, cut into
    thin sticks

2 beef fillets, 4 oz/115 g each,
    sliced thinly

1 green bell pepper, seeded
    and sliced

5¹/₂ oz/150 g canned bamboo
    shoots

4 oz/115 g bean sprouts

2 tbsp Thai magic paste
    (see below)

1 tbsp Thai red curry paste

handful of fresh cilantro,
    chopped

few sprigs Thai basil

boiled rice, to serve

thai magic paste

whole bulb of garlic, peeled

bunch of fresh cilantro
    leaves and roots, coarsely
    chopped

¹/₂ cup white peppercorns

method

1 To make the Thai magic paste, pulse all the ingredients briefly in a blender or food processor to form a thick paste, or pound with a pestle until well mixed. Store in the refrigerator for 3–4 days or freeze in small amounts.

2 Heat the oil in a wok and stir-fry the onions, garlic, and gingerroot for 1 minute.

3 Add the beef strips and stir-fry over high heat until browned all over.

4 Add the vegetables and the magic and curry pastes and cook for 2–3 minutes until blended and cooked.

5 Stir in the cilantro and basil and serve immediately with rice.

stir-fried beef with broccoli & gingerroot

ingredients

SERVES 4–6

12 oz/350 g tenderloin steak, cut into thin strips

1 medium head broccoli, cut into florets

2 tbsp vegetable or peanut oil

1 garlic clove, finely chopped

1 tsp finely chopped fresh gingerroot

1 small onion, finely sliced

1 tsp salt

1 tsp light soy sauce

marinade

1 tbsp light soy sauce

1 tsp sesame oil

1 tsp Shaoxing rice wine

1 tsp sugar

pinch of white pepper

method

1 Combine the marinade ingredients in a bowl, then mix in the beef. Cover and let stand for 1 hour, basting occasionally. Blanch the broccoli in a large pan of boiling water for 30 seconds. Drain and set aside.

2 In a preheated wok or deep pan, heat 1 tablespoon of the oil and stir-fry the garlic, gingerroot, and onion for 1 minute. Add the broccoli and stir-fry for an additional minute. Remove from the wok and set aside.

3 In the clean preheated wok or deep pan, heat the remaining oil and stir-fry the beef until it has changed color. Return the broccoli mixture to the pan with the salt and light soy sauce and stir until cooked through. Serve immediately.

stir-fried beef with bean sprouts

ingredients

SERVES 4

1 bunch of scallions

2 tbsp corn oil

1 garlic clove, crushed

1 tsp finely chopped fresh
     gingerroot

1 lb 2 oz/500 g lean beef fillet,
     cut into thin strips

1 large red bell pepper,
     seeded and sliced

1 small fresh red chile, seeded
     and chopped

3 cups fresh bean sprouts

1 small lemongrass stem,
     finely chopped

2 tbsp smooth peanut butter

4 tbsp coconut milk

1 tbsp rice vinegar or white
     wine vinegar

1 tbsp soy sauce

1 tsp brown sugar

9 oz/250 g medium egg
     noodles

salt and pepper

method

1 Thinly slice the scallions, reserving some slices to use as a garnish.

2 Heat the oil in a skillet or preheated wok over high heat. Add the scallions, garlic, and gingerroot and stir-fry for 2–3 minutes to soften. Add the beef and continue stir-frying for 4–5 minutes, or until evenly browned.

3 Add the bell pepper and stir-fry for an additional 3–4 minutes. Add the chile and bean sprouts and stir-fry for 2 minutes. Mix the lemongrass, peanut butter, coconut milk, rice vinegar, soy sauce, and sugar together in a bowl, then stir into the skillet.

4 Meanwhile, cook the egg noodles in boiling salted water for 4 minutes, or according to the package directions. Drain and stir into the skillet, tossing to mix evenly. Season to taste with salt and pepper. Sprinkle with the reserved scallions and serve hot.

gingerroot beef with yellow bell peppers

ingredients

SERVES 4

1 lb 2 oz/500 g beef fillet,
   cut into 1-inch/2.5-cm
   cubes
2 tsp peanut oil
2 garlic cloves, crushed
2 tbsp grated fresh gingerroot
pinch of chile flakes
2 yellow bell peppers, sliced
   thinly
4 1/2 oz/125 g baby corn
6 oz/175 g snow peas
hot noodles drizzled with
   sesame oil, to serve

marinade
2 tbsp soy sauce
2 tsp peanut oil
1 1/2 tsp superfine sugar
1 tsp cornstarch

method

1 To make the marinade, mix the soy sauce, peanut oil, sugar, and cornstarch in a bowl. Stir in the beef cubes, then cover with plastic wrap and set aside to marinate for 30 minutes.

2 Heat the peanut oil in a skillet or wok over medium heat. Add the garlic, gingerroot, and chile flakes and cook for 30 seconds. Stir in the yellow bell peppers and baby corn, and stir-fry for 2 minutes. Add the snow peas and cook for another minute.

3 Remove the vegetables from the skillet. Put the beef cubes and marinade into the skillet and stir-fry for 3–4 minutes or until cooked to taste. Return the vegetables to the skillet, mix well, and cook until all the ingredients are heated through. Remove from the heat and serve over noodles.

mussaman curry

ingredients

SERVES 4

1 tbsp vegetable or peanut oil

1 lb/450 g beef top round,
  cut into cubes

2 tbsp Mussaman curry paste

2 large onions, cut into
  wedges

2 large potatoes, cut into
  chunks

1³/₄ cups coconut milk

²/₃ cup water

2 cardamom pods

2 tbsp tamarind paste

2 tsp jaggery or soft light
  brown sugar

¹/₂ cup unsalted peanuts,
  toasted or dry-fried

1 fresh red chile, sliced thinly

boiled rice, to serve

method

1 Heat the oil in a wok and cook the meat, in batches, until browned all over. Remove with a slotted spoon and set aside.

2 Add the curry paste to the wok and stir-fry for 1–2 minutes. Add the onions and potatoes and stir-fry for 4–5 minutes, until golden brown. Remove with a slotted spoon and set aside.

3 Pour the coconut milk into the wok with the measured water and bring to a boil. Reduce the heat and let simmer for 8–10 minutes.

4 Return the meat and cooked vegetables to the wok. Add the cardamom, tamarind paste, and sugar, and let simmer for 15–20 minutes, until the meat is tender. Stir in the peanuts and chile and serve with rice.

spicy beef with potato

ingredients

SERVES 4

1 lb/450 g beef fillet

2 tbsp Thai soy sauce

2 tbsp fish sauce

2 tbsp vegetable or peanut oil

3–4 cilantro roots, chopped

1 tbsp crushed black
    peppercorns

2 garlic cloves, chopped

1 tbsp jaggery or soft light
    brown sugar

12 oz/350 g potatoes, diced

2/3 cup water

bunch of scallions, chopped

5 cups baby spinach leaves

cooked rice or noodles,
    to serve

method

1 Cut the beef into thick slices and place in a shallow dish. Put the soy sauce, fish sauce, 1 tablespoon of the oil, the cilantro roots, peppercorns, garlic, and sugar in a food processor and process to a thick paste. Scrape the paste into the dish and toss the beef to coat. Cover with plastic wrap and set aside to marinate in the refrigerator for at least 3 hours, and preferably overnight.

2 Heat the remaining oil in a wok. Lift the beef out of the marinade, reserving the marinade, and cook for 3–4 minutes on each side, until browned. Add the reserved marinade and the potatoes with the measured water and gradually bring to a boil. Let simmer for 6–8 minutes, or until the potatoes are tender.

3 Add the scallions and spinach. Cook gently until the greens have wilted. Serve immediately with rice or noodles.

beef with onions & broccoli

ingredients

SERVES 4

2 tbsp vegetable or peanut oil

2 tbsp Thai green curry paste

2 sirlion steaks, 6 oz/175 g
   each, sliced thinly

2 onions, sliced

6 scallions, chopped

2 shallots, chopped finely

1 medium head broccoli,
   cut into florets

1³/₄ cups coconut milk

3 kaffir lime leaves, chopped
   coarsely

4 tbsp chopped fresh cilantro

few Thai basil leaves

method

1 Heat the oil in a wok and stir-fry the curry paste for 1–2 minutes. Add the meat, in batches if necessary, and stir-fry until starting to brown.

2 Add the onions, scallions, and shallots, and stir-fry for 2–3 minutes. Add the broccoli and stir-fry for 2–3 minutes.

3 Pour in the coconut milk, add the lime leaves, and bring to a boil. Let simmer gently for 8–10 minutes, until the meat is tender. Stir in the cilantro and basil and serve immediately.

ma po doufu

ingredients

SERVES 4

1 lb/450 g bean curd

2 tbsp vegetable or peanut oil

1 tsp Sichuan peppers

3$^{1}/_{2}$ oz/100 g ground beef

2 tbsp chili bean sauce

1 tsp fermented black beans,
    rinsed and lightly mashed

scant ½ cup hot chicken stock

pinch of sugar

1 tsp light soy sauce

pinch of salt

2 tbsp thinly sliced scallion,
    cut on the diagonal

method

1 Cut the bean curd into ³/4-inch/2-cm cubes and arrange in a large pan. Pour over enough boiling water to cover and let rest.

2 In a preheated wok, heat the oil until almost smoking. Throw in the Sichuan peppers and stir until fragrant. Add the beef and stir-fry until brown and crispy.

3 Lower the heat and add the chili bean sauce and black beans and stir for about 30 seconds, or until the oil is richly red.

4 Pour in the hot chicken stock and gently add the drained bean curd. Season with the sugar, light soy sauce, and salt. Simmer for about 5 minutes.

5 Finally, toss in the scallion. Transfer into 1 large or 4 individual bowls and serve.

beef noodles with oyster sauce

ingredients

SERVES 4

10^1/2 oz/300 g boneless sirloin steak, thinly sliced

9 oz/250 g dried thick Chinese egg noodles

2 tbsp peanut or corn oil

8 oz/225 g fresh asparagus spears, woody ends cut off and chopped

2 large garlic cloves, finely chopped

^{1}/2-inch/1-cm piece fresh gingerroot, peeled and finely chopped

^{1}/2 red onion, thinly sliced

4 tbsp beef or vegetable stock

1^1/2 tbsp rice wine

2–3 tbsp bottled oyster sauce

toasted sesame seeds, to garnish

marinade

1 tbsp light soy sauce

1 tsp toasted sesame oil

2 tsp rice wine

method

1 To make the marinade, stir the ingredients together in a nonmetallic bowl. Stir in the steak so all the slices are coated, then set aside to marinate for at least 15 minutes.

2 Meanwhile, boil the noodles in a pan of boiling water for 4 minutes, or according to the package instructions, until soft. Drain, rinse, and drain again, then set aside.

3 When you are ready to stir-fry, heat a wok or large skillet over high heat. Add 1 tablespoon of the oil and heat. Add the asparagus and stir-fry for 1 minute. Tip the beef and marinade into the wok, standing back because it will splutter, and continue stir-frying until the beef is cooked to your taste, about 1^1/2 minutes for medium. Remove the beef and asparagus from the wok and set aside.

4 Heat the remaining oil and stir-fry the garlic, gingerroot, and onion for about 1 minute, until the onion is soft. Add the stock, rice wine, and oyster sauce and bring to a boil, stirring. Return the beef and asparagus to the wok, along with the noodles. Use 2 forks to mix all the ingredients together and stir around until the noodles are hot. Sprinkle with toasted sesame seeds.

beef chow mein

ingredients

SERVES 4

10 oz/280 g tenderloin steak,
    cut into slivers

8 oz/225 g dried egg noodles

2 tbsp vegetable or peanut oil

1 onion, finely sliced

1 green bell pepper, finely
    sliced

5 oz/140 g bean sprouts,
    trimmed

1 tsp salt

pinch of sugar

2 tsp Shaoxing rice wine

2 tbsp light soy sauce

1 tbsp dark soy sauce

1 tbsp finely shredded scallion

marinade

1 tsp light soy sauce

dash of sesame oil

$1/2$ tsp Shaoxing rice wine

pinch of white pepper

method

1 Combine all the marinade ingredients in a bowl and marinate the beef for at least 20 minutes.

2 Cook the noodles according to the directions on the package. When cooked, rinse under cold water and set aside.

3 In a preheated wok, heat the oil and stir-fry the beef for about 1 minute, or until the meat has changed color, then add the onion and cook for 1 minute, followed by the bell pepper and bean sprouts. Evaporate off any water from the vegetables. Add the salt, sugar, Shaoxing, and soy sauces. Stir in the noodles and toss for 1 minute. Finally, stir in the scallion and serve.

rice sticks with beef in black bean sauce

ingredients

SERVES 4–6

8 oz/225 g rump steak, finely sliced

8 oz/225 g rice sticks

2–3 tbsp vegetable or peanut oil

1 small onion, finely sliced

1 green bell pepper, finely sliced

1 red bell pepper, finely sliced

2 tbsp black bean sauce

2–3 tbsp light soy sauce

marinade

1 tbsp dark soy sauce

1 tsp Shaoxing rice wine

1/2 tsp sugar

1/2 tsp white pepper

method

1 Combine all the marinade ingredients in a bowl, add the beef, and let marinate for at least 20 minutes.

2 Cook the rice sticks according to the directions on the package. When cooked, drain and set aside.

3 In a preheated wok or deep pan, heat the oil and stir-fry the beef for 1 minute, or until the meat has changed color. Drain the meat and set aside.

4 Pour off any excess oil from the wok and stir-fry the onion and bell peppers for 1 minute. Add the black bean sauce and stir well, then pour in the light soy sauce. Toss the rice sticks in the vegetables and when fully incorporated, add the beef and stir until warmed through. Serve immediately.

red-hot beef with cashew nuts

ingredients

SERVES 4

1 lb 2 oz/500 g lean boneless
    beef sirloin
1 tsp vegetable oil

marinade
1 tbsp sesame seeds
1 garlic clove, chopped
1 tbsp finely chopped fresh
    gingerroot
1 fresh red Thai chile,
    chopped
2 tbsp dark soy sauce
1 tsp Thai red curry paste

to finish
1 tsp sesame oil
4 tbsp unsalted cashew nuts
1 scallion, thickly sliced
    diagonally
cucumber slices, to garnish

method

1 Using a sharp knife, cut the beef into
1/2-inch/1-cm wide strips. Place them in a
large, nonmetallic bowl.

2 To make the marinade, toast the sesame
seeds in a heavy-bottom skillet over medium
heat for 2–3 minutes, or until golden brown,
shaking the skillet occasionally.

3 Place the seeds in a mortar with the garlic,
gingerroot, and chile and, using a pestle, grind
to a smooth paste. Add the soy sauce and curry
paste and mix well.

4 Spoon the paste over the beef strips and
toss to coat the meat evenly. Cover and let
marinate in the refrigerator for at least
2–3 hours or overnight.

5 Heat a heavy-bottom skillet or ridged grill
pan until very hot and brush with vegetable
oil. Place the beef strips in the skillet and cook
quickly, turning frequently, until lightly browned.
Remove the skillet from the heat and spoon the
beef into a pile on a hot serving dish.

6 Heat the sesame oil in a small skillet. Add
the cashew nuts and quickly cook until golden.
Add the scallion and stir-fry for 30 seconds.
Sprinkle the mixture on top of the beef strips,
then garnish with cucumber slices and serve
immediately.

hot beef & coconut curry

ingredients

SERVES 4

1³/₄ cups coconut milk

2 tbsp Thai red curry paste

2 garlic cloves, crushed

1 lb 2 oz/500 g braising steak

2 fresh kaffir lime leaves,
   shredded

3 tbsp lime juice

2 tbsp Thai fish sauce

1 large fresh red chile, seeded
   and sliced

¹/₂ tsp ground turmeric

salt and pepper

2 tbsp chopped fresh basil
   leaves

2 tbsp chopped cilantro leaves

shredded coconut, to garnish

freshly cooked rice, to serve

method

1 Place the coconut milk in a large pan and bring to a boil. Reduce the heat and simmer gently for 10 minutes, or until it has thickened. Stir in the curry paste and garlic and simmer for an additional 5 minutes.

2 Cut the beef into ³/₄-inch/2-cm chunks. Add to the pan and bring to a boil, stirring constantly. Reduce the heat and add the kaffir lime leaves, lime juice, fish sauce, sliced chile, turmeric, and ¹/₂ teaspoon of salt.

3 Cover the pan and continue simmering for 20–25 minutes, or until the meat is tender, adding a little water if the sauce looks too dry.

4 Stir in the basil and cilantro and season to taste with salt and pepper. Sprinkle with shredded coconut and serve with freshly cooked rice.

egg-fried rice with seven-spice beef

ingredients

SERVES 4

8 oz/225 g long-grain white
    rice
2¹/₂ cups water
12 oz/350 g beef tenderloin
2 tbsp dark soy sauce
2 tbsp ketchup
1 tbsp seven-spice seasoning
2 tbsp peanut oil
1 onion, diced
3 small carrots, diced
generous ³/₄ cup frozen peas
2 eggs, beaten
2 tbsp cold water

method

1 Rinse the rice under cold running water, then drain thoroughly. Place the rice in a pan with the water, bring to a boil, cover, and let simmer for 12 minutes. Turn the cooked rice out onto a cookie sheet and let cool.

2 Using a sharp knife, thinly slice the beef tenderloin and place in a large, shallow dish. Mix the soy sauce, ketchup, and seven-spice seasoning. Spoon over the beef and toss well to coat.

3 Heat the peanut oil in a preheated wok. Add the beef and stir-fry for 3–4 minutes. Add the onion, carrots, and peas and stir-fry for an additional 2–3 minutes. Add the cooked rice to the wok and mix together.

4 Beat the eggs with 2 tablespoons of cold water. Drizzle the egg mixture over the rice and stir-fry for 3–4 minutes, or until the rice is heated through and the egg has set. Transfer the rice and beef to a warm serving bowl and serve immediately.

beef with fresh noodles

ingredients

SERVES 4

6 dried black cloud Chinese
    mushrooms
2 tbsp vegetable or peanut oil
2 sirloin steaks, 8 oz/225 g
    each, sliced thickly
1 onion, cut into thin wedges
2 garlic cloves, chopped
1 green bell pepper, seeded
    and chopped
3 celery stalks, sliced
2 tbsp Thai green curry paste
1¼ cups beef stock
4 tbsp black bean sauce
8 oz/225 g fresh egg noodles
4 tbsp chopped fresh parsley

method

1 Put the dried mushrooms in a bowl, cover with boiling water, and let soak for 30 minutes. Drain, then break up any larger pieces.

2 Heat the oil in a wok and stir-fry the steak over high heat until browned. Add the mushrooms, onion, garlic, bell pepper, and celery, and stir-fry for 3–4 minutes. Add the curry paste, beef stock, and black bean sauce, and stir-fry for 2–3 minutes.

3 Meanwhile, cook the noodles in boiling water for 3–4 minutes, drain well, and stir into the wok. Sprinkle the parsley over and stir. Serve immediately.

dan dan mian

ingredients

SERVES 4

1 tbsp vegetable or peanut oil

1 large dried chile, seeded
    and snipped into 3 pieces

1/2 tsp Sichuan peppers

31/2 oz/100 g ground beef

2 tsp light soy sauce

101/2 oz/300 g fine white
    noodles

1 tbsp roasted peanuts,
    chopped

s a u c e

1 tbsp preserved vegetables

1/2 tsp Sichuan peppers, lightly
    roasted and crushed

scant 1/2 cup chicken stock

1 tsp black Chinese vinegar

1 tsp chili oil

1 tsp dark soy sauce

1 tbsp light soy sauce

1 tbsp sesame paste

few drops of sesame oil

2 scallions, finely chopped

method

1 Heat the oil in a preheated wok and toss in the chile and peppers, then add the meat and stir rapidly. When the meat has changed color, add the light soy sauce and continue to cook until the meat is well browned. Carefully mix the sauce ingredients together and pour into 4 noodle bowls.

2 Cook the noodles according to the directions on the package. When cooked, drain and divide among the bowls.

3 Top with the meat mixture, then sprinkle with the roasted peanuts and serve at once. Mix well before eating.

chirashi sushi with soy-glazed steak

ingredients

SERVES 4

8 dried shiitake mushrooms

2-inch/5-cm piece of daikon (long white radish), peeled

2-inch/5-cm piece of carrot, peeled

1 tbsp soy sauce

1 tsp mirin

1 tsp brown sugar

7 oz/200 g tenderloin steak, trimmed

1 quantity freshly cooked sushi rice

2 tsp wasabi paste

1 sheet of toasted nori, cut into strips

pickled gingerroot, to serve

method

1 Soak the mushrooms in boiling water for 20 minutes, then simmer them in the same liquid for 3 minutes. Lift them out and squeeze them dry. Chop 4 mushrooms finely and halve the rest.

2 Shred the daikon and carrot using the finest setting on a mandolin or a very sharp knife. If you are using a knife, then cut the daikon and carrot into long, thin slices and cut each slice along its length as finely as you can. Rinse, drain, and refrigerate.

3 Preheat the broiler to its highest setting. Mix together the soy sauce, mirin, and brown sugar, then brush the mixture all over the steak. Broil the coated steak for 3 minutes on each side. Let it rest for a minute, then cut into strips.

4 Mix the sushi rice with the chopped shiitake mushrooms. Divide the mushroom rice between 4 serving bowls and arrange the broiled steak and halved mushrooms on top. Add a neat pile of shredded daikon and carrot to each bowl, together with 1/2 tsp of the wasabi. Garnish each bowl with nori strips, and serve with pickled gingerroot on the side.

spicy sichuan pork

ingredients

SERVES 4

10 oz/280 g pork belly, thinly
   sliced

1 tbsp vegetable or peanut oil

1 tbsp chili bean sauce

1 tbsp fermented black beans,
   rinsed and lightly mashed

1 tsp sweet red bean paste
   (optional)

1 green bell pepper, finely
   sliced

1 red bell pepper, finely sliced

1 tsp sugar

1 tsp dark soy sauce

pinch of white pepper

method

1 Bring a pan of water to a boil and place the pork slices in the pan, then cover and let simmer for about 20 minutes, skimming occasionally. Let the pork cool and rest before slicing thinly.

2 In a preheated wok or deep pan, heat the oil and stir-fry the pork slices until they begin to shrink. Stir in the chili bean sauce, then add the black beans and the red bean paste, if using. Finally, toss in the bell peppers and the remaining ingredients and stir-fry for a couple of minutes.

sichuan-style pork & bell pepper

ingredients

SERVES 4

1 lb 2 oz/500 g pork
    tenderloin, cubed
2 tbsp cornstarch
3 tbsp soy sauce
1 tbsp white wine vinegar
scant 1½ cups water
2 tbsp peanut oil
2 leeks, sliced thinly
1 red bell pepper, cut into thin
    strips
1 zucchini, cut into thin strips
1 carrot, cut into thin strips
pinch of salt
freshly cooked white and wild
    rice, to serve

marinade
1 tbsp soy sauce
pinch of chile flakes

method

1 To make the marinade, mix the soy sauce and chile flakes in a bowl. Add the pork cubes and toss to coat. Cover with plastic wrap and let stand for 30 minutes.

2 Combine the cornstarch, soy sauce, and white wine vinegar in a small bowl. Stir in the water gradually, then set aside.

3 Heat 1 tablespoon of the oil in a wok or skillet. Add the pork and marinade mixture and stir-fry for 2–3 minutes. Remove the pork from the skillet with a slotted spoon and set aside.

4 Heat the remaining oil in the skillet, add the leeks and red bell pepper, and stir-fry for 2 minutes. Then add the zucchini, carrot, and salt and stir-fry for an additional 2 minutes.

5 Stir in the pork and the cornstarch mixture and bring to a boil, stirring constantly until the sauce thickens. Remove from the heat and serve immediately with freshly cooked white and wild rice.

ants climbing a tree

ingredients

SERVES 4

9 oz/250 g dried thick rice
   noodles

1 tbsp cornstarch

3 tbsp soy sauce

1½ tbsp rice wine

1½ tsp sugar

1½ tsp toasted sesame oil

12 oz/350 g/lean fresh ground
   pork

1½ tbsp peanut or toasted
   sesame oil

2 large garlic cloves, finely
   chopped

1 large fresh red chile,
   or to taste, seeded and
   thinly sliced

3 scallions, finely chopped

finely chopped fresh cilantro
   or parsley, to garnish

method

1 Soak the rice noodles in enough lukewarm water to cover for 20 minutes, until soft, or cook according to the package instructions. Drain well and set aside.

2 Meanwhile, put the cornstarch in another large bowl, then stir in the soy sauce, rice wine, sugar, and sesame oil, stirring so that no lumps form. Add the ground pork and use your hands to toss the ingredients together without squeezing the pork; set aside to marinate for 10 minutes.

3 Heat a wok or large skillet over high heat. Add the oil and heat until it shimmers. Add the garlic, chile, and scallions and stir around for about 30 seconds. Tip in the ground pork together with any marinade left in the bowl and stir-fry for about 5 minutes, or until the pork is no longer pink. Add the noodles and use 2 forks to mix together. Sprinkle with the chopped herbs and serve.

pork lo mein

ingredients

SERVES 4–6

6 oz/175 g boneless lean pork,
　shredded
8 oz/225 g egg noodles
1½ tbsp vegetable or
　peanut oil
2 tsp finely chopped garlic
1 tsp finely chopped fresh
　gingerroot
1 carrot, julienned
4 cups finely sliced
　mushrooms
1 green bell pepper,
　thinly sliced
1 tsp salt
½ cup hot chicken soup
7 oz/200 g bean sprouts,
　trimmed
2 tbsp finely chopped scallions

m a r i n a d e
1 tsp light soy sauce
dash of sesame oil
pinch of white pepper

method

1 Combine all the marinade ingredients in a bowl, add the pork, and let marinate for at least 20 minutes.

2 Cook the noodles according to the package instructions. When cooked, drain and set aside.

3 In a preheated wok or deep pan, heat 1 teaspoon of the oil and stir-fry the pork until it has changed color. Remove and set aside.

4 In the clean wok or pan, heat the remaining oil and stir-fry the garlic and gingerroot until fragrant. Add the carrot and cook for 1 minute, then add the mushrooms and cook for an additional 1 minute. Toss in the bell pepper and cook for 1 minute more. Add the pork, salt, and stock and heat through. Finally, toss in the noodles, followed by the bean sprouts, and stir well. Sprinkle with the scallions and serve.

singapore noodles

ingredients

SERVES 4

7 oz/200 g dried rice vermicelli noodles

1 tbsp mild, medium, or hot curry paste, to taste

1 tsp ground turmeric

6 tbsp water

2 tbsp peanut or corn oil

1/2 onion, very thinly sliced

2 large garlic cloves, thinly sliced

1/2 medium head broccoli, cut into very small florets

3 oz/85 g green beans, trimmed, and cut into 1-inch/2.5-cm pieces

3 oz/85 g pork tenderloin, cut in half lengthwise, and then into thin strips, or skinless, boneless chicken breast, thinly sliced

3 oz/85 g small cooked shelled shrimp, thawed if frozen

2/3 cup thinly shredded Chinese cabbage or romaine lettuce

1/4 Thai chile, or to taste, seeded and thinly sliced

2 scallions, light green parts only, thinly shredded

fresh cilantro, to garnish

method

1 Soak the noodles in enough lukewarm water to cover for 20 minutes, or according to the package instructions, until soft. Drain and set aside until required. While the noodles are soaking, put the curry paste and turmeric in a small bowl and stir in 4 tablespoons of the water, then set aside.

2 Heat a wok or large skillet over high heat. Add the oil and heat until it shimmers. Add the onion and garlic and stir-fry for 1 minute, or until the onion softens. Add the broccoli florets and beans to the wok with the remaining 2 tablespoons water and continue stir-frying for 2 minutes. Add the pork and stir-fry for 1 more minute. Add the shrimp, cabbage, and chile to the wok and continue stir-frying for an additional 2 minutes, until the meat is cooked through and the vegetables are tender, but still with a little bite. Scoop out of the wok and keep warm.

3 Add the scallions, noodles, and curry paste mixture to the wok. Use 2 forks to mix the noodles and onions together, and continue stir-frying for about 2 minutes, until the noodles are hot and have picked up a dark golden color from the turmeric. Return the other ingredients to the wok and continue stir-frying and mixing for 1 minute. Garnish with fresh cilantro.

sour-&-spicy pork

ingredients

SERVES 4

2 oz/55 g dried Chinese
    cloud ear mushrooms,
    soaked in boiling water
    for 20 minutes

3¹/₂ oz/100 g baby corn,
    halved lengthwise

2 tbsp honey

1 tbsp tamarind paste

4 tbsp boiling water

2 tbsp dark soy sauce

1 tbsp rice vinegar

2 tbsp peanut or corn oil

1 large garlic clove, very finely
    chopped

¹/₂-inch/1-cm piece fresh
    gingerroot, peeled and very
    finely chopped

¹/₂ tsp dried red pepper flakes,
    or to taste

12 oz/350 g pork tenderloin,
    thinly sliced

4 scallions, thickly sliced
    diagonally

1 green bell pepper, cored,
    seeded, and sliced

9 oz/250 g fresh Hokkien
    noodles

chopped fresh cilantro,
    to garnish

method

1 Drain the mushrooms well, then cut off and discard any thick stems, and slice the cups if they are large. Meanwhile, bring a large pan of lightly salted water to a boil, add the baby corn, and blanch for 3 minutes. Drain the corn and run them under cold running water to stop the cooking, then set aside.

2 Put the honey and tamarind paste in a small bowl and stir in the water, stirring until the paste dissolves. Then stir in the soy sauce and rice vinegar and set aside.

3 Heat a wok or large skillet over high heat. Add 1 tablespoon of the oil and heat until it shimmers. Add the garlic, gingerroot, and red pepper flakes and stir-fry for about 30 seconds. Add the pork and continue stir-frying for 2 minutes.

4 Add the remaining oil to the wok and heat. Add the scallions, bell pepper, mushrooms, and baby corn, along with the tamarind mixture, and stir-fry for an additional 2–3 minutes, until the pork is cooked through and the vegetables are tender, but still firm to the bite. Add the noodles and use 2 forks to mix all the ingredients together. When the noodles and sauce are hot, sprinkle with cilantro.

hoisin pork with garlic noodles

ingredients

SERVES 4

9 oz/250 g dried thick Chinese
   egg noodles, or Chinese
   whole wheat egg noodles
1 lb/450 g pork tenderloin,
   thinly sliced
1 tsp sugar
1 tbsp peanut or corn oil
4 tbsp rice vinegar
4 tbsp white wine vinegar
4 tbsp bottled hoisin sauce
2 scallions, sliced diagonally
about 2 tbsp garlic-flavored
   corn oil
2 large garlic cloves, thinly
   sliced

method

1 Cook the noodles in a pan of boiling water for 3 minutes, or according to the package instructions, until soft. Drain well, rinse under cold water to stop the cooking, and drain again, then set aside.

2 Sprinkle the pork slices with the sugar and use your hands to toss together. Heat a wok or large skillet over high heat. Add the oil and heat until it shimmers. Add the pork and stir-fry for about 3 minutes, until the pork is cooked through and is no longer pink. Use a slotted spoon to remove the pork from the wok and keep warm. Add both vinegars to the wok and boil until they are reduced to about 5 tablespoons. Pour in the hoisin sauce with the scallions and let bubble until reduced by half. Add to the pork and stir together.

3 Quickly wipe out the wok and reheat. Add the garlic-flavored oil and heat until it shimmers. Add the garlic slices and stir around for about 30 seconds, until they are golden and crisp, then use a slotted spoon to scoop them out of the wok and set aside.

4 Add the noodles to the wok and stir to warm through. Divide the noodles among 4 plates, top with the pork and onion mixture, and sprinkle with cooked garlic slices.

katsudon

ingredients

SERVES 4

4 tbsp all-purpose flour
1 egg, lightly beaten
4 oz/115 g Tonkatsu (panko)
    breadcrumbs
4 pork chops, about
    5^1/$_2$ oz/150 g each,
    bones removed
oil, for pan-frying
2^1/$_2$ cups dashi stock
4 tbsp shoyu (Japanese
    soy sauce)
2 tbsp mirin
1 onion, sliced
4 eggs
3 cups cooked Japanese
    short-grain rice

method

1 Put the flour, egg, and breadcrumbs separately into 3 shallow bowls large enough to fit a pork chop. Roll a rolling pin over each chop to thin it a little.

2 Dip each chop first in the flour, then in the egg, and finally in the breadcrumbs to coat. Cover with plastic wrap and let chill in the refrigerator for 10 minutes, then dip again in the egg and breadcrumbs.

3 Preheat a wok over high heat. Add oil to a depth of about ^{3}/$_4$ inch/2 cm and heat until very hot. Add the chops, one at a time, reduce the heat to medium, and cook for 4 minutes on each side, or until the pork is cooked through and the breadcrumbs are golden. Remove and slice.

4 Meanwhile, put the stock, soy sauce, and mirin in a pan and bring to a simmer. Add the onion and let simmer for 5 minutes. Beat the eggs in a bowl, then pour over the onions in the stock. Cover and cook for 1 minute.

5 Divide the rice between 4 bowls. Lay the pork slices on top, then ladle some of the egg, onion, and stock over the pork and rice. Serve immediately.

fried rice with pork & shrimp

ingredients

SERVES 4

3 tsp vegetable or peanut oil

1 egg, lightly beaten

3$\frac{1}{2}$ oz/100 g shrimp, shelled, deveined and cut into 2 pieces

3$\frac{1}{2}$ oz/100 g cha siu (roast honeyed pork), finely chopped

2 tbsp finely chopped scallions

1$\frac{1}{2}$ cups cooked rice, chilled

1 tsp salt

method

1 In a preheated wok or deep pan, heat 1 teaspoon of the oil and pour in the egg. Cook until scrambled. Remove and set aside.

2 Add the remaining oil and stir-fry the shrimp, cha siu, and scallions for about 2 minutes. Add the rice and salt, breaking up the rice into grains, and cook for an additional 2 minutes. Finally, stir in the cooked egg. Serve immediately.

red curry pork with bell peppers

ingredients

SERVES 4

2 tbsp vegetable or peanut oil

1 onion, coarsely chopped

2 garlic cloves, chopped

1 lb/450 g pork tenderloin,
    sliced thickly

1 red bell pepper, seeded and
    cut into squares

6 oz/175 g mushrooms,
    quartered

2 tbsp Thai red curry paste

4 oz/115 g block creamed
    coconut, chopped

1¼ cups pork or vegetable
    stock

2 tbsp Thai soy sauce

4 tomatoes, peeled, seeded,
    and chopped

handful of fresh cilantro,
    chopped

boiled noodles or rice, to serve

method

1 Heat the oil in a wok or large skillet and sauté the onion and garlic for 1–2 minutes, until they are softened but not browned.

2 Add the pork slices and stir-fry for 2–3 minutes until browned all over. Add the bell pepper, mushrooms, and curry paste.

3 Dissolve the coconut in the hot stock and add to the wok with the soy sauce. Bring to a boil and let simmer for 4–5 minutes until the liquid has reduced and thickened.

4 Add the tomatoes and cilantro and cook for 1–2 minutes before serving with noodles or rice.

pad thai

ingredients

SERVES 4

8 oz/225 g thick rice-stick
  noodles
2 tbsp vegetable or peanut oil
2 garlic cloves, chopped
2 fresh red chiles, seeded and
  chopped
6 oz/175 g pork tenderloin,
  sliced thinly
4 oz/115 g shrimp, shelled
  and chopped
8 fresh Chinese chives,
  chopped
2 tbsp fish sauce
juice of 1 lime
2 tsp jaggery or soft light
  brown sugar
2 eggs, beaten
3/4 cup bean sprouts
4 tbsp chopped fresh cilantro
3/4 cup unsalted peanuts,
  chopped, plus extra
  to serve
crispy fried onions, to serve

method

1 Soak the noodles in warm water for
10 minutes, drain well, and set aside.

2 Heat the oil in a wok and stir-fry the
garlic, chiles, and pork for 2–3 minutes.
Add the shrimp and stir-fry for an additional
2–3 minutes.

3 Add the chives and noodles, then cover and
cook for 1–2 minutes. Add the fish sauce,
lime juice, sugar, and eggs. Cook, stirring and
tossing constantly to mix in the eggs.

4 Stir in the bean sprouts, cilantro, and
peanuts, and serve with small dishes of crispy
fried onions and extra chopped peanuts.

pork with vegetables

ingredients

SERVES 4

8 tbsp vegetable or peanut oil

4 oz/115 g rice vermicelli
    noodles

4 belly pork strips, sliced
    thickly

1 red onion, sliced

2 garlic cloves, chopped

1-inch/2.5-cm piece fresh
    gingerroot, sliced thinly

1 large fresh red chile, seeded
    and chopped

4 oz/115 g baby corn, halved
    lengthwise

1 red bell pepper, seeded and
    sliced

1 medium head broccoli,
    cut into florets

$5^{1}/_{2}$ oz/150 g black bean
    sauce

$^{3}/_{4}$ cup bean sprouts

method

1 Heat the oil in a wok and cook the rice noodles, in batches, for 15–20 seconds, until they puff up. Remove with a slotted spoon, drain on paper towels, and set aside.

2 Pour off all but 2 tablespoons of the oil and stir-fry the pork, onion, garlic, gingerroot, and chile for 4–5 minutes, or until the meat has browned.

3 Add the corn, red bell pepper, and broccoli and stir-fry for 3–4 minutes, until the vegetables are just tender. Stir in the black bean sauce and bean sprouts, then cook for an additional 2–3 minutes. Serve immediately, topped with the crispy noodles.

pork with bell peppers

ingredients

SERVES 4

1 tbsp vegetable or peanut oil

1 tbsp chili oil

1 lb/450 g pork tenderloin,
    sliced thinly

2 tbsp green chili sauce

6 scallions, sliced

1-inch/2.5-cm piece fresh
    gingerroot, sliced thinly

1 red bell pepper, seeded
    and sliced

1 yellow bell pepper, seeded
    and sliced

1 orange bell pepper, seeded
    and sliced

1 tbsp fish sauce

2 tbsp Thai soy sauce

juice of $1/2$ lime

4 tbsp chopped fresh parsley

cooked flat rice noodles,
    to serve

method

1 Heat both the oils in a wok. Add the pork, in batches, and stir-fry until browned all over. Remove with a slotted spoon and set aside.

2 Add the chili sauce, scallions, and gingerroot to the wok and stir-fry for 1–2 minutes. Add the bell peppers and stir–fry for 2–3 minutes.

3 Return the meat to the wok, stir well, and add the fish sauce, soy sauce, and lime juice. Cook for an additional 1–2 minutes, then stir in the parsley and serve with flat rice noodles.

spicy fried ground pork

ingredients

SERVES 4

2 tbsp corn oil

2 garlic cloves

3 shallots

1-inch/2.5-cm piece fresh
gingerroot

1 lb 2 oz/500 g ground lean
pork

2 tbsp Thai fish sauce

1 tbsp dark soy sauce

1 tbsp Thai red curry paste

4 dried kaffir lime leaves,
crumbled

4 plum tomatoes, chopped

3 tbsp chopped cilantro

salt and pepper

freshly cooked fine egg
noodles, to serve

cilantro sprigs and scallion
tassels, to garnish

method

1 Heat the oil in a large skillet or preheated wok over medium heat. Add the garlic, shallots, and gingerroot and stir-fry for 2 minutes. Stir in the pork and continue stir-frying until golden brown.

2 Stir in the fish sauce, soy sauce, curry paste, and lime leaves and stir-fry for an additional 1–2 minutes over high heat.

3 Add the chopped tomatoes and cook for an additional 5–6 minutes, stirring occasionally. Stir in the chopped cilantro and season to taste with salt and pepper.

4 Serve hot, spooned onto freshly cooked fine egg noodles, garnished with cilantro sprigs and scallion tassels.

five-spice crispy pork with egg-fried rice

ingredients

SERVES 4

9^1/$_2$ oz/275 g long-grain white
   rice
2^1/$_2$ cups cold water
salt and pepper
12 oz/350 g pork tenderloin
2 tsp Chinese five-spice
   powder
4 tbsp cornstarch
3 extra-large eggs
2 tbsp raw brown sugar
2 tbsp corn oil
1 onion, chopped
2 garlic cloves, minced
1 large carrot, diced
1 red bell pepper, seeded and
   diced
1 cup peas
1 tbsp butter

method

1 Rinse the rice in a strainer under cold running water. Place in a large pan, add the cold water and a pinch of salt. Bring to a boil, cover, then reduce the heat, and let simmer for about 9 minutes, or until all of the liquid has been absorbed and the rice is tender.

2 Meanwhile, slice the pork into very thin, even-size pieces, using a sharp knife or meat cleaver. Set aside.

3 Stir together the Chinese five-spice powder, cornstarch, 1 egg, and the raw brown sugar. Toss the pork in the mixture until coated.

4 Heat the oil in a preheated wok or skillet. Add the pork and cook over high heat until the pork is cooked through and crispy. Remove the pork from the wok or skillet with a slotted spoon and keep warm.

5 Add the onion, garlic, carrot, bell pepper, and peas to the wok or skillet and stir-fry for 5 minutes. Return the pork to the wok, together with the cooked rice, and stir-fry for 5 minutes.

6 Heat the butter in a skillet. Beat the remaining eggs, add to the skillet, and cook until set. Turn out onto a clean board and slice thinly. Toss the strips of egg into the rice mixture and serve immediately.

spareribs in a sweet-&-sour sauce

ingredients

SERVES 4

1 lb/450 g spareribs, cut into
   bite-size pieces (you or
   your butcher can cut ribs
   into pieces with a cleaver)
vegetable or peanut oil,
   for deep-frying

marinade
2 tsp light soy sauce
1/2 tsp salt
pinch of white pepper

sauce
3 tbsp white rice vinegar
2 tbsp sugar
1 tbsp light soy sauce
1 tbsp ketchup
1 1/2 tbsp vegetable or
   peanut oil
1 green bell pepper, coarsely
   chopped
1 small onion, coarsely
   chopped
1 small carrot, finely sliced
1/2 tsp finely chopped garlic
1/2 tsp finely chopped
   gingerroot
3 1/2 oz/100 g pineapple
   chunks

method

1 Combine the marinade ingredients in a bowl with the pork and let marinate for at least 20 minutes.

2 Heat enough oil for deep-frying in a wok or deep-fat fryer until it reaches 350–375°F/ 180–190°C, or until a cube of bread browns in 30 seconds. Deep-fry the spareribs for 8 minutes. Drain and set aside.

3 To prepare the sauce, first mix together the vinegar, sugar, light soy sauce, and ketchup. Set aside.

4 In a preheated wok, heat 1 tablespoon of the oil and stir-fry the bell pepper, onion, and carrot for 2 minutes. Remove and set aside.

5 In the clean preheated wok, heat the remaining oil and stir-fry the garlic and gingerroot until fragrant. Add the vinegar mixture. Bring back to a boil and add the pineapple chunks. Finally add the spareribs and the bell pepper, onion, and carrot. Stir until warmed through and serve immediately.

xinjiang rice pot with lamb

ingredients

SERVES 6–8

2 tbsp vegetable or peanut oil

10$\frac{1}{2}$ oz/300 g lamb or
    mutton, cut into bite-size
    cubes

2 carrots, coarsely chopped

2 onions, coarsely chopped

1 tsp salt

1 tsp ground gingerroot

1 tsp Sichuan peppers, lightly
    roasted and lightly crushed

generous 2 cups short-or
    medium-grain rice

3$\frac{1}{2}$ cups water

method

1 In a large casserole, heat the oil and stir-fry the meat for 1–2 minutes, or until the pieces are sealed on all sides. Add the carrot and onion and stir-fry until the vegetables are beginning to soften. Add the salt, gingerroot, and Sichuan peppers and mix well.

2 Finally, add the rice and water and bring to a boil. Cover the pan and cook over low heat for 30 minutes, or until the rice has absorbed all the water. Serve alone or as part of a meal.

xinjiang lamb casserole

ingredients

SERVES 5–6

1–2 tbsp vegetable or peanut
    oil

14 oz/400 g lamb or mutton,
    cut into bite-size cubes

1 onion, coarsely chopped

1 green bell pepper, coarsely
    chopped

1 carrot, coarsely chopped

1 turnip, coarsely chopped

2 tomatoes, coarsely chopped

1-inch/2.5-cm piece of fresh
    gingerroot, finely sliced

1¼ cups water

1 tsp salt

method

1 In a preheated wok or deep pan, heat the oil and stir-fry the lamb for 1–2 minutes, or until the meat is sealed on all sides.

2 Transfer the meat to a large casserole and add all the other ingredients. Bring to a boil, then cover and let simmer over low heat for 35 minutes.

red lamb curry

ingredients

SERVES 4

2 tbsp vegetable oil

1 large onion, sliced

2 garlic cloves, crushed

1 lb 2 oz/500 g lean boneless
   leg of lamb

2 tbsp Thai red curry paste

$^2/_3$ cup coconut milk

1 tbsp brown sugar

1 large red bell pepper,
   seeded and thickly sliced

$^1/_2$ cup lamb or beef stock

1 tbsp Thai fish sauce

2 tbsp lime juice

generous 1 cup canned water
   chestnuts, drained

2 tbsp chopped cilantro

2 tbsp chopped fresh basil

salt and pepper

fresh basil leaves, to garnish

freshly cooked jasmine rice,
   to serve

method

1 Heat the oil in a large skillet or preheated wok over high heat. Add the onion and garlic and stir-fry for 2–3 minutes to soften. Add the meat and stir-fry the mixture quickly until lightly browned.

2 Stir in the curry paste and cook for a few seconds, then add the coconut milk and sugar and bring to a boil. Reduce the heat and simmer for 15 minutes, stirring occasionally.

3 Stir in the bell pepper, stock, fish sauce, and lime juice, then cover and simmer for an additional 15 minutes, or until the meat is tender.

4 Add the water chestnuts, cilantro, and basil and season to taste with salt and pepper. Transfer to serving plates, then garnish with basil leaves and serve with jasmine rice.

lamb with lime leaves

ingredients

SERVES 4

2 fresh red Thai chiles

2 tbsp peanut oil

2 garlic cloves, crushed

4 shallots, chopped

2 lemongrass stems, sliced

6 fresh kaffir lime leaves

1 tbsp tamarind paste

2 tbsp palm sugar

1 lb/450 g lean boneless lamb
   (leg or loin fillet)

2$\frac{1}{2}$ cups coconut milk

6 oz/175 g cherry tomatoes,
   halved

1 tbsp chopped cilantro

freshly cooked Thai fragrant
   rice, to serve

method

1 Using a sharp knife, seed and very finely chop the chiles. Reserve until required.

2 Heat the oil in a large, preheated wok. Add the garlic, shallots, lemongrass, lime leaves, tamarind paste, sugar, and chiles to the wok and stir-fry for 2 minutes.

3 Using a sharp knife, cut the lamb into thin strips or cubes.

4 Add the lamb to the wok and stir-fry for 5 minutes, tossing well so that the lamb is evenly coated in the spice mixture.

5 Pour the coconut milk into the wok and bring to a boil. Reduce the heat and let simmer for 20 minutes.

6 Add the cherry tomatoes and chopped cilantro to the wok and simmer for 5 minutes. Transfer to serving plates and serve hot with fragrant rice.

stir-fried lamb with mint

ingredients

SERVES 4

2 tbsp vegetable oil

2 garlic cloves, finely sliced

2 fresh red chiles, seeded and
  cut into thin strips

1 onion, thinly sliced

1 1/2 tbsp Madras curry paste

1 lb 2 oz/500 g lamb fillet,
  cut into thin strips

8 oz/225 g canned baby corn
  cobs, drained

4 scallions, finely chopped

generous 1/3 cup fresh mint
  leaves

1 tbsp Thai fish sauce

freshly cooked rice, to serve

method

1 Heat half the oil in a preheated wok or large skillet. Add the garlic and chiles and cook until soft. Remove and reserve. Add the onion and cook for 5 minutes, or until soft. Remove and reserve.

2 Heat the remaining oil in the wok. Add the curry paste and cook for 1 minute. Add the lamb, in batches if necessary, and cook for 5–8 minutes, or until cooked through and tender.

3 Return the onion to the wok with the baby corn cobs, scallions, mint, and fish sauce. Cook until heated through. Sprinkle the garlic and chiles over and serve with rice.

shredded chile chicken pouches

ingredients

MAKES 8 PIECES

4 sheets of abura-age
  (deep-fried bean curd)

3/4 cup dashi stock

3 tbsp Japanese soy sauce

2 tbsp superfine sugar

1 tbsp sake

1 skinless, boneless chicken
  breast, about 5 1/2 oz/150 g

1 tbsp vegetable oil

1 tsp red chile flakes

2 tbsp pine nuts, toasted

1 tbsp chopped flat-leaf
  parsley

1/4 quantity freshly cooked
  sushi rice

method

1 Put the bean curd in a bowl and pour boiling water over it to remove any excess oil. Drain and let cool. Cut each piece in half and gently open out each half into a bag.

2 Place the dashi stock, soy sauce, sugar, and sake in a pan, stir, and bring to a boil. Add the bean curd bags and let simmer for 10–15 minutes, until almost all the liquid has been absorbed. Remove from the heat, drain, and let cool. Press any remaining liquid out of the bags with a clean dish towel (the bags should be moist but not wet).

3 While the bags are simmering, cut the chicken into thin strips. Heat the oil in a wok or large skillet, then add the chile flakes. Heat for a few seconds, then add the chicken strips. Cook for 3–4 minutes, until the chicken is cooked through. Drain on kitchen towels and then chop very finely. Let cool.

4 Gently stir the chile chicken, toasted pine nuts, and parsley into the sushi rice. Fill the seasoned bean curd bags with the rice mixture and fold over the tops to enclose them. Serve them at room temperature.

thai-style chicken chunks

ingredients

SERVES 4

4 skinless, boneless chicken
  breasts, cut into small
  chunks
freshly cooked jasmine rice,
  to serve
chopped fresh cilantro,
  to garnish

marinade

1 red chile and 1 green chile,
  seeded and finely chopped
2 garlic cloves, chopped
3 cups chopped fresh cilantro
1 tbsp finely chopped fresh
  lemongrass
$1/2$ tsp ground turmeric
$1/2$ tsp garam masala
2 tsp brown sugar
2 tbsp Thai fish sauce
1 tbsp lime juice
salt and pepper

method

1 To make the marinade, put the red and green chiles, garlic, cilantro, and lemongrass into a food processor and process until coarsely chopped. Add the turmeric, garam masala, sugar, fish sauce, and lime juice, season to taste with salt and pepper and blend until smooth.

2 Put the chicken chunks into a nonmetallic bowl, which will not react with acid. Pour over enough marinade to cover the chicken, then cover with plastic wrap and chill for at least $2^1/2$ hours. Cover the remaining marinade with wrap and chill until the chicken is ready.

3 When the chicken chunks are thoroughly marinated, lift them out and barbecue them over hot coals for 20 minutes, or until cooked right through, turning them frequently and basting with the remaining marinade. Arrange the chicken on serving plates with some freshly cooked jasmine rice. Garnish with chopped fresh cilantro and serve.

gingered chicken kebabs

ingredients

SERVES 4

3 skinless, boneless chicken breasts, cut into cubes

juice of 1 lime

1-inch/2.5-cm piece gingerroot, peeled and chopped

1 fresh red chile, seeded and sliced

2 tbsp vegetable or peanut oil

1 onion, sliced

2 garlic cloves, chopped

1 eggplant, cut into chunks

2 zucchini, cut into thick slices

1 red bell pepper, seeded and cut into squares

2 tbsp Thai red curry paste

2 tbsp Thai soy sauce

1 tsp jaggery or soft light brown sugar

boiled rice, with chopped cilantro, to serve

method

1 Put the chicken cubes in a shallow dish. Mix the lime, gingerroot, and chile together and pour over the chicken pieces. Stir gently to coat. Cover and let chill for at least 3 hours to marinate.

2 Thread the chicken pieces onto soaked wooden skewers and cook under a hot broiler for 3–4 minutes, turning often, until cooked through.

3 Meanwhile, heat the oil in a wok or large skillet and sauté the onion and garlic for 1–2 minutes, until softened but not browned. Add the eggplant, zucchini, and bell pepper and cook for 3–4 minutes, until cooked but still firm. Add the curry paste, soy sauce, and sugar, and cook for 1 minute.

4 Serve hot with boiled rice, stirred through with chopped cilantro.

ground chicken skewers

ingredients

SERVES 4

2 cups ground chicken

1 onion, chopped finely

1 fresh red chile, seeded and
    chopped

2 tbsp Thai red curry paste

1 tsp jaggery or soft light
    brown sugar

1 tsp ground coriander

1 tsp ground cumin

1 egg white

8 lemongrass stalks

boiled rice with chopped
    scallion, to serve

method

1 Preheat the broiler to a high heat. Combine the chicken, onion, chile, curry paste, and sugar in a bowl and stir well to make a thick paste. Stir in the ground coriander, cumin, and egg white, and mix again.

2 Divide the mixture into 8 equal portions and squeeze them around each of the lemongrass stalks. Arrange on a broiler pan and cook under high heat, turning frequently, until browned and cooked through. Serve hot with the rice with the scallion stirred through it.

chirashi sushi with teriyaki chicken

ingredients

SERVES 4

4 skinless, boneless chicken
    breasts, weighing about
    5$\frac{1}{2}$ oz/150 g each
1 tbsp vegetable oil
1 quantity freshly cooked
    sushi rice
finely chopped scallion, green
    parts only, and sticks of
    cucumber, to garnish
sweet chili sauce, to serve

teriyaki marinade

4 tbsp Japanese soy sauce
2 tbsp mirin
2 tbsp sake
2 tsp superfine sugar
1 tsp shredded gingerroot
    (optional)
1 garlic clove, crushed
    (optional)

method

1 Combine all the ingredients for the marinade in a bowl that is large enough to take the chicken as well. Add the chicken and turn to coat. Cover and let marinate in the refrigerator for 30 minutes.

2 Heat the oil in a skillet. Remove the chicken from the marinade, add to the skillet, and cook for 4 minutes. Turn over, brush with marinade, and cook for another 4–6 minutes, or until the chicken is tender and the juices run clear when a skewer is inserted into the thickest part of the meat. Once you have brushed on the marinade, do not add on any more during the cooking process.

3 Transfer the cooked chicken to a chopping board and cut into thin diagonal slices, holding your knife at a 4-degree angle to the board.

4 Divide the rice between 4 serving bowls. Top with the sliced chicken and garnish with chopped scallion and cucumber sticks. Serve with the sweet chili sauce.

chicken fried rice

ingredients

SERVES 4

$^1/_2$ tbsp sesame oil

6 shallots, peeled and cut into
    fourths

1 lb/450g cooked, cubed
    chicken meat

3 tbsp soy sauce

2 carrots, diced

1 stalk celery, diced

1 red bell pepper, diced

$1^1/_2$ cups fresh shelled peas

$3^1/_2$ oz/100 g canned corn
    kernels

$1^1/_2$ cups cooked
    long-grain rice

2 large eggs, scrambled

method

1 Heat the oil in a large skillet over medium heat. Add the shallots and fry until soft, then add the chicken and 2 tablespoons of the soy sauce and stir-fry for 5–6 minutes.

2 Stir in the carrots, celery, red bell pepper, peas, and corn and stir-fry for an additional 5 minutes. Add the rice and stir thoroughly.

3 Finally, stir in the scrambled eggs and the remaining tablespoon of soy sauce. Serve immediately.

sweet-&-sour chicken

ingredients

SERVES 4–6

1 lb/450 g lean chicken meat, cubed

5 tbsp vegetable or peanut oil

1/2 tsp minced garlic

1/2 tsp finely chopped fresh gingerroot

1 green bell pepper, coarsely chopped

1 onion, coarsely chopped

1 carrot, finely sliced

1 tsp sesame oil

1 tbsp finely chopped scallions

marinade

2 tsp light soy sauce

1 tsp Shaoxing rice wine

pinch of white pepper

1/2 tsp salt

dash of sesame oil

sauce

8 tbsp rice vinegar

4 tbsp sugar

2 tsp light soy sauce

6 tbsp ketchup

method

1 Place all the marinade ingredients in a bowl and marinate the chicken pieces for at least 20 minutes.

2 To prepare the sauce, heat the vinegar in a pan and add the sugar, light soy sauce, and ketchup. Stir to dissolve the sugar, then set aside.

3 In a preheated wok or deep pan, heat 3 tablespoons of the oil and stir-fry the chicken until it starts to turn golden brown. Remove and set aside.

4 In the clean wok or deep pan, heat the remaining oil and cook the garlic and gingerroot until fragrant. Add the vegetables and cook for 2 minutes. Add the chicken and cook for 1 minute. Finally add the sauce and sesame oil, then stir in the scallions and serve.

gong bao chicken

ingredients

SERVES 4

2 boneless chicken breasts, with or without skin, cut into 1/2-inch/1-cm cubes

1 tbsp vegetable or peanut oil

10 dried red chiles or more, to taste, snipped into 2–3 pieces

1 tsp Sichuan peppers

3 garlic cloves, finely sliced

1-inch/2.5-cm piece of fresh gingerroot, finely sliced

1 tbsp coarsely chopped scallions, white part only

generous 1/2 cup peanuts, roasted

marinade

2 tsp light soy sauce

1 tsp Shaoxing rice wine

1/2 tsp sugar

sauce

1 tsp light soy sauce

1 tsp dark soy sauce

1 tsp black Chinese rice vinegar

a few drops of sesame oil

2 tbsp chicken stock

1 tsp sugar

method

1 Combine all the ingredients for the marinade in a bowl and marinate the chicken, covered, for at least 20 minutes. Combine all the ingredients for the sauce and set aside.

2 In a preheated wok or deep pan, heat the oil and stir-fry the chiles and peppers until crisp and fragrant. Toss in the chicken pieces. When they begin to turn white, add the garlic, gingerroot, and scallions. Stir-fry for about 5 minutes, or until the chicken is cooked.

3 Pour in the sauce, and when everything is well mixed, stir in the peanuts. Serve at once.

bang bang chicken

ingredients

SERVES 4

12 oz/350 g boneless, skinless chicken meat

few drops of sesame oil

2 tbsp sesame paste

1 tbsp light soy sauce

1 tbsp chicken stock

1/2 tsp salt

pinch of sugar

8 tbsp shredded lettuce leaves and 1 tbsp sesame seeds, roasted, to serve

method

1 Place the chicken in a pan of cold water, then bring to a boil and let simmer for 8–10 minutes. Drain and let cool a little, then cut or tear the chicken into bite-size pieces.

2 Mix together the sesame oil, sesame paste, light soy sauce, chicken stock, salt, and sugar and whisk until the sauce is thick and smooth. Toss in the chicken.

3 To serve, put the shredded lettuce on a large plate and spoon the chicken and sauce on top. Sprinkle with the sesame seeds and serve at room temperature.

chicken with cashew nuts

ingredients

SERVES 4–6

1 lb/450 g boneless chicken
  meat, cut into bite-size
  pieces
3 dried Chinese mushrooms,
  soaked in warm water for
  20 minutes
2 tbsp vegetable or peanut oil
4 slices of fresh gingerroot
1 tsp finely chopped garlic
1 red bell pepper, cut into
  1-inch/2.5-cm squares
generous 1/2 cup cashew nuts,
  roasted

marinade
3 tbsp light soy sauce
1 tsp Shaoxing rice wine
pinch of sugar
1/2 tsp salt

method

1 Marinate the chicken in 2 tablespoons of the light soy sauce, Shaoxing, sugar, and salt for at least 20 minutes.

2 Squeeze any excess water from the mushrooms and finely slice, discarding any tough stems. Reserve the soaking water.

3 In a preheated wok or deep pan, heat 1 tablespoon of the oil. Add the gingerroot and stir-fry until fragrant. Stir in the chicken and cook for 2 minutes, or until it begins to turn brown. Before the chicken is cooked through, remove and set aside.

4 In the clean wok or deep pan, heat the remaining oil and stir-fry the garlic until fragrant. Add the mushrooms and red bell pepper and stir-fry for 1 minute. Add about 2 tablespoons of the mushroom soaking water and cook for about 2 minutes, or until the water has evaporated. Return the chicken to the wok, then add the remaining light soy sauce and the cashew nuts and stir-fry for 2 minutes, or until the chicken is thoroughly cooked through.

gingerroot chicken with toasted sesame seeds

ingredients

SERVES 4

1 lb 2 oz/500 g chicken breasts, skinned, cut into strips
2 tbsp peanut oil
1 leek, sliced thinly
1 head of broccoli, cut into small florets
2 carrots, sliced thinly
1/2 cauliflower, cut into small florets
1 tsp grated fresh gingerroot
5 tbsp white wine
2 tbsp sesame seeds
1 tbsp cornstarch
1 tbsp water
freshly cooked rice, to serve

marinade
4 tbsp soy sauce
4 tbsp water

method

1 In a medium dish, combine the soy sauce with 4 tablespoons of water. Toss and coat the chicken strips in the sauce. Cover the dish with plastic wrap and let chill in the refrigerator for 1 hour.

2 Remove the chicken from the marinade with a slotted spoon. Heat the oil in a skillet or wok and stir-fry the chicken and leek until the chicken is browned and the leek is beginning to soften. Stir in the vegetables, gingerroot, and wine. Reduce the heat, cover, and let simmer for 5 minutes.

3 Place the sesame seeds on a cookie sheet under a hot broiler. Stir them once to make sure they toast evenly. Set aside to cool.

4 In a small bowl, combine the cornstarch with 1 tablespoon of water and whisk until smooth. Gradually add the liquid to the skillet, stirring constantly until thickened.

5 Pile onto a bed of hot rice, top with the sesame seeds, and serve.

sweet-&-sour noodles with chicken

ingredients

SERVES 4

9 oz/250 g dried medium
Chinese egg noodles

2 tbsp peanut or corn oil

1 onion, thinly sliced

4 boneless chicken thighs,
skinned and cut into thin
strips

1 carrot, peeled and cut into
thin half-moon slices

1 red bell pepper, cored,
seeded, and finely
chopped

3$\frac{1}{2}$ oz/100 g canned bamboo
shoots, drained weight

generous $\frac{1}{2}$ cup cashew nuts

sweet-&-sour sauce

$\frac{1}{2}$ cup water

1$\frac{1}{2}$ teaspoons arrowroot

4 tbsp rice vinegar

3 tbsp brown sugar

2 tsp dark soy sauce

2 tsp tomato paste

2 large garlic cloves,
very finely chopped

$\frac{1}{2}$-inch/1-cm piece fresh
gingerroot, peeled and very
finely chopped

pinch of salt

method

1 Cook the noodles in a large pan of boiling water for 3 minutes, or according to the package instructions, until soft. Drain, rinse, and drain again, then set aside.

2 Meanwhile, to make the sauce, stir half the water into the arrowroot, and set aside. Stir the remaining sauce ingredients and the remaining water together in a small pan and bring to a boil. Stir in the arrowroot mixture and continue boiling until the sauce becomes clear, glossy, and thick. Remove from the heat and set aside.

3 Heat a wok or large skillet over high heat. Add the oil and heat it until it shimmers. Add the onion and stir-fry for 1 minute. Stir in the chicken, carrot, and bell pepper and continue stir-frying for about 3 minutes, or until the chicken is cooked through. Add the bamboo shoots and cashew nuts and stir them round to lightly brown the nuts. Stir the sauce into the wok and heat until it starts to bubble. Add the noodles and use 2 forks to mix them with the chicken and vegetables.

chicken & green vegetables

ingredients

SERVES 4

9 oz/250 g dried medium
   Chinese egg noodles
2 tbsp peanut or corn oil
1 large garlic clove, crushed
1 fresh green chile, seeded
   and sliced
1 tbsp Chinese five-spice
   powder
2 skinless, boneless chicken
   breasts, cut into thin strips
2 green bell peppers, cored,
   seeded, and sliced
1 small head broccoli
2 oz/55 g green beans,
   trimmed and cut into
   1¹/₂-inch/4-cm pieces
5 tbsp vegetable or chicken
   stock
2 tbsp oyster sauce
2 tbsp soy sauce
1 tbsp rice wine or dry sherry
3¹/₂ oz/100 g bean sprouts

method

1 Cook the noodles in a pan of boiling water for 4 minutes, or according to the package instructions, until soft. Drain, rinse, and drain again, then set aside.

2 Heat a wok or large skillet over high heat. Add 1 tablespoon of the oil and heat until it shimmers. Add the garlic, chile, and five-spice powder and stir-fry for about 30 seconds. Add the chicken and stir-fry for 3 minutes, or until it is cooked through. Use a slotted spoon to remove the chicken from the wok and set aside.

3 Add the remaining oil to the wok and heat until it shimmers. Add the bell peppers, broccoli, and beans and stir-fry for about 2 minutes. Stir in the stock, oyster sauce, soy sauce, and rice wine and return the chicken to the wok. Continue stir-frying for about 1 minute, until the chicken is reheated and the vegetables are tender but still firm to the bite. Add the noodles and bean sprouts and use 2 forks to mix all the ingredients together.

chicken chow mein

ingredients

SERVES 4

9 oz/250 g dried medium
   Chinese egg noodles
2 tbsp sunflower oil
10 oz/280 g cooked chicken
   breasts, shredded
1 garlic clove, finely chopped
1 red bell pepper, seeded and
   thinly sliced
3½ oz/100 g shiitake
   mushrooms, sliced
6 scallions, sliced
3½ oz/100 g bean sprouts
3 tbsp soy sauce
1 tbsp sesame oil

method

1 Place the egg noodles in a large bowl or dish and break them up slightly. Pour enough boiling water over the noodles to cover and let stand while preparing the other ingredients.

2 Preheat a wok over medium heat. Add the sunflower oil and swirl it around to coat the sides of the wok. When the oil is hot, add the shredded chicken, garlic, bell pepper, mushrooms, scallions, and bean sprouts to the wok and stir-fry for about 5 minutes.

3 Drain the noodles thoroughly then add them to the wok, toss well, and stir-fry for an additional 5 minutes. Drizzle over the soy sauce and sesame oil and toss until thoroughly combined.

4 Transfer to warmed serving bowls and serve immediately.

chicken chow mein baskets

ingredients

SERVES 4

9 oz/250 g fresh thin or
medium Chinese egg
noodles

peanut or corn oil, for
deep-frying

6 tbsp water

3 tbsp soy sauce

1 tbsp cornstarch

3 tbsp peanut or corn oil

4 boneless chicken thighs,
skinned and chopped

1-inch/2.5-cm piece fresh
gingerroot, peeled and
finely chopped

2 large garlic cloves, crushed

2 celery stalks, thinly sliced

1 3/4 cups thinly sliced white
mushrooms

method

1 Dip a large wire strainer in oil, then line it completely and evenly with one fourth of the tangled noodles. Dip a smaller wire strainer in oil, then position it inside the larger strainer. Heat 4 inches/10 cm of oil in a wok to 350– 375°F/180–190°C, or until a cube of bread browns in 30 seconds. Lower the strainers into the oil and deep-fry the noodles for 2–3 minutes, until golden brown. Remove from the oil and drain on paper towels. Carefully remove the small strainer and remove the noodle basket. Repeat to make 3 more baskets. Let cool.

2 Stir the water and soy sauce into the cornstarch in a small bowl and set aside.

3 Heat a wok or large skillet over high heat. Add 2 tablespoons of the oil and heat until it shimmers. Add the chicken and stir-fry for about 3 minutes, or until it is cooked through. Remove the chicken from the wok.

4 Add the remaining oil, then add the gingerroot, garlic, and celery and stir-fry for 2 minutes. Add the mushrooms and continue stir-frying for 2 minutes. Remove the vegetables and add them to the chicken.

5 Pour the cornstarch mixture into the wok and bring to a boil, stirring until it thickens. Return the chicken and vegetables to the wok and reheat in the sauce. Divide the chicken mixture among the noodle baskets to serve.

cross the bridge noodles

ingredients

SERVES 4

10½ oz/300 g thin Chinese
  egg or rice sticks

7 oz/200 g choi sum or similar
  green vegetable

8 cups chicken stock

½-inch/1-cm piece of fresh
  gingerroot, peeled

1–2 tsp salt

1 tsp sugar

1 boneless, skinless chicken
  breast, finely sliced
  diagonally

7 oz/200 g white fish fillet,
  finely sliced diagonally

1 tbsp light soy sauce

method

1 Cook the noodles according to the directions on the package. When cooked, rinse under cold water and set aside. Blanch the choi sum in a large pan of boiling water for 30 seconds. Rinse under cold water and set aside.

2 In a large pan, bring the chicken stock to a boil, then add the gingerroot, 1 teaspoon of the salt, and the sugar and skim the surface. Add the chicken and cook for about 4 minutes, then add the fish slices and simmer for an additional 4 minutes, or until the fish and chicken are cooked through.

3 Add the noodles and choi sum with the light soy sauce and bring back to a boil. Taste and adjust the seasoning if necessary. Serve immediately in large individual noodle bowls.

chicken & peanut curry

ingredients

SERVES 4

1 tbsp vegetable or peanut oil

2 red onions, sliced

2 tbsp Penang curry paste

1³/₄ cups coconut milk

²/₃ cup chicken stock

4 kaffir lime leaves,
    torn coarsely

1 lemongrass stalk, chopped
    finely

6 skinless, boneless chicken
    thighs, chopped

1 tbsp fish sauce

2 tbsp Thai soy sauce

1 tsp jaggery or soft, light
    brown sugar

¹/₂ cup unsalted peanuts,
    roasted and chopped,
    plus extra to garnish

6 oz/175 g fresh pineapple,
    chopped coarsely

6-inch/15-cm piece
    cucumber, peeled, seeded,
    and sliced thickly, plus
    extra to garnish

method

1 Heat the oil in a wok and stir-fry the onions for 1 minute. Add the curry paste and stir-fry for 1–2 minutes.

2 Pour in the coconut milk and stock. Add the lime leaves and lemongrass and let simmer for 1 minute. Add the chicken and gradually bring to a boil. Let simmer for 8–10 minutes, until the chicken is tender.

3 Stir in the fish sauce, soy sauce, and sugar, and let simmer for 1–2 minutes. Stir in the peanuts, pineapple, and cucumber, and cook for 30 seconds. Serve immediately, sprinkled with extra nuts and cucumber.

green chicken curry

ingredients

SERVES 4

1 tbsp vegetable or peanut oil

1 onion, sliced

1 garlic clove, chopped finely

2–3 tbsp Thai green curry
   paste

1³/₄ cups coconut milk

²/₃ cup chicken stock

4 kaffir lime leaves

4 skinless, boneless chicken
   breasts, cut into cubes

1 tbsp fish sauce

2 tbsp Thai soy sauce

grated rind and juice of
   ¹/₂ lime

1 tsp jaggery or soft light
   brown sugar

4 tbsp chopped fresh cilantro,
   to garnish

method

1 Heat the oil in a wok or large skillet and stir-fry the onion and garlic for 1–2 minutes, until starting to soften. Add the curry paste and stir-fry for 1–2 minutes.

2 Add the coconut milk, stock, and lime leaves, bring to a boil and add the chicken. Reduce the heat and let simmer gently for 15–20 minutes, until the chicken is tender.

3 Add the fish sauce, soy sauce, lime rind and juice, and sugar. Cook for 2–3 minutes, until the sugar has dissolved. Serve immediately, garnished with chopped cilantro.

thai red chicken curry

ingredients

SERVES 4

6 garlic cloves, chopped

2 fresh red chiles, chopped

2 tbsp chopped fresh lemongrass

1 tsp finely grated lime rind

1 tbsp chopped fresh kaffir lime leaves

1 tbsp Thai red curry paste

1 tbsp coriander seeds, toasted and crushed

1 tbsp chili oil

4 skinless, boneless chicken breasts, sliced

1 1/4 cups coconut milk

1 1/4 cups chicken stock

1 tbsp soy sauce

1/3 cup shelled, unsalted peanuts, toasted and ground

3 scallions, diagonally sliced

1 red bell pepper, seeded and sliced

3 Thai eggplants, sliced

2 tbsp chopped fresh Thai basil or fresh cilantro

fresh cilantro, to garnish

freshly cooked jasmine rice, to serve

method

1 Place the garlic, chiles, lemongrass, lime rind, lime leaves, curry paste, and coriander seeds in a food processor and process until the mixture is smooth.

2 Heat the oil in a preheated wok or large skillet over high heat. Add the chicken and the garlic mixture and stir-fry for 5 minutes. Add the coconut milk, stock, and soy sauce and bring to a boil. Reduce the heat and cook, stirring, for an additional 3 minutes. Stir in the ground peanuts and let simmer for 20 minutes.

3 Add the scallions, bell pepper, and eggplants and let simmer, stirring occasionally, for an additional 10 minutes. Remove from the heat, stir in the basil, and garnish with cilantro. Serve immediately with freshly cooked jasmine rice.

chicken with yellow curry sauce

ingredients

SERVES 4

spice paste

6 tbsp Thai yellow curry paste

²/₃ cup plain yogurt

1³/₄ cups water

handful of fresh cilantro,
    chopped

handful of fresh Thai basil
    leaves, shredded

stir-fry

2 tbsp vegetable or peanut oil

2 onions, cut into thin wedges

2 garlic cloves, chopped finely

2 skinless, boneless chicken
    breasts, cut into strips

6 oz/175 g baby corn, halved
    lengthwise

to garnish

chopped fresh cilantro

shredded fresh basil

method

1 To make the spice paste, stir-fry the yellow curry paste in a wok for 2–3 minutes, then stir in the yogurt, water, and herbs. Bring to a boil, then let simmer for 2–3 minutes.

2 Meanwhile, heat the oil in a wok and stir-fry the onions and garlic for 2–3 minutes. Add the chicken and corn and stir-fry for 3–4 minutes, until the meat and corn are tender.

3 Stir in the spice paste and bring to a boil. Let simmer for 2–3 minutes, until heated through. Serve immediately, garnished with extra herbs if desired.

spiced cilantro chicken

ingredients

SERVES 4

4 skinless, boneless chicken
    breasts
2 garlic cloves
1 fresh green chile, seeded
3/4-inch/2-cm piece fresh
    gingerroot
4 tbsp chopped cilantro
finely grated rind of 1 lime
3 tbsp lime juice
2 tbsp light soy sauce
1 tbsp superfine sugar
3/4 cup coconut milk

to garnish
finely chopped cilantro
cucumber slices
radish slices
1/2 fresh red chile, seeded and
    sliced into rings
freshly cooked rice, to serve

method

1 Using a sharp knife, cut 3 deep slashes into the skinned side of each chicken breast. Place the breasts in a single layer in a nonmetallic dish.

2 Place the garlic, chile, gingerroot, cilantro, lime rind and juice, soy sauce, sugar, and coconut milk in a food processor and process to a smooth paste.

3 Spread the paste over both sides of the chicken breasts, coating them evenly. Cover with plastic wrap and let marinate in the refrigerator for 1 hour.

4 Preheat the broiler to medium. Lift the chicken from the marinade, then drain off the excess and place on a broiler pan. Cook under the hot broiler for 12–15 minutes, or until thoroughly and evenly cooked.

5 Meanwhile, place the remaining marinade in a pan and bring to a boil. Reduce the heat and simmer for several minutes. Transfer the chicken breasts to serving plates. Garnish with chopped cilantro, cucumber slices, radish slices, and chile rings and serve with rice.

chicken with vegetables & cilantro rice

ingredients

SERVES 4

3 tbsp vegetable or peanut oil

2 red onions, chopped

2 garlic cloves, chopped

1-inch/2.5-cm piece
   gingerroot, peeled and
   chopped

2 skinless, boneless chicken
   breasts, cut into strips

4 oz/115 g white mushrooms

1¾ cups coconut milk

2 oz/55 g sugar snap peas,
   trimmed and halved
   lengthwise

3 tbsp Thai soy sauce

1 tbsp fish sauce

3 cups rice, cooked and
   cooled

8 oz/250 g bok choy, torn into
   large pieces

handful of fresh cilantro,
   chopped

method

1 Heat the oil in a wok or large skillet and sauté the onions, garlic, and gingerroot together for 1–2 minutes.

2 Add the chicken and mushrooms and cook over high heat until browned. Add the coconut milk, sugar snap peas, and sauces, and bring to a boil. Let simmer gently for 4–5 minutes until tender.

3 Heat the oil for the rice in a separate wok or large skillet and cook the onion until softened but not browned.

4 Add the cooked rice, bok choy, and fresh cilantro, and heat gently until the leaves have wilted and the rice is hot. Sprinkle over the soy sauce and serve immediately with the chicken.

chicken steamed with rice in lotus leaves

ingredients

SERVES 4–8

1 lb/450 g glutinous rice,
soaked in cold water for
2 hours

2 cups cold water

1 tsp salt

1 tsp vegetable or peanut oil

4 dried lotus leaves, soaked in
hot water for 1 hour

filling

3¹/₂ oz/100 g small shrimp,
shelled and deveined

2-inch/5-cm piece of very
fresh gingerroot

7 oz/200 g lean chicken meat,
cut into bite-size strips

2 tsp light soy sauce

2 oz/55 g dried Chinese
mushrooms, soaked in
warm water for 20 minutes

1 tbsp vegetable or peanut oil,
for frying

7 oz/200 g cha siu or pork loin

1 tbsp Shaoxing rice wine

1 tsp dark soy sauce

¹/₂ tsp white pepper

1 tsp sugar

method

1 For the filling, steam the shrimp for 5 minutes and set aside. Finely grate the gingerroot, discarding the fibrous parts on the grater and reserving the liquid that drips through. Marinate the chicken in the light soy sauce and gingerroot juices for at least 20 minutes. Steam for a few minutes in the marinade. Set aside.

2 Drain the rice and place in a pan with the water. Bring to a boil, then add the salt and oil. Cover and cook over very low heat for 15 minutes. Divide into 8 portions and set aside.

3 Squeeze out any excess water from the mushrooms, then finely slice, discarding any tough stems. Reserve the soaking water.

4 In a preheated wok or deep pan, heat the oil and stir-fry the pork, shrimp, and mushrooms for 2 minutes. Stir in the Shaoxing, dark soy sauce, pepper, and sugar. Add the reserved mushroom soaking water, if necessary.

5 Rinse and dry the lotus leaves. Place a portion of rice in the center of each and flatten out to form a 4-inch/10-cm square. Top with the pork mixture and some pieces of chicken. Top with another portion of rice, then fold the lotus leaf to form a tight package. Steam for about 15 minutes. Let rest for 5 minutes, then serve.

hainan chicken rice

ingredients

SERVES 4–6

1 chicken, weighing
   3 lb 5 oz/1.5 kg
2 oz/55 g fresh young
   gingerroot, smashed
2 garlic cloves, smashed
1 scallion, tied in a knot
1 tsp salt
2 tbsp vegetable or peanut oil
chili or soy dipping sauce,
   to serve

rice

2 tbsp vegetable or peanut oil
5 garlic cloves, finely chopped
5 shallots, finely chopped
12 oz/350 g long-grain rice
3¾ cups chicken stock
1 tsp salt

method

1 Wash the chicken and dry thoroughly. Stuff the body cavity with the gingerroot, garlic, scallion, and salt.

2 In a large pan, bring enough water to a boil to submerge the chicken. Place the chicken in the pan, breast-side down. Bring the water back to a boil, then turn down the heat and simmer, covered, for 30–40 minutes. Turn the chicken over once.

3 Remove the chicken and wash in running cold water for 2 minutes to stop the cooking. Drain, then rub the oil into the skin. Set aside.

4 To prepare the rice, heat the oil in a preheated wok or deep pan. Stir-fry the garlic and shallots until fragrant. Add the rice and cook for 3 minutes, stirring rapidly. Transfer to a large pan and add the chicken stock and salt. Bring to a boil, then turn down the heat and let simmer, covered, for 20 minutes. Turn off the heat and let steam for an additional 5–10 minutes, or until the rice is perfectly cooked.

5 To serve, chop the chicken horizontally through the bone and skin into chunky wedges. Serve with the rice and a chili or soy dipping sauce.

egg-fried rice with chicken

ingredients

SERVES 4

generous 1 cup jasmine rice

3 skinless, boneless chicken
    breasts, cut into cubes

1³/4 cups canned coconut milk

1³/4 oz/50 g block creamed
    coconut, chopped

2–3 cilantro roots, chopped

thinly pared rind of 1 lemon

1 fresh green chile, seeded
    and chopped

3 fresh Thai basil leaves

1 tbsp fish sauce

1 tbsp oil

3 eggs, beaten

fresh chives and sprigs fresh
    cilantro, to garnish

method

1 Cook the rice in boiling water for
12–15 minutes, drain well, then let cool and
chill overnight.

2 Put the chicken into a pan and cover with
the coconut milk. Add the creamed coconut,
cilantro roots, lemon rind, and chile, and bring
to a boil. Let simmer for 8–10 minutes, until the
chicken is tender. Remove from the heat. Stir in
the basil and fish sauce.

3 Meanwhile, heat the oil in a wok and stir-fry
the rice for 2–3 minutes. Pour in the eggs and
stir until they have cooked and mixed with the
rice. Line 4 small ovenproof bowls or ramekins
with plastic wrap and pack with the rice. Turn
out carefully onto serving plates and remove
the plastic wrap. Garnish with long chives and
sprigs of cilantro. Serve with the chicken.

gingerroot chicken with noodles

ingredients

SERVES 4

2 tbsp vegetable or peanut oil

1 onion, sliced

2 garlic cloves, chopped finely

2-inch/5-cm piece fresh
    gingerroot, sliced thinly

2 carrots, sliced thinly

4 skinless, boneless chicken
    breasts, cut into cubes

1¼ cups chicken stock

4 tbsp Thai soy sauce

8 oz/225 g canned bamboo
    shoots, drained and rinsed

2¾ oz/75 g flat rice noodles

4 scallions, chopped and
    4 tbsp chopped fresh
    cilantro, to garnish

method

1 Heat the oil in a wok and stir-fry the onion, garlic, gingerroot, and carrots for 1–2 minutes, until softened. Add the chicken and stir-fry for 3–4 minutes, until the chicken is cooked through and lightly browned.

2 Add the stock, soy sauce, and bamboo shoots, and gradually bring to a boil. Let simmer for 2–3 minutes. Meanwhile, soak the noodles in boiling water for 6–8 minutes. Drain well. Garnish with the scallions and cilantro and serve immediately, with the chicken stir-fry.

chinese chicken rice

ingredients

SERVES 4

12 oz/350 g long-grain white
rice

1 tsp ground turmeric

salt

2 tbsp corn oil

12 oz/350 g skinless, boneless
chicken thighs, sliced

1 red bell pepper, seeded and
sliced

1 green bell pepper, seeded
and sliced

1 fresh green chile, seeded
and finely chopped

1 carrot, grated coarsely

5^1/$_2$ oz/150 g bean sprouts

6 scallions, sliced, plus extra
to garnish

2 tbsp light soy sauce

method

1 Place the rice and turmeric in a large pan of lightly salted water and cook until the grains of rice are just tender, about 10 minutes. Drain the rice thoroughly and press out any excess water with paper towels.

2 Heat the corn oil in a large preheated skillet. Add the strips of chicken and stir-fry over high heat until just starting to turn a golden color. Add the sliced bell peppers and green chile to the wok and stir-fry for 2–3 minutes.

3 Add the cooked rice to the wok, a little at a time, tossing well after each addition until well mixed and the grains of rice are separated. Add the carrot, bean sprouts, and scallions to the wok and stir-fry for an additional 2 minutes. Drizzle with the soy sauce and toss to mix.

4 Transfer the Chinese chicken rice to a warmed serving dish, garnish with extra scallions, if you like, and serve immediately.

yaki soba

ingredients

SERVES 2

14 oz/400 g ramen noodles

1 onion, finely sliced

7 oz/200 g bean sprouts

1 red bell pepper, seeded and
    finely shredded

1 boneless, skin-on cooked
    chicken breast, about
    5¹/₂ oz/150 g, cooked and
    sliced

12 cooked shelled shrimp

1 tbsp oil

2 tbsp shoyu (Japanese
    soy sauce)

¹/₂ tbsp mirin

1 tsp sesame oil

1 tsp roasted sesame seeds

2 scallions, finely sliced

method

1 Cook the noodles according to the package instructions, drain well, and tip into a bowl.

2 Mix the onion, bean sprouts, red bell pepper, chicken, and shrimp together in a separate bowl. Stir through the noodles.

3 Preheat a wok over high heat. Add the oil and heat until very hot. Add the noodle mixture and stir-fry for 4 minutes, or until golden, then add the shoyu, mirin, and sesame oil and toss together.

4 Divide the mixture between 2 plates, sprinkle with the sesame seeds and scallions, and serve at once.

teriyaki chicken with sesame noodles

ingredients

SERVES 4

4 boneless chicken breasts,
    about 6 oz/175 g each,
    with or without skin,
    as you like
about 4 tbsp teriyaki sauce
peanut or corn oil

sesame noodles
9 oz/250 g dried thin
    buckwheat noodles
1 tbsp toasted sesame oil
2 tbsp toasted sesame seeds
2 tbsp finely chopped fresh
    parsley
salt and pepper

method

1 Using a sharp knife, score each chicken breast diagonally across 3 times and rub all over with teriyaki sauce. Set aside to marinate for at least 10 minutes, or cover and let chill all day.

2 When you are ready to cook the chicken, preheat the broiler to high. Bring a pan of water to a boil, add the buckwheat noodles, and boil for 3 minutes, until soft. Alternatively, cook according to the package instructions. Drain and rinse well in cold water to stop the cooking and remove excess starch, then drain again.

3 Lightly brush the broiler rack with oil. Add the chicken breasts, skin-side up, and brush again with a little extra teriyaki sauce. Broil the chicken breasts about 4 inches/10 cm from the heat, brushing occasionally with extra teriyaki sauce, for 15 minutes, or until cooked through and the juices run clear.

4 Meanwhile, heat a wok over high heat. Add the sesame oil and heat until it shimmers. Add the noodles and stir round to heat through, then stir in the sesame seeds and parsley. Finally, add salt and pepper to taste.

5 Transfer the chicken breasts to plates and add a portion of noodles to each.

noodle baskets with chicken lime salad

ingredients

SERVES 4

peanut or corn oil,
  for deep-frying
9 oz/250 g fresh thin or
  medium Chinese egg
  noodles

chicken-lime salad
6 tbsp sour cream
6 tbsp mayonnaise
1-inch/2.5-cm piece fresh
  gingerroot, peeled
  and grated
grated rind and juice of 1 lime
4 skinless, boneless chicken
  thighs, poached and
  cooled, then cut into
  thin strips
1 carrot, peeled and grated
1 cucumber, cut in half
  lengthwise, seeds removed
  and sliced
salt and pepper
1 tbsp finely chopped
  fresh cilantro
1 tbsp finely chopped
  fresh mint
1 tbsp finely chopped
  fresh parsley
several fresh basil leaves, torn

method

1 To shape noodle baskets, you will need a special set of 2 long-handled wire baskets that clip inside each other, available from gourmet kitchen stores. Dip the larger wire basket in oil, then line it completely and evenly with one-fourth of the tangled noodles. Dip the smaller wire basket in oil, then position it inside the larger basket and clip it into position.

2 Heat 4 inches/10 cm of oil in a wok or deep-fat fryer to 350–375°F/180–190°C, or until a cube of bread browns in 30 seconds. Lower the baskets into the oil and deep-fry for 2–3 minutes, or until the noodles are golden brown. Remove the baskets from the oil and drain on paper towels. Unclip the 2 wire baskets and carefully remove the small one. Use a round-bladed knife, if necessary, to pry the noodle basket from the wire frame. Repeat to make 3 more baskets. Let the noodle baskets cool.

3 To make the salad, combine the sour cream, mayonnaise, gingerroot, and lime rind. Gradually add the lime juice until you get the flavor you like. Stir in the chicken, carrot, cucumber, and seasoning to taste. Cover and let chill. Just before serving, stir in the herbs and spoon the salad into the noodle baskets.

426 meat & poultry

chicken with water chestnuts & plum sauce

ingredients

SERVES 4–6

1 tbsp vegetable or peanut oil

3¹/₂ oz/100 g chicken,
    finely chopped

1 oz/25 g water chestnuts,
    finely chopped

1 tsp finely chopped
    Chinese chives

1 oz/25 g pine nuts,
    lightly toasted

1 tsp salt

¹/₂ tsp white pepper

6 lettuce leaves, washed

3 tsp plum sauce, to serve

method

1 In a preheated wok or deep pan, heat the oil and stir-fry the chicken for 1 minute. Add the water chestnuts and chives and cook for 2 minutes. Add the pine nuts and cook for 1 minute. Add the salt and pepper and stir.

2 To serve, place a spoonful in the center of each lettuce leaf, top with the plum sauce, and fold the lettuce leaf to make a small roll.

turkey with bamboo shoots & water chestnuts

ingredients

SERVES 4

marinade

4 tbsp sweet sherry

1 tbsp lemon juice

1 tbsp soy sauce

2 tsp grated fresh gingerroot

1 clove garlic, crushed

stir-fry

1 tbsp sesame oil

2 tbsp vegetable oil

1 lb/450 g turkey breast,
    cubed

125 g/4^1/$_2$ oz small
    mushrooms,
    cut into halves

1 green bell pepper,
    cut into strips

1 zucchini, sliced thinly

4 scallions, cut into fourths

4 oz/115 g canned bamboo
    shoots, drained

4 oz/115 g canned sliced
    water chestnuts, drained

cooked noodles or rice,
    to serve

method

1 Blend the sherry, lemon juice, soy sauce, gingerroot, and garlic in a bowl, then add the turkey and stir. Cover the dish with plastic wrap and refrigerate to marinate for 3–4 hours.

2 In a wok, add the sesame oil and vegetable oil and heat slowly. Remove the turkey from the marinade with a slotted spoon (reserving the marinade) and stir-fry a few pieces at a time until browned. Remove the turkey from the wok and set aside.

3 Add the mushrooms, green bell pepper, and zucchini to the wok and stir-fry for 3 minutes. Add the scallions and stir-fry for 1 minute more. Add the bamboo shoots and water chestnuts to the wok, then the turkey along with half of the reserved marinade. Stir over a medium–high heat for another 2–3 minutes, or until the ingredients are evenly coated and the marinade has reduced.

4 Serve immediately over noodles or rice.

duck & hoisin hand rolls

ingredients

MAKES 6 PIECES

1/4 prepared barbecued or
   Peking duck

4 tbsp hoisin or plum sauce

3 sheets of toasted nori

1/4 quantity freshly cooked
   sushi rice

3 scallions, halved lengthwise
   and shredded, plus extra,
   to garnish

method

1 Pull the flesh and skin off the duck and slice into strips. If you have lots of skin, just keep the crispiest bits. Discard any excess fat.

2 Put half the hoisin or plum sauce into a large bowl, add the duck strips, and toss to coat.

3 Fold a nori sheet in half lengthwise, press along the fold, and then tear it into 2 pieces. Lay a half-sheet smooth-side down on a work surface and place a heaping tbsp of rice on the left-hand side. Lay a sixth of the duck and duck skin on the rice, scatter with some of the shredded scallion, then drizzle over 1 tsp of the remaining hoisin or plum sauce.

4 Fold the bottom left-hand corner of the nori over the rice and filling, so that the folded edge forms a right angle with the bottom edge. Continue folding along that line to make a cone with a sharp point at the bottom. Place a drop of vinegared water on the underside of the join to seal it.

5 Repeat with the rest of the ingredients to make 6 cones in total, transfer to a serving plate, and garnish with the remaining shredded scallions.

duck with mixed bell peppers

ingredients

SERVES 4

1 tbsp vegetable or peanut oil

2 duck breasts, skin on

1 onion, sliced

2 garlic cloves, chopped

1 red bell pepper, seeded and
    chopped

1 green bell pepper, seeded
    and chopped

1 yellow bell pepper, seeded
    and chopped

4 tomatoes, peeled, seeded,
    and chopped

2/3 cup stock

3 tbsp Thai soy sauce

boiled noodles, garnished with
    chopped scallion, to serve

method

1 Heat the oil in a wok and cook the duck breasts over high heat until crisp and brown. Turn over and cook until cooked through. Lift out and keep warm.

2 Pour off any excess fat and stir-fry the onion and garlic for 2–3 minutes, until softened and lightly browned.

3 Add the bell peppers and stir-fry for 2–3 minutes, until tender. Add the tomatoes, stock, and soy sauce, and let simmer for 1–2 minutes. Transfer to a serving plate. Slice the duck thickly and arrange on top, spooning any sauce over it. Serve with noodles.

chinese crispy duck

ingredients

SERVES 4

3 tbsp soy sauce

1/4 tsp Chinese five-spice powder

1/4 tsp pepper and pinch of salt

4 duck legs or breasts, cut into pieces

3 tbsp vegetable oil

1 tsp dark sesame oil

1 tsp finely chopped gingerroot

1 large garlic clove, finely chopped

4 scallions, white part thickly sliced, green part shredded

2 tbsp rice wine or dry sherry

1 tbsp oyster sauce

3 whole star anise

2 tsp black peppercorns

2–2 1/2 cups chicken stock or water

6 dried shiitake mushrooms, soaked in warm water for 20 minutes

8 oz/225 g canned water chestnuts, drained

2 tbsp cornstarch

method

1 Combine 1 tablespoon of the soy sauce, the five-spice powder, pepper, and salt and rub over the duck pieces. Place 2 1/2 tablespoons of vegetable oil in a flameproof casserole, add the duck pieces and cook until browned, then transfer to a plate and set aside.

2 Drain the fat from the casserole and wipe out. Add the sesame oil and remaining vegetable oil and heat. Add the gingerroot and garlic and cook for a few seconds. Add the sliced white scallions and cook for a few more seconds. Return the duck to the casserole. Add the rice wine, oyster sauce, star anise, peppercorns, and remaining soy sauce. Pour in enough stock to just cover the duck. Bring to a boil, cover, and let simmer gently for 1 1/2 hours, adding more stock if necessary.

3 Drain the mushrooms and squeeze dry. Slice the caps, add to the duck with the water chestnuts, and let simmer for an additional 20 minutes.

4 Mix the cornstarch with 2 tablespoons of the cooking liquid to form a smooth paste. Add to the remaining liquid, stirring, until thickened. To serve, garnish with green scallion shreds.

436 meat & poultry

peking duck

ingredients

SERVES 6–10

1 duck, weighing
    4 lb 8 oz/2 kg

7 cups boiling water

1 tbsp honey

1 tbsp Shaoxing rice wine

1 tsp white rice vinegar

1 cucumber, peeled, seeded,
    and julienned

10 scallions, white part only,
    shredded

30 Peking duck pancakes

plum or hoisin sauce, or both

method

1 To prepare the duck, massage the skin to separate it from the meat.

2 Pour the boiling water into a large pan, then add the honey, Shaoxing, and vinegar and lower in the duck. Baste for about 1 minute. Remove the duck and hang it to dry for a few hours or overnight.

3 Preheat the oven to 400°F/200°C. Place the duck on a rack above a roasting pan and roast for at least 1 hour, or until the skin is very crispy and the duck cooked through.

4 Bring the duck to the table, together with the cucumber, scallions, and pancakes, and carve off the skin first. On a pancake, arrange a little skin with some cucumber and scallion pieces. Top with a little plum or hoisin sauce, or both. Roll up and eat. Repeat the process with the lean meat.

duck breasts with chili sauce & lime

ingredients

SERVES 4

4 boneless duck breasts

2 garlic cloves, crushed

4 tsp brown sugar

3 tbsp lime juice

1 tbsp soy sauce

1 tsp chili sauce

1 tsp vegetable oil

2 tbsp plum jelly

1/2 cup chicken stock

salt and pepper

freshly cooked rice and crisp
   salad greens, to serve

method

1 Using a small, sharp knife, cut deep slashes in the skin of the duck to make a diamond pattern. Place the duck breasts in a wide, nonmetallic dish.

2 Mix the garlic, sugar, lime juice, soy sauce, and chili sauce together in a bowl, then spoon over the duck breasts, turning well to coat evenly. Cover and let marinate in the refrigerator for at least 3 hours or overnight.

3 Drain the duck, reserving the marinade. Heat a large, heavy-bottom skillet until very hot and brush with the oil. Add the duck breasts, skin-side down, and cook for 5 minutes, or until the skin is browned and crisp. Tip away the excess fat. Turn the duck breasts over.

4 Continue cooking on the other side for 2–3 minutes to brown. Add the reserved marinade, plum jelly, and stock and simmer for 2 minutes. Season to taste with salt and pepper. Transfer to individual serving plates, then spoon over the pan juices and serve hot with freshly cooked rice and crisp salad greens.

fish & seafood

When it comes to fish and shellfish, finding authentic ingredients may be difficult for the Western cook. Fortunately, many types are as popular and easily available in the West as in the East—tuna, shrimp, crab, squid, and scallops, for example. It is sometimes possible to find more exotic species in Asian grocers and specialty stores, usually deep-frozen, but it's rarely necessary as the recipes work well with a wide variety of more easily available fish.

Of all the countries of Asia, Japan must take the crown for its fish dishes. Not only is the country made up of a group of islands, but for many years the government prohibited the population from eating meat, so fish and shellfish occupied the central place in the Japanese diet. No one will repeat the mistake of thinking that fish is only ever eaten raw in Japan after tasting any of the fabulous traditional ways in which it is cooked.

Many other Asian countries are also made up of islands—Indonesia comprises nearly 14,000 of them—and China's coastline is immensely long, so fish and shellfish are important ingredients in all Asian kitchens. As fish can easily dry out during cooking, it is especially well suited to the speedy method of stir-frying or the moist techniques of steaming or braising. Wrapping whole fish in a banana leaf parcel before cooking it is a popular Southeast Asian method of retaining its delicate texture. Westerners may have to rely on the more prosaic wrappings of waxed paper or foil.

444 fish & seafood

mixed sashimi

ingredients

SERVES 2

1 fresh mackerel, cleaned and
    filleted
1/3 cup rice vinegar
3 scallops, in their shells
5 1/2 oz/150 g sashimi-grade
    tuna, trimmed
5 1/2 oz/150 g sashimi-grade
    salmon, trimmed
2 oz/55 g daikon (long white
    radish), shredded
whole trimmed chives to
    garnish
Japanese wasabi paste
soy sauce, and pickled
    gingerroot, to serve

method

1 Place the mackerel fillets in a shallow, non-metallic dish, pour over the rice vinegar, and cover with plastic wrap. Let marinate in the refrigerator for 1 hour.

2 Remove the mackerel from the marinade, pat dry with paper towels, and take off the skin. Holding a wet, very sharp knife at a 45-degree angle to the chopping board, cut the fish into 1/3-inch/8-mm thick, diagonal slices.

3 To prepare the scallops, insert a short, strong knife between the shells and twist to prise apart. Separate the scallops from their shells. Remove and discard any corals and black matter, the white frills, and membranes. Slice the scallops in half horizontally.

4 Put the halved scallops into a heatproof dish and cover with boiling water. Remove with a slotted spoon straight away. Pat the scallops dry with paper towels.

5 Slice the tuna and salmon into 1/3-inch/8-mm thick rectangles, using a wet, very sharp knife and cutting across the grain. Wipe your knife on a damp cloth between each cut.

6 Place the shredded daikon on a serving platter, place the scallops on top, and arrange the sliced fish around it. Garnish with fresh chives. Add a mound of wasabi paste and serve with soy sauce and pickled gingerroot.

clams in black bean sauce

ingredients

SERVES 4

2 lb/900 g small clams

1 tbsp vegetable or peanut oil

1 tsp finely chopped fresh gingerroot

1 tsp finely chopped garlic

1 tbsp fermented black beans, rinsed and coarsely chopped

2 tsp Shaoxing rice wine

1 tbsp finely chopped scallions

1 tsp salt (optional)

method

1 Start by washing the clams thoroughly, then let them soak in clean water until it is time to drain them and toss them in the wok.

2 In a preheated wok or deep pan, heat the oil and stir-fry the gingerroot and garlic until fragrant. Add the black beans and cook for 1 minute.

3 Over high heat, add the drained clams and Shaoxing and stir-fry for 2 minutes to mix everything together. Cover and cook for about 3 minutes. Add the scallions and salt, if necessary, and serve immediately.

chiles stuffed with fish paste

ingredients

SERVES 4–6

8 oz/225 g white fish, minced
2 tbsp lightly beaten egg
4–6 mild red and green chiles
vegetable or peanut oil, for
    shallow-frying
2 garlic cloves, finely chopped
1/2 tsp fermented black beans,
    rinsed and lightly mashed
1 tbsp light soy sauce
pinch of sugar
1 tbsp water

marinade
1 tsp finely chopped fresh
    gingerroot
pinch of salt
pinch of white pepper
1/2 tsp vegetable or peanut oil

method

1 Combine all the ingredients for the marinade in a bowl and marinate the fish for 20 minutes. Add the egg and mix by hand to create a smooth paste.

2 To prepare the chiles, cut in half lengthwise and scoop out the seeds and loose flesh. Cut into bite-size pieces. Spread each piece of chile with about 1/2 teaspoon of the fish paste.

3 In a preheated wok or deep pan, heat plenty of the oil and cook the chile pieces on both sides until beginning to turn golden brown. Drain and set aside.

4 Heat 1 tablespoon of the oil in a wok or deep pan and stir-fry the garlic until aromatic. Stir in the black beans and mix well. Add the light soy sauce and sugar and stir, then add the chile pieces. Add the water, then cover and let simmer over low heat for 5 minutes. Serve immediately.

chirashi sushi on scallop shells

ingredients

MAKES 8 SHELLS

8 scallops with their shells

1 tbsp vegetable oil

zest and juice of $1/2$ lime

$1/3$ quantity freshly cooked
  sushi rice

small handful of fresh cilantro
  leaves

pickled gingerroot and wasabi
  paste, to garnish

3 tbsp Japanese mayonnaise

method

1 Remove the scallops from their shells. Clean the shells to use for serving.

2 Clean each scallop by pulling off the small, white shiny muscle and its membrane. Leave the roe attached, but snip off the black vein, if present, with a pair of kitchen scissors.

3 Heat the oil in a skillet and sauté the scallops for 2–3 minutes on each side, until they are lightly browned and cooked through. Squeeze a little lime juice over the scallops and let cool.

4 Mix the sushi rice with the remaining lime juice and zest.

5 Divide the lime-flavored sushi rice between the 8 scallop shells. Arrange a scallop along with a few cilantro leaves on top of the rice in each shell, then garnish with a piece of pickled gingerroot, a tiny amount of wasabi, and a heaping tsp of mayonnaise. Serve on a platter with a pile of chopsticks.

simple stir-fried scallops

ingredients

SERVES 4

1 lb/450 g scallops

2 tbsp sesame oil

1 tbsp chopped fresh cilantro

1 tbsp chopped flat-leaf
    parsley

rice noodles, to serve

s a u c e

2 tbsp lemon juice

2 tbsp soy sauce

1 tbsp honey

1 tbsp minced fresh gingerroot

1 tbsp fish sauce

1 clove garlic, peeled and
    flattened

method

1 Combine the lemon juice, soy sauce, honey, gingerroot, fish sauce, and garlic in a bowl and stir well to dissolve the honey. Add the scallops and toss to coat.

2 Heat a heavy skillet or wok over the highest heat for 3 minutes. Add the oil and heat for 30 seconds.

3 Add the scallops with their sauce and the cilantro and parsley to the skillet. Stir constantly, cooking for about 3 minutes (less time if the scallops are small). Serve immediately with rice noodles.

stir-fried scallops with asparagus

ingredients

SERVES 4

8 oz/225 g scallops

2 tsp salt

8 oz/225 g asparagus

3 tbsp vegetable or peanut oil

1/2 cup fresh or canned
   bamboo shoots, rinsed and
   thinly sliced (if using fresh
   shoots, boil in water first for
   30 minutes)

1 small carrot, finely sliced

4 thin slices of fresh gingerroot

pinch of white pepper

2 tbsp Shaoxing rice wine

2 tbsp chicken stock

1 tsp sesame oil

method

1 Sprinkle the scallops with 1 teaspoon of the salt and let stand for 20 minutes.

2 Trim the asparagus, discarding the tough ends. Cut into 2-inch/5-cm pieces and blanch in a large pan of boiling water for 30 seconds. Drain and set aside.

3 In a preheated wok, heat 1 tablespoon of the oil and cook the scallops for 30 seconds. Drain and set aside.

4 In the clean wok, heat another tablespoon of the oil and stir-fry the asparagus, bamboo shoots, and carrot for 2 minutes. Season with the remaining salt. Drain and set aside.

5 In the clean wok, heat the remaining oil, then add the gingerroot and stir-fry until fragrant. Return the scallops and vegetables to the wok and sprinkle with the pepper, Shaoxing, and stock. Cover and continue cooking for 2 minutes, then toss through the sesame oil and serve.

spicy scallops with lime & chile

ingredients

SERVES 4

16 large scallops, shelled

1 tbsp butter

1 tbsp vegetable oil

1 tsp crushed garlic

1 tsp grated fresh gingerroot

1 bunch of scallions, finely
    sliced

finely grated rind of 1 lime

1 small fresh red chile, seeded
    and very finely chopped

3 tbsp lime juice

lime wedges, to garnish

freshly cooked rice, to serve

method

1 Using a sharp knife, trim the scallops to remove any black intestine, then wash and pat dry with paper towels. Separate the corals from the white parts, then slice each white part in half horizontally, making 2 circles.

2 Heat the butter and oil in a skillet or preheated wok.

3 Add the garlic and gingerroot and stir-fry for 1 minute without browning. Add the scallions and stir-fry for an additional 1 minute.

4 Add the scallops and continue stir-frying over high heat for 4–5 minutes. Stir in the lime rind, chile, and lime juice and cook for an additional 1 minute.

5 Transfer the scallops to serving plates, then spoon over the pan juices and garnish with lime wedges. Serve hot with freshly cooked rice.

shrimp tempura & lettuce wraps

ingredients

MAKES 6 PIECES

6 large shrimp, shelled and
   deveined
1⅓ oz/38 g prepared tempura
   mix
vegetable oil, for deep-frying
3 sheets of toasted nori
¼ quantity freshly cooked
   sushi rice
handful of iceberg lettuce
   leaves, shredded
1 red and 1 green chile,
   seeded and cut into very
   fine strips (optional)
tempura dipping sauce,
   to serve

method

1 Cut a few slits on the underside of the shrimp to keep them straight as they cook.

2 Blend the tempura batter with water according to the package instructions. The batter should be lumpy with plenty of air bubbles. Heat the vegetable oil in a deep-fryer to 350–375°F/180–190°C, or until a cube of bread browns in 30 seconds.

3 Dip the prepared shrimp in the batter mix, then drop them into the oil 3 at a time. Cook for 2–3 minutes, until golden. Remove from the oil and drain on paper towels. Let cool.

4 Halve the nori sheets. Lay a half-sheet of nori smooth-side down on a work surface and place a heaping tbsp of rice on the left-hand side. Top with shredded lettuce and 1 tempura shrimp, then add a strip of red and a strip of green chile, if using.

5 Fold the bottom left-hand corner of the nori over the rice and filling, so that the folded edge forms a right angle with the bottom edge. Continue folding along that line to make a cone with a sharp point at the bottom. Place a drop of vinegared water on the underside of the join to seal it. Repeat with the rest of the ingredients to make 6 cones in total. Serve with the tempura dipping sauce.

chirashi sushi with shrimp, crab & avocado

ingredients

SERVES 4

1 tbsp vegetable oil

6 large shrimp, shelled and deveined

1 cooked prepared crab

1 quantity freshly cooked sushi rice

juice and zest of 1 lemon

1 ripe avocado, pitted, peeled, and cut into strips

$1/2$ cucumber, peeled and cut into slices

Japanese soy sauce, pickled gingerroot, and wasabi paste, to serve

method

1 Heat the oil in a wok or skillet and stir-fry the shrimp for 2 minutes on each side. Once they are cooked, let cool, then cut in half lengthwise. Lift the crabmeat out of the shell.

2 Mix the sushi rice with the lemon juice and lemon zest, then divide between 4 serving bowls. Arrange the cooked shrimp, crabmeat, and avocado and cucumber slices on top of the rice. Serve with soy sauce, pickled gingerroot, and wasabi paste.

gingerroot shrimp with oyster mushrooms

ingredients

SERVES 4

about 3 tbsp vegetable oil

3 carrots, sliced thinly

12 oz/350 g oyster
   mushrooms, sliced thinly

1 large red bell pepper, sliced
   thinly

1 lb/450g large shrimp,
   shelled

2 garlic cloves, crushed

fresh cilantro leaves,
   to garnish

sauce

$2/3$ cup chicken stock

2 tsp sesame seeds

3 tsp grated fresh gingerroot

1 tbsp soy sauce

$1/4$ tsp hot pepper sauce

1 tsp cornstarch

method

1 In a small bowl, stir together the chicken stock, sesame seeds, gingerroot, soy sauce, hot pepper sauce, and cornstarch until well blended. Set aside.

2 In a large skillet or wok, heat 2 tablespoons of the oil. Stir-fry the carrots for 3 minutes, then remove from the skillet and set aside.

3 Add another 1 tablespoon of the oil to the skillet and fry the mushrooms for 2 minutes. Remove from the skillet and set aside.

4 Add more oil if needed and stir-fry the bell pepper with the shrimp and garlic for 3 minutes, until the shrimp turn pink and opaque.

5 Stir the sauce again and pour it into the skillet. Cook until the mixture bubbles, then return the carrots and mushrooms to the skillet. Cover and cook for an additional 2 minutes, until heated through. Serve garnished with cilantro.

shrimp, snow peas & cashew nuts

ingredients

SERVES 4

generous ½ cup cashew nuts

3 tbsp peanut oil

4 scallions, slivered

2 celery stalks, sliced thinly

3 carrots, sliced finely

3½ oz/100 g baby corn,
    halved

6 oz/175 g mushrooms, sliced
    finely

1 clove of garlic, chopped
    coarsely

1 lb/450 g shrimp, shelled

1 tsp cornstarch

2 tbsp soy sauce

¼ cup chicken stock

8 oz/225 g savoy cabbage,
    shredded

6 oz/175 g snow peas

freshly cooked rice, to serve

method

1 Put a skillet or wok over medium heat, add the cashew nuts, and toast them until they begin to brown. Remove with a slotted spoon and set aside.

2 Add the oil to the skillet and heat. Add the scallions, celery, carrots, and baby corn and cook, stirring occasionally, over medium-high heat for 3–4 minutes.

3 Add the mushrooms and cook until they become brown. Mix in the garlic and shrimp, stirring until the shrimp turn pink.

4 Mix the cornstarch with the soy sauce and chicken stock until smooth. Add the liquid to the shrimp mixture and stir. Then add the savoy cabbage, snow peas, and all but a few of the cashew nuts and cook for 2 minutes.

5 Garnish with the reserved cashew nuts and serve on a bed of rice.

curried noodles with shrimp & straw mushrooms

ingredients

SERVES 4

1 tbsp vegetable or peanut oil

3 shallots, chopped

1 fresh red chile, seeded and
   chopped

1 tbsp red curry paste

1 lemongrass stalk (white part
   only), chopped finely

8 oz/225 g cooked shelled
   shrimp

14 oz/400 g canned straw
   mushrooms, drained

2 tbsp fish sauce

2 tbsp Thai soy sauce

8 oz/225 g fresh egg noodles

fresh cilantro, chopped,
   to garnish

method

1 Heat the oil in a wok and stir-fry the shallots and chile for 2–3 minutes. Add the curry paste and lemongrass and stir-fry for 2–3 minutes.

2 Add the shrimp, mushrooms, fish sauce, and soy sauce, and stir well to mix.

3 Meanwhile, cook the noodles in boiling water for 3–4 minutes, drain, and transfer to warmed plates.

4 Top with the shrimp curry, sprinkle the cilantro over, and serve immediately.

shrimp & pineapple curry

ingredients

SERVES 4

1/2 fresh pineapple

1 3/4 cups coconut cream

2 tbsp Thai red curry paste

2 tbsp fish sauce

2 tsp sugar

12 oz/350 g jumbo shrimp

2 tbsp chopped cilantro

steamed jasmine rice, to serve

method

1 Peel the pineapple and chop the flesh. Heat the coconut cream, pineapple, curry paste, fish sauce, and sugar until almost boiling.

2 Shell and devein the shrimp. Add the shrimp and cilantro to the pan and simmer for 3 minutes, or until the shrimp have turned a bright pink color.

3 Serve the shrimp with steamed jasmine rice.

noodles with shrimp & green bell peppers

ingredients

SERVES 4

9 oz/250 g rice noodles

1 tbsp vegetable oil

2 garlic cloves, crushed

1 fresh red chile, seeded and
   thinly sliced

1 green bell pepper, seeded
   and thinly sliced

6 scallions, coarsely chopped

2 tsp cornstarch

2 tbsp oyster sauce

1 tbsp Thai fish sauce

1 tsp sugar

1 cup chicken stock

9 oz/250 g small cooked
   shrimp, shelled

method

1 Prepare the noodles according to the package directions. Drain, then rinse under cold water and drain again.

2 Heat the oil in a preheated wok. Add the garlic, chile, bell pepper, and scallions. Cook for 1 minute, then transfer to a plate and reserve.

3 Blend the cornstarch with a little water and add to the wok with the oyster sauce, fish sauce, sugar, and stock. Stir over medium heat until the mixture boils and thickens.

4 Return the bell pepper and scallion mixture to the wok with the shrimp and noodles. Cook, stirring, for 2 minutes, or until heated through. Transfer to a heated serving bowl and serve immediately.

shrimp with noodles

ingredients

SERVES 4

1 lb/450 g jumbo shrimp

1 tbsp vegetable or peanut oil

3 shallots, chopped finely

2 garlic cloves, chopped finely

1-inch/2.5-cm piece fresh
   gingerroot, sliced thinly

1³/₄ cups canned coconut milk

1 tbsp green curry paste

3–4 fresh Thai basil leaves

1 tsp jaggery or soft light
   brown sugar

8 oz/225 g flat rice noodles

2 tsp sesame oil

2 tbsp sesame seeds, toasted

sprigs fresh Thai basil,
   to garnish

method

1 Remove and discard the heads and shell the shrimp. Cut a slit along the back of each and remove and discard the dark vein.

2 Heat the oil in a wok and stir-fry the shallots, garlic, and gingerroot for 2–3 minutes. Add the coconut milk and curry paste and let simmer for 2–3 minutes.

3 Add the shrimp, basil leaves, and sugar, and cook until the shrimp turn pink.

4 Meanwhile, cook the noodles in boiling water according to the package instructions, then drain well. Stir in the sesame oil and seeds, garnish with the sprigs of basil, and serve immediately with the shrimp.

shrimp with coconut rice

ingredients

SERVES 4

1 cup dried Chinese
    mushrooms

2 tbsp vegetable or peanut oil

6 scallions, chopped

scant $1/2$ cup dry unsweetened
    coconut

1 fresh green chile, seeded
    and chopped

generous 1 cup jasmine rice

$2/3$ cup fish stock

$13/4$ cups coconut milk

12 oz/350 g cooked shelled
    shrimp

6 sprigs fresh Thai basil

method

1 Place the mushrooms in a small bowl, cover with hot water, and set aside to soak for 30 minutes. Drain, then cut off and discard the stalks and slice the caps.

2 Heat 1 tablespoon of the oil in a wok and stir-fry the scallions, coconut, and chile for 2–3 minutes, until lightly browned. Add the mushrooms and stir-fry for 3–4 minutes.

3 Add the rice and stir-fry for 2–3 minutes, then add the stock and bring to a boil. Reduce the heat and add the coconut milk. Let simmer for 10–15 minutes, until the rice is tender. Stir in the shrimp and basil, heat through, and serve.

shrimp with scallions & straw mushrooms

ingredients

SERVES 4

2 tbsp vegetable or peanut oil

bunch of scallions, chopped

2 garlic cloves, chopped finely

6 oz/175 g block creamed
   coconut, chopped coarsely

2 tbsp red curry paste

scant 2 cups fish stock

2 tbsp fish sauce

2 tbsp Thai soy sauce

6 sprigs fresh Thai basil

14 oz/400 g canned straw
   mushrooms, drained

12 oz/350 g large cooked
   shelled shrimp

boiled jasmine rice, to serve

method

1 Heat the oil in a wok and stir-fry the scallions and garlic for 2–3 minutes. Add the creamed coconut, red curry paste, and stock, and heat gently until the coconut has dissolved.

2 Stir in the fish sauce and soy sauce, then add the basil, mushrooms, and shrimp. Gradually bring to a boil and serve immediately with jasmine rice.

malaysian-style coconut noodles with shrimp

ingredients

SERVES 4

2 tbsp vegetable oil

1 small red bell pepper, seeded and diced

7 oz/200 g bok choy, stalks thinly sliced and leaves chopped

2 large garlic cloves, chopped

1 tsp ground turmeric

2 tsp garam masala

1 tsp chili powder (optional)

1/2 cup hot vegetable stock

2 heaping tbsp smooth peanut butter

1 1/2 cups coconut milk

1 tbsp soy sauce

9 oz/250 g thick rice noodles

10 oz/280 g cooked shelled jumbo shrimp

2 scallions, finely shredded and 1 tbsp sesame seeds, to garnish

method

1 Heat the oil in a preheated wok or large, heavy-bottom skillet over high heat. Add the red bell pepper, bok choy stalks, and garlic and stir-fry for 3 minutes. Add the turmeric, garam masala, chili powder, if using, and bok choy leaves, and stir-fry for 1 minute.

2 Mix the hot stock and peanut butter together in a heatproof bowl until the peanut butter has dissolved, then add to the stir-fry with the coconut milk and tamari. Cook for 5 minutes over medium heat, or until reduced and thickened.

3 Meanwhile, immerse the noodles in a bowl of just boiled water. Let stand for 4 minutes, then drain and refresh the noodles under cold running water. Add the cooked noodles and shrimp to the coconut curry and cook for an additional 2–3 minutes, stirring frequently, until heated through.

4 Serve the noodle dish sprinkled with scallions and sesame seeds.

shrimp laksa

ingredients

SERVES 4

20–24 large unshelled shrimp
2 cups fish stock
pinch of salt
1 tsp peanut oil
2 cups coconut milk
2 tsp nam pla (Thai fish sauce)
1/2 tablespoon lime juice
4 oz/115 g dried medium
    rice-flour noodles
1/2 cup bean sprouts
fresh cilantro, chopped,
    to garnish

laksa paste

6 fresh cilantro stalks with
    leaves
3 large garlic cloves, crushed
1 fresh red chile, seeded and
    chopped
1 lemongrass stalk, center part
    only, chopped
1-inch/2.5-cm piece fresh
    gingerroot, peeled and
    chopped
1 1/2 tbsp shrimp paste
1/2 tsp ground turmeric
2 tbsp peanut oil

method

1 Remove the heads and shells from the shrimp, leaving the tails intact, and devein. Reserve the heads and shells. Put the fish stock, salt, and the shrimp heads and shells in a pan over high heat and slowly bring to a boil. Lower the heat and let simmer for 10 minutes.

2 Meanwhile, make the laksa paste. Put all the ingredients, except the oil, in a food processor and blend. With the motor running, slowly add up to 2 tablespoons of peanut oil just until a paste forms. (If your food processor is too large to work efficiently with this small quantity, use a mortar and pestle.)

3 Heat 1 teaspoon of peanut oil in a large pan over high heat. Add the paste and stir-fry until it is fragrant. Strain the fish stock through a strainer lined with cheesecloth. Stir the stock into the laksa paste, along with the coconut milk, nam pla, and lime juice. Bring to a boil, then cover and let simmer for 30 minutes.

4 Meanwhile, soak the noodles in a large bowl with enough lukewarm water to cover for 20 minutes, until soft. Drain and set aside.

5 Add the shrimp and bean sprouts to the soup and continue simmering just until the shrimp turn opaque and curl. Divide the noodles among 4 bowls and ladle the soup over. Garnish with chopped cilantro and serve.

thai fisherman's catch

ingredients

SERVES 4

20 cooked jumbo shrimp

20 cooked mussels in their
shells (be sure to discard
any mussels that remain
closed after cooking)

2 oz/55 g oyster mushrooms,
wiped clean

2 scallions, finely sliced

3 kaffir lime leaves, thinly
sliced

1 lemongrass stalk, center part
only, finely chopped

1/2 red onion, very thinly sliced

31/2 oz/100 g dried medium
rice noodles

thai coconut
dressing

1/2 cup creamed coconut

3 tbsp lime juice

11/2 tbsp nam pla (Thai fish
sauce)

11/2 tbsp brown sugar

1–2 fresh red chiles, to taste,
seeded and thinly sliced

1 small garlic clove, crushed

method

1 To make the dressing, stir all the ingredients together in a large bowl until the sugar dissolves. Add the shrimp, mussels, mushrooms, scallions, lime leaves, lemongrass, and red onion, then cover and let chill until required.

2 Meanwhile, soak the noodles in a bowl with enough lukewarm water to cover for 20 minutes, until soft, or cook according to the package instructions. Drain well.

3 To serve, divide the noodles among 4 bowls. Spoon the seafood salad over them, adding any extra dressing.

shrimp fu yung

ingredients

SERVES 4–6

1 tbsp vegetable or peanut oil

4 oz/115 g shrimp, peeled and
  deveined

4 eggs, lightly beaten

1 tsp salt

pinch of white pepper

2 tbsp finely chopped Chinese
  chives

method

1 In a preheated wok, heat the oil and stir-fry the shrimp until they begin to turn pink.

2 Season the beaten eggs with the salt and pepper and pour over the shrimp. Stir-fry for 1 minute, then add the chives.

3 Cook for an additional 4 minutes, stirring all the time, until the eggs are cooked through but still soft in texture, and serve immediately.

wok-fried jumbo shrimp in spicy sauce

ingredients

SERVES 4

3 tbsp vegetable or peanut oil

1 lb/450 g jumbo shrimp, deveined but unpeeled

2 tsp finely chopped fresh gingerroot

1 tsp finely chopped garlic

1 tbsp chopped scallion

2 tbsp chili bean sauce

1 tsp Shaoxing rice wine

1 tsp sugar

$1/2$ tsp light soy sauce

1–2 tbsp chicken stock

method

1 In a preheated wok, heat the oil, then toss in the shrimp and stir-fry over high heat for about 4 minutes. Arrange the shrimp on the sides of the wok out of the oil, then throw in the gingerroot and garlic and stir until fragrant. Add the scallion and chili bean sauce. Stir the shrimp into this mixture.

2 Lower the heat slightly and add the Shaoxing, sugar, light soy sauce, and a little chicken stock. Cover and cook for an additional minute. Serve immediately.

somen noodles with shrimp

ingredients

SERVES 2

1 tbsp oil

16 shrimp, shelled and deveined

3 shiitake mushrooms, finely sliced

1/4 white or green cabbage, shredded

1 carrot, shredded

2 bundles of somen noodles

6 shiso leaves, shredded

dressing

3 tbsp oil

1 tbsp sesame seeds, toasted

1/2 cup Japanese rice vinegar

1 tbsp sugar

1 tbsp usukuchi shoyu (Japanese light soy sauce)

salt

method

1 To make the dressing, mix all the dressing ingredients together, with salt to taste, in a nonmetallic bowl.

2 Preheat a wok over high heat. Add the 1 tablespoon of oil and heat until very hot. Add the shrimp and cook, tossing occasionally, until they have turned pink.

3 Add the mushrooms to the wok and stir-fry for 1 minute, then add the cabbage and carrot and toss together. Remove from the heat and let cool.

4 Cook the noodles according to the package instructions, then drain. Put in a large bowl with the shrimp mixture. Add the dressing and toss well. Sprinkle with the shiso leaves and serve.

crab soufflé

ingredients

SERVES 4–6

3 tbsp butter, plus extra for greasing

1/4 cup dried breadcrumbs

1 small onion, finely chopped

1 garlic clove, crushed

2 tsp mustard powder

scant 1/2 cup all-purpose flour

1 cup milk

scant 1/2 cup grated Gruyère cheese

3 eggs, separated

8 oz/225 g fresh crabmeat, thawed if frozen

2 tbsp snipped fresh chives

pinch of cayenne pepper

salt and pepper

method

1 Preheat the oven to 400°F/200°C. Generously grease a 6-cup soufflé dish. Add the breadcrumbs and shake around the dish to coat completely, shaking out any excess. Set aside on a cookie sheet.

2 Melt the butter in a large pan over low heat, add the onion, and cook, stirring occasionally, for 8 minutes, until softened but not browned. Add the garlic and cook, stirring, for 1 minute. Then add the mustard powder and flour and continue stirring for another minute. Gradually add the milk, stirring constantly, until smooth. Increase the heat slightly and bring slowly to a boil, stirring constantly. Let simmer gently for 2 minutes. Remove from the heat and stir in the cheese. Let cool slightly.

3 Lightly beat in the egg yolks, then fold in the crabmeat, chives, cayenne, salt, and pepper.

4 Whisk the egg whites in a large, clean, greasefree bowl until they hold stiff peaks. Add a large spoonful of the egg whites to the crab mixture and fold together to slacken. Add the remaining egg whites and fold together carefully but thoroughly. Spoon into the prepared dish.

5 Cook in the preheated oven for 25 minutes until well risen and golden. Serve at once.

thai-style chirashi sushi with crabmeat

ingredients

SERVES 4

6 oz/175 g cooked crabmeat

juice of 2 limes, plus 4 thin
    slices of lime to garnish

2 large red chiles, seeded and
    finely chopped

1 cup shelled fresh peas

salt

1 quantity freshly cooked
    sushi rice

2 tbsp chopped fresh cilantro

1 sheet of toasted nori, cut
    into thin strips

method

1 Put the crabmeat in a bowl and squeeze over the lime juice. Stir in the chopped chile.

2 Place the peas in a pan of boiling salted water for 2 minutes or until just tender, then plunge into ice-cold water to stop the cooking. Drain well.

3 Add the peas to the sushi rice, turning the rice to mix evenly. Divide the mixture between 4 serving bowls.

4 Top each bowl with a quarter of the crab mixture and sprinkle with 1/2 tbsp of the chopped cilantro. Add a quarter of the nori strips, and garnish with a slice of lime.

fried fish with pine nuts

ingredients

SERVES 4–6

1/2 tsp salt

1 lb/450 g thick white fish
fillets, cut into 1-inch/
2.5-cm cubes

2 dried Chinese mushrooms,
soaked in warm water
for 20 minutes

3 tbsp vegetable or peanut oil

1-inch/2.5-cm piece of fresh
gingerroot, finely shredded

1 tbsp chopped scallions

1 red bell pepper, cut into
1-inch/2.5-cm squares

1 green bell pepper, cut into
1-inch/2.5-cm squares

25 g/1 oz fresh or canned
bamboo shoots, rinsed
and cut into small cubes (if
using fresh shoots, boil in
water first for 30 minutes)

2 tsp Shaoxing rice wine

2 tbsp pine nuts, toasted

method

1 Sprinkle the salt over the fish and set aside for 20 minutes. Squeeze out any excess water from the mushrooms and finely slice, discarding any tough stems.

2 In a preheated wok, heat 2 tablespoons of the oil and fry the fish for 3 minutes. Drain and set aside.

3 In a clean, preheated wok, heat the remaining oil and toss in the gingerroot. Stir until fragrant, then add the scallions, peppers, bamboo shoots, mushrooms, and Shaoxing and cook for 1–2 minutes.

4 Finally add the fish and stir to warm through. Sprinkle with the pine nuts and serve.

whole deep-fried fish with soy & gingerroot

ingredients

SERVES 4–6

6 dried Chinese mushrooms, soaked in warm water for 20 minutes

3 tbsp rice vinegar

2 tbsp brown sugar

3 tbsp dark soy sauce

3-inch/7.5-cm piece fresh gingerroot, finely chopped

4 scallions, sliced diagonally

2 tsp cornstarch

2 tbsp lime juice

1 sea bass, cleaned and scaled, about 2 lb 4 oz/ 1 kg

4 tbsp all-purpose flour

sunflower oil, for deep-frying

salt and pepper

shredded Napa cabbage and radish slices, to serve

1 radish, sliced but left whole, to garnish

method

1 Drain the mushrooms, reserving scant 1/2 cup of the liquid. Cut the mushrooms into thin slices. Mix the reserved mushroom liquid with the vinegar, sugar, and soy sauce. Put in a pan with the mushrooms and bring to a boil. Reduce the heat and let simmer for 3–4 minutes. Add the gingerroot and scallions and let simmer for 1 minute.

2 Blend the cornstarch and lime juice together, stir into the pan, and cook, stirring constantly, for 1–2 minutes until the sauce thickens and clears. Set aside.

3 Season the fish inside and out with salt and pepper, then dust lightly with flour.

4 Heat 1 inch/2.5 cm of oil in a wide, heavy-bottom pan to 350–375°F/180–190°C, or until a cube of bread browns in 30 seconds. Lower the fish carefully into the oil and deep-fry on one side for 3–4 minutes until golden brown. Use 2 metal spatulas to turn the fish carefully and deep-fry on the other side for an additional 3–4 minutes, until golden brown.

5 Remove the fish, drain off the excess oil, and put on a serving plate. Reheat the sauce until boiling, then spoon it over the fish. Serve at once with shredded Napa cabbage and sliced radishes, garnished with a sliced whole radish.

shrimp & haddock with rice

ingredients

SERVES 4–6

1/2 cup brown rice

salt and pepper

a few saffron threads

10 1/2 oz/300 g undyed
    smoked haddock fillets

1 bay leaf

1 large onion

2/3 cup milk

4 oz/115 g green beans,
    chopped

2 tbsp olive oil

1–2 garlic cloves, crushed

2/3 cup fish stock

scant 3/4 cup corn kernels,
    thawed if frozen

2 tomatoes, chopped

8 oz/225 g jumbo shrimp,
    shelled

1 tbsp chopped fresh cilantro

method

1 Cook the rice in a pan of lightly salted boiling water with the saffron for 25 minutes, or until tender. Drain and set aside.

2 Meanwhile, rinse the haddock and put into a skillet with the bay leaf. Cut a few slices off the onion and add to the skillet. Pour over the milk and bring to a boil, then reduce the heat and let simmer for 10 minutes, or until the fish is cooked. Drain and let cool slightly. When cool enough to handle, remove and discard the skin and any remaining bones and flake the flesh into small pieces.

3 Cook the beans in a pan of lightly salted boiling water for 5 minutes, drain, then plunge into cold water. Drain again and set aside.

4 Finely chop the remaining onion. Heat the oil in a large skillet over medium heat, add the onion and garlic, and cook for 5 minutes, stirring frequently. Add the cooked rice, stock, haddock, beans, corn, tomatoes, and jumbo shrimp. Cook, stirring occasionally, for 10 minutes, or until the shrimp are cooked and have turned pink. Add salt and pepper to taste, stir in the cilantro, and serve.

five-willow fish

ingredients

SERVES 4–6

1 whole sea bass or similar,
   weighing 1 lb–1 lb 8 oz/
   450–675 g, gutted

2 tsp salt

6 tbsp vegetable or peanut oil

2 slices fresh gingerroot

2 garlic cloves, finely sliced

2 scallions, coarsely chopped

1 green bell pepper, thinly
   sliced

1 red bell pepper, thinly sliced

1 carrot, finely sliced

1/2 cup fresh or canned
   bamboo shoots, rinsed and
   thinly sliced (if using fresh
   shoots, boil in water first for
   30 minutes)

2 tomatoes, peeled, seeded,
   and thinly sliced

1 tbsp Shaoxing rice wine

2 tbsp white rice vinegar

1 tbsp light soy sauce

1 tbsp sugar

method

1 To prepare the fish, clean and dry it thoroughly. Score the fish on both sides with deep, diagonal cuts. Press 1/2 teaspoon of the salt into the skin.

2 In a preheated wok or deep pan, heat 4 tablespoons of the oil and cook the fish for about 4 minutes on each side, or until the flesh is soft. Drain, then set aside and keep warm.

3 In a preheated wok or deep pan, heat the remaining oil and stir-fry the gingerroot, garlic, and scallions until fragrant. Toss in the vegetables with the remaining salt and stir rapidly for 2–3 minutes. Add the remaining ingredients and mix well for 2–3 minutes. Pour the sauce over the fish and serve immediately.

steamed sole with black bean sauce

ingredients

SERVES 3–4

1 sole, gutted

$1/2$ tsp salt

2 tsp fermented black beans, rinsed and chopped

2 tsp finely chopped garlic

1 tsp finely shredded fresh gingerroot

1 tbsp shredded scallions

1 tbsp light soy sauce

1 tsp Shaoxing rice wine

1 tsp vegetable or peanut oil

dash of sesame oil

$1/2$ tsp sugar

pinch of white pepper

method

1 Place the fish on a plate or create a small dish with foil.

2 Arrange all the other ingredients on top of the fish. Place in a steamer for about 10–12 minutes, or until the fish is cooked through.

deep-fried river fish with chili bean sauce

ingredients

SERVES 4–6

1 whole freshwater fish, such as trout or carp, weighing 14 oz/400 g, gutted

1 heaped tbsp all-purpose flour

pinch of salt

scant 1/2 cup water

vegetable or peanut oil, for deep-frying

sauce

scant 1/2 cup vegetable or peanut oil

1 tsp dried chile flakes

1 garlic clove, finely chopped

1 tsp finely chopped fresh gingerroot

1 tbsp chili bean sauce

1/2 tsp white pepper

2 tsp sugar

1 tbsp white rice vinegar

1 tsp finely chopped scallions

method

1 To prepare the fish, clean and dry thoroughly. Mix together the flour, salt, and water to create a light batter. Coat the fish.

2 Heat enough oil for deep-frying in a wok, deep-fat fryer, or large heavy-bottom pan until it reaches 350–375°F/180–190°C, or until a cube of bread browns in 30 seconds. Deep-fry the fish on one side at a time until the skin is crisp and golden brown. Drain, then set aside and keep warm.

3 To make the sauce, heat all but 1 tablespoon of the oil in a small pan and, when smoking, pour over the dried chile flakes. Set aside.

4 In a preheated wok or deep pan, heat the remaining oil and stir-fry the garlic and gingerroot until fragrant. Stir in the chili bean sauce, then add the oil and chile flake mixture. Season with the pepper, sugar, and vinegar. Turn off the heat and stir in the scallions. Tip over the fish and serve immediately.

lemon pepper crab sushi boats

ingredients

MAKES 8 PIECES

1 small cooked prepared crab

1 tsp grated lemon zest

2 tbsp Japanese mayonnaise

salt and black pepper

$1/3$ quantity freshly cooked
   sushi rice

2 sheets of toasted nori, each
   cut into 4 strips lengthwise

juice of 1 lemon

2 lemons, cut into wedges,
   to garnish

method

1 Lift the crabmeat out of the shell and mix with the grated lemon zest and mayonnaise. Season with salt and plenty of black pepper.

2 Divide the rice into 8 equal batches. Wet your hands to stop the rice sticking, then shape each batch of the rice into an oval. Carefully wrap a strip of nori round each oval of rice, trimming off any excess. Place a drop of vinegared water on the underside of the join to seal it.

3 Top the sushi boat with a sixth of the crab mixture, then squeeze over a few drops of lemon juice. Repeat with the remaining ingredients, and serve with lemon wedges on the side.

pork & romaine lettuce in egg & lemon sauce

ingredients

SERVES 4

4 pork loin steaks

salt and pepper

2 tbsp olive oil

bunch scallions, white parts
    only, sliced thinly

1 romaine lettuce, sliced thinly
    widthwise

1 tbsp chopped fresh dill

1 cup chicken stock

2 eggs

juice of 1 large lemon

method

1 Season the pork steaks with pepper. Heat the oil in a large, heavy-bottom skillet, add the scallions and fry until softened. Add the pork steaks and fry for 10 minutes, turning the steaks several times, until browned on both sides and tender.

2 When the pork steaks are cooked, add the lettuce, dill, and stock to the skillet. Bring to a boil, cover, and then simmer for 4–5 minutes or until the lettuce has wilted.

3 Meanwhile, put the eggs and lemon juice in a large bowl and whisk together.

4 When the lettuce has wilted, remove the pork steaks and lettuce from the skillet with a slotted spoon, put in a warmed serving dish, and keep warm in a low oven. Strain the cooking liquid into a measuring pitcher.

5 Gradually add 4 tablespoons of the hot cooking liquid to the lemon mixture, whisking all the time. Pour the egg mixture into the skillet and simmer for 2–3 minutes, whisking all the time, until the sauce thickens. (Do not boil or the sauce will curdle.) Season with salt and pepper. Pour the sauce over the pork steaks and lettuce and serve hot.

stir-fried fresh crab with gingerroot

ingredients

SERVES 4

3 tbsp vegetable or peanut oil

2 large fresh crabs, cleaned, broken into pieces and legs cracked with a cleaver

1½–inch/4-cm piece fresh gingerroot, julienned

3½ oz/100 g scallions, chopped into 2-inch/5-cm lengths

2 tbsp light soy sauce

1 tsp sugar

pinch of white pepper

method

1 In a preheated wok or deep pan, heat 2 tablespoons of the oil and cook the crab over high heat for 3–4 minutes. Remove and set aside.

2 In the clean wok or deep pan, heat the remaining oil, then toss in the gingerroot and stir until fragrant. Add the scallions, then stir in the crab pieces. Add the light soy sauce, sugar, and pepper. Cover and let simmer for 1 minute, then serve immediately.

chirashi sushi with lobster & wasabi mayonnaise

ingredients

SERVES 4

1 cooked prepared lobster

5 tbsp pickled gingerroot

1 quantity freshly cooked
    sushi rice

1/2 cucumber, cut into slices

1 ripe avocado, peeled, pitted,
    and cut into slices

2 tsp wasabi paste

wasabi mayonnaise

2 tbsp Japanese mayonnaise

1 tsp wasabi paste, or to taste

method

1 Take the meat out of the lobster shell, keeping it in as large pieces as you can. If your lobster is whole, the best way to do this is to twist off the head and halve the body down the center with a big sharp knife or cleaver. The claws will have to be smashed open to get at the meat. Cover them with a cloth and hit them hard with a rolling pin.

2 Make the wasabi mayonnaise by mixing together the mayonnaise and wasabi.

3 Chop 1 tablespoon of the pickled gingerroot very finely and mix it with the sushi rice.

4 Divide the rice between 4 serving bowls. Arrange the lobster, cucumber, and avocado on top of the rice and spoon the wasabi mayonnaise into the gaps. Garnish each bowl with 1 tbsp of the pickled gingerroot and 1/2 teaspoon of the wasabi paste.

baby squid stuffed with pork & mushrooms

ingredients

SERVES 6–8

14 oz/400 g squid

4 dried Chinese mushrooms, soaked in warm water for 20 minutes

2 cups ground pork

4 water chestnuts, finely chopped

1/2 tsp sesame oil

1 tsp salt

1/2 tsp white pepper

dark soy sauce and 1 red Thai chile, chopped (optional), to serve

method

1 Clean the squid thoroughly, removing all the tentacles. Squeeze out any excess water from the mushrooms and finely chop, discarding any tough stems.

2 Mix the mushrooms with the pork, water chestnuts, sesame oil, salt, and pepper.

3 Force the stuffing into the squid, pressing firmly but leaving enough room to secure each one with a toothpick.

4 Steam for 15 minutes. Serve with a good soy sauce for dipping, adding the chile, if you like.

sweet chile squid

ingredients

SERVES 4

1 tbsp sesame seeds, toasted

$2^1/2$ tbsp sesame oil

10 oz/280 g squid, cut into
strips

2 red bell peppers, sliced
thinly

3 shallots, sliced thinly

$1^1/2$ cups thinly sliced
mushrooms

1 tbsp dry sherry

4 tbsp soy sauce

1 tsp sugar

1 tsp hot chile flakes,
or to taste

1 clove of garlic, crushed

freshly cooked rice, to serve

method

1 Place the sesame seeds on a cookie sheet, toast under a hot broiler, and set aside.

2 Heat 1 tablespoon of the oil in a skillet or wok over medium heat. Add the squid and cook for 2 minutes, then remove and set aside.

3 Add the other 1 tablespoon of oil to the skillet and fry the bell peppers and shallots over medium heat for 1 minute. Add the mushrooms and fry for an additional 2 minutes.

4 Return the squid to the skillet and add the sherry, soy sauce, sugar, chile flakes, and garlic, stirring thoroughly. Cook for an additional 2 minutes.

5 Sprinkle with the toasted sesame seeds, drizzle over the remaining sesame oil and mix. Serve on a bed of rice.

stir-fried squid with hot black bean sauce

ingredients

SERVES 4

1 lb 10 oz/750 g squid, cleaned and tentacles discarded

1 large red bell pepper, seeded

scant 1 cup snow peas

1 head bok choy

3 tbsp black bean sauce

1 tbsp Thai fish sauce

1 tbsp rice wine or dry sherry

1 tbsp dark soy sauce

1 tsp brown sugar

1 tsp cornstarch

1 tbsp water

1 tbsp corn oil

1 tsp sesame oil

1 small fresh red Thai chile, chopped

1 garlic clove, finely chopped

1 tsp grated fresh gingerroot

2 scallions, chopped

method

1 Cut the squid body cavities into fourths lengthwise. Use the tip of a small, sharp knife to score a diamond pattern into the flesh, without cutting all the way through. Pat dry with paper towels.

2 Cut the bell pepper into long, thin slices. Cut the snow peas in half diagonally. Coarsely shred the bok choy.

3 Mix the black bean sauce, fish sauce, rice wine, soy sauce, and sugar together in a bowl. Blend the cornstarch with the water and stir into the other sauce ingredients. Reserve until required.

4 Heat the oils in a preheated wok. Add the chile, garlic, gingerroot, and scallions and stir-fry for 1 minute. Add the bell pepper slices and stir-fry for 2 minutes.

5 Add the squid and stir-fry over high heat for an additional 1 minute. Stir in the snow peas and bok choy and stir for an additional 1 minute, or until wilted.

6 Stir in the sauce ingredients and cook, stirring constantly, for 2 minutes, or until the sauce thickens and clears. Serve immediately.

squid & red bell peppers

ingredients

SERVES 4

spice paste

2 tbsp vegetable or peanut oil

1 tbsp chili oil with shrimp

2 shallots, chopped

2–3 large fresh red chiles,
    seeded and chopped
    coarsely

2 tbsp ground coriander

2 tbsp ground cumin

1-inch piece fresh gingerroot,
    chopped

1 tbsp finely chopped
    lemongrass

3–4 cilantro roots, chopped

1 tsp salt

1 tsp jaggery or soft light
    brown sugar

stir-fry

2 red bell peppers, seeded
    and diced

2/3 cup plain yogurt

1 lb 10 oz/750 g squid,
    cleaned and sliced

juice of 1 lime

4 oz/115 g block creamed
    coconut, chopped

2/3 cup hot water

method

1 Put all the ingredients for the spice paste into a food processor and process until chopped finely.

2 Scrape the spice paste into a wok and stir-fry gently for 3–4 minutes. Add the red bell peppers and stir-fry for 1–2 minutes.

3 Add the yogurt and bring to a boil. Add the squid and let simmer for 2–3 minutes, then stir in the lime juice, coconut, and water. Let simmer for an additional 1–2 minutes, until the coconut dissolves. Serve immediately.

squid & red onion stir-fry

ingredients

SERVES 4

1 lb/450 g squid rings
2 tbsp all-purpose flour
$1/2$ tsp salt
1 green bell pepper
2 tbsp peanut oil
1 red onion, sliced
$5^3/4$ oz/160 g black bean
  sauce

method

1 Rinse the squid rings under cold running water and pat dry with paper towels.

2 Place the all-purpose flour and salt in a bowl and mix together. Add the squid rings and toss until they are finely coated.

3 Using a sharp knife, seed the bell pepper and slice into thin strips.

4 Heat the peanut oil in a large preheated wok. Add the bell pepper and red onion to the wok and stir-fry for 2 minutes, or until the vegetables are just beginning to soften. Add the squid rings to the wok and cook for an additional 5 minutes, or until the squid is cooked through.

5 Add the black bean sauce to the wok and heat through until the juices are bubbling. Transfer to warmed bowls and serve at once.

salt & pepper squid wraps

ingredients

MAKES 6 PIECES

4 tbsp all-purpose flour

1 tsp Sichuan pepper or black pepper, crushed

1 tsp sea salt, crushed

12 squid rings, membranes removed, cut in half

vegetable oil, for frying

3 sheets of toasted nori

1/4 quantity freshly cooked sushi rice

4 tbsp Japanese mayonnaise

method

1 Mix the flour with the crushed Sichuan or black pepper and salt. Put the seasoned flour into a plastic bag with the squid, and shake until the squid is thoroughly coated.

2 Heat about 3/4 inch/2 cm of oil in a wok until it is very hot. Add the seasoned squid in batches and cook, stirring, for 1 minute, or until the coating is browned. Drain on paper towels to get rid of any excess oil.

3 Fold a nori sheet in half lengthwise, press along the fold, and then tear it into 2 pieces. Lay a half-sheet smooth-side down on a work surface and place a heaping tbsp of rice on the left. Lay 4 cooked squid halves on the rice, and spoon over 2/3 tsp of the mayonnaise.

4 Fold the bottom left-hand corner of the nori over the rice and filling, so that the folded edge forms a right angle with the bottom edge. Continue folding along that line to make a cone with a sharp point at the bottom. Place a drop of vinegared water on the underside of the seam to seal it.

5 Repeat with the rest of the ingredients to make 6 cones in total.

rice with seafood & squid

ingredients

SERVES 4

2 tbsp vegetable or peanut oil

3 shallots, chopped finely

2 garlic cloves, chopped finely

generous 1 cup jasmine rice

1¼ cups fish stock

4 scallions, chopped

2 tbsp Thai red curry paste

8 oz/225 g baby squid,
    cleaned and sliced thickly

8 oz/225 g white fish fillets,
    skinned and cut into cubes

8 oz/225 g salmon fillets,
    skinned and cut into cubes

4 tbsp chopped fresh cilantro

method

1 Heat 1 tablespoon of the oil in a wok and stir-fry the shallots and garlic for 2–3 minutes, until softened. Add the rice and stir-fry for 2–3 minutes.

2 Add a ladleful of the stock and let simmer, adding more stock as needed, for 12–15 minutes, until tender. Transfer to a dish, let cool, and chill overnight.

3 Heat the remaining oil in a wok and stir-fry the scallions and curry paste for 2–3 minutes. Add the squid and fish and stir-fry gently to avoid breaking up the fish. Stir in the rice and cilantro, heat through gently, and serve.

congee with fish fillet

ingredients

SERVES 6–8

8 oz/225 g short-grain rice

12 cups water

7 oz/200 g firm white fish fillet,
    flaked

2 tsp salt

1/2 tsp white pepper

1 head lettuce, finely
    shredded

2 tbsp finely shredded
    scallions

2 tbsp finely shredded fresh
    gingerroot

3 tbsp light soy sauce, to serve

method

1 Wash the rice and place in a large pan with the water. Cover, and cook for about 2 hours, stirring regularly.

2 Add the fish fillet, salt, and pepper. Stir well, then return to a boil and cook for a couple more minutes.

3 To serve, divide the lettuce, scallions, and gingerroot among large individual bowls. Pour the congee on top. Finally, sprinkle with 1–2 teaspoons of good-quality soy sauce.

seafood chow mein

ingredients

SERVES 4

3 oz/85 g squid, cleaned

3–4 fresh scallops

3 oz/85 g shrimp, shelled

1/2 egg white, lightly beaten

2 tsp cornstarch, mixed to a
   paste with 2 1/2 tsp water

9 1/2 oz/275 g dried thin
   Chinese egg noodles

5–6 tbsp vegetable oil

2 tbsp light soy sauce

2 oz/55 g snow peas

1/2 tsp salt

1/2 tsp sugar

1 tsp Chinese rice wine

2 scallions, shredded finely

a few drops of sesame oil

method

1 Open up the squid and score the inside in a crisscross pattern, then cut into pieces about 1 inch/2.5 cm square. Soak the squid in a bowl of boiling water until all the pieces curl up. Rinse in cold water and drain.

2 Cut each scallop into 3–4 slices. Cut the shrimp in half lengthwise if large. Mix the scallops and shrimp with the egg white and cornstarch paste.

3 Cook the noodles in boiling water according to the package instructions, then drain and rinse under cold water. Drain well, then toss with about 1 tablespoon of the oil.

4 Heat 3 tablespoons of the oil in a preheated wok. Add the noodles and 1 tablespoon of the soy sauce and stir-fry for 2–3 minutes. Remove to a large serving dish.

5 Heat the remaining oil in the wok and add the snow peas and seafood. Stir-fry for about 2 minutes, then add the salt, sugar, rice wine, remaining soy sauce, and about half the scallions. Blend well and add a little water if necessary. Pour the seafood mixture on top of the noodles and sprinkle with sesame oil. Garnish with the remaining scallions and serve immediately.

mixed seafood curry

ingredients

SERVES 4

1 tbsp vegetable or peanut oil

3 shallots, chopped finely

1-inch piece fresh galangal,
    peeled and sliced thinly

2 garlic cloves, chopped finely

1³/₄ cups canned coconut milk

2 lemongrass stalks, snapped
    in half

4 tbsp fish sauce

2 tbsp chili sauce

8 oz/225 g jumbo shrimp,
    shelled

8 oz/225 g baby squid,
    cleaned and sliced thickly

8 oz/225 g salmon fillet,
    skinned and cut into
    chunks

6 oz/175 g tuna steak, cut into
    chunks

8 oz/225 g fresh mussels,
    scrubbed and debearded

fresh Chinese chives,
    to garnish

boiled rice, to serve

method

1 Heat the oil in a large wok and stir-fry the shallots, galangal, and garlic for 1–2 minutes, until they start to soften. Add the coconut milk, lemongrass, fish sauce, and chili sauce. Bring to a boil, reduce the heat, and let simmer for 1–2 minutes.

2 Add the shrimp, squid, salmon, and tuna, and let simmer for 3–4 minutes, until the shrimp have turned pink and the fish is cooked.

3 Add the mussels and cover with a lid. Let simmer for 1–2 minutes, until they have opened. Discard any mussels that remain closed. Garnish with Chinese chives and serve immediately with rice.

fish curry

ingredients

SERVES 4

juice of 1 lime

4 tbsp fish sauce

2 tbsp Thai soy sauce

1 fresh red chile, seeded and
chopped

12 oz/350 g angler fish fillet,
cut into cubes

12 oz/350 g salmon fillets,
skinned and cut into cubes

1³/₄ cups coconut milk

3 kaffir lime leaves

1 tbsp Thai red curry paste

1 lemongrass stalk (white part
only), chopped finely

2 cups jasmine rice, boiled

4 tbsp chopped fresh cilantro

method

1 Combine the lime juice, half the fish sauce, and the soy sauce in a shallow, nonmetallic dish. Add the chile and the fish, stir to coat, cover with plastic wrap, and chill for 1–2 hours, or overnight.

2 Bring the coconut milk to a boil in a pan and add the lime leaves, curry paste, the remaining fish sauce, and the lemongrass. Let simmer gently for 10–15 minutes.

3 Add the fish and the marinade and let simmer for 4–5 minutes, until the fish is cooked. Serve hot with boiled rice with chopped cilantro stirred through it.

fish curry with rice noodles

ingredients

SERVES 4

2 tbsp vegetable or peanut oil

1 large onion, chopped

2 garlic cloves, chopped

3 oz/75 g white mushrooms

8 oz/225 g angler fish, cut into
    cubes, each about 1 inch

8 oz/225 g salmon fillets,
    cut into cubes,
    each about 1 inch

8 oz/225 g cod, cut into
    cubes, each about 1 inch

2 tbsp Thai red curry paste

1³/₄ cups canned coconut milk

handful of fresh cilantro,
    chopped

1 tsp jaggery or soft light
    brown sugar

1 tsp fish sauce

4 oz/115 g rice noodles

3 scallions, chopped

¹/₂ cup bean sprouts

few Thai basil leaves

method

1 Heat the oil in a wok or large skillet and gently sauté the onion, garlic, and mushrooms until softened but not browned.

2 Add the fish, curry paste, and coconut milk and bring gently to a boil. Let simmer for 2–3 minutes before adding half the the cilantro, the sugar, and fish sauce. Keep warm.

3 Meanwhile, soak the noodles for 3–4 minutes or until tender, and drain well through a colander. Put the colander and noodles over a pan of simmering water. Add the scallions, bean sprouts, and most of the basil and steam on top of the noodles for 1–2 minutes or until just wilted.

4 Pile the noodles onto warmed serving plates and top with the fish curry. Sprinkle the remaining cilantro and basil over the top and serve immediately.

stir-fried rice noodles with marinated fish

ingredients

SERVES 4

1 lb angler fish or cod, cubed

8 oz/225 g salmon fillets,
   cubed

4 tbsp vegetable or peanut oil

2 fresh green chiles, seeded
   and chopped

grated rind and juice of 1 lime

1 tbsp fish sauce

4 oz/115 g wide rice noodles

2 shallots, sliced

2 garlic cloves, chopped finely

1 fresh red chile, seeded and
   chopped

2 tbsp Thai soy sauce

2 tbsp chili sauce

cilantro leaves, to garnish

method

1 Place the fish in a shallow bowl. To make the marinade, mix 2 tablespoons of the oil, the green chiles, lime juice and rind, and fish sauce together and pour over the fish. Cover and chill for 2 hours.

2 Put the noodles in a bowl and cover with boiling water. Let stand for 8–10 minutes (check the package instructions) and drain well.

3 Heat the remaining oil in a wok or large skillet and sauté the shallots, garlic, and red chile until lightly browned. Add the soy sauce and chili sauce. Add the fish and the marinade to the wok and stir-fry gently for 2–3 minutes until cooked through.

4 Add the drained noodles and stir gently. Sprinkle with cilantro and serve immediately.

fish in coconut

ingredients

SERVES 4

2 tbsp vegetable or peanut oil

6 scallions, chopped coarsely

1-inch/2.5-cm piece fresh
    gingerroot, grated

2–3 tbsp Thai red curry paste

1³/₄ cups coconut milk

²/₃ cup fish stock

4 kaffir lime leaves

1 lemongrass stalk,
    broken in half

12 oz/350 g white fish fillets,
    skinned and cut into
    chunks

8 oz/225 g squid rings and
    tentacles

8 oz/225 g large cooked
    shelled shrimp

1 tbsp fish sauce

2 tbsp Thai soy sauce

4 tbsp chopped fresh Chinese
    chives

boiled jasmine rice with
    chopped fresh cilantro,
    to serve

method

1 Heat the oil in a wok or large skillet and stir-fry the scallions and gingerroot for 1–2 minutes. Add the curry paste and stir-fry for 1–2 minutes.

2 Add the coconut milk, fish stock, lime leaves, and lemongrass. Bring to a boil, then reduce the heat and let simmer for 1 minute.

3 Add the fish, squid, and shrimp, and let simmer for 2–3 minutes, until the fish is cooked. Add the fish and soy sauces and stir in the chives. Serve immediately with jasmine rice with fresh cilantro stirred through it.

spiced steamed fish

ingredients

SERVES 4–6

1-inch/2.5-cm piece fresh
gingerroot, finely grated

1 lemongrass stem
(base only), thinly sliced

6 fresh red chiles, seeded and
coarsely chopped

1 small red onion, finely
chopped

1 tbsp Thai fish sauce

2 lb/900 g whole fish, cleaned

2 fresh kaffir lime leaves,
thinly sliced

2 fresh basil sprigs

freshly cooked rice and
cucumber, cut into
thin sticks

method

1 Place the gingerroot, lemongrass, chiles, onion, and fish sauce in a food processor. Process to a coarse paste, adding a little water, if needed.

2 Cut 3–4 deep slits crosswise on each side of the fish. Spread over the spice paste, rubbing it well into the slits. Place the fish in a dish deep enough to hold the liquid that collects during steaming. Sprinkle over the lime leaves and basil.

3 Set up a steamer or place a rack into a wok or deep pan. Bring about 2 inches/5 cm of water to a boil in the steamer or wok.

4 Place the dish of fish into the steamer or on to the rack. Reduce the heat to a simmer, then cover tightly and steam the fish for 15–20 minutes, or until the fish is cooked through. Serve with freshly cooked rice and cucumber sticks.

steamed yellow fish fillets

ingredients

SERVES 4

1 lb 2 oz/500 g firm fish fillets, such as red snapper, sole, or angler fish

1 red bird chile

1 small onion, chopped

3 garlic cloves, chopped

2 cilantro sprigs

1 tsp coriander seeds

$1/2$ tsp ground turmeric

$1/2$ tsp pepper

1 tbsp Thai fish sauce

2 tbsp coconut milk

1 small egg, beaten

2 tbsp rice flour

fresh red and green chile strips, to garnish

stir-fried vegetables, to serve

method

1 Using a sharp knife, remove any skin from the fish and cut the fillets diagonally into 3/4-inch/2-cm wide strips.

2 Place the bird chile, onion, garlic, cilantro, and coriander seeds in a mortar and, using a pestle, grind to a smooth paste.

3 Transfer the paste to a bowl and add the turmeric, pepper, fish sauce, coconut milk, and beaten egg, stirring to mix evenly. Spread the rice flour out on a large plate. Dip the fish strips into the paste mixture, then into the rice flour to coat lightly.

4 Bring the water in the bottom of a steamer to a boil, then arrange the fish strips in the top of the steamer. Cover and steam for 12–15 minutes, or until the fish is just firm.

5 Garnish the fish with the chile strips and serve immediately with stir-fried vegetables.

chirashi sushi with salmon

ingredients

SERVES 4

8 large shrimp, heads
    removed
salt
1 tbsp sake
1 tbsp rice vinegar
9 oz/250 g sashimi-grade
    salmon
3-inch/7.5-cm piece of
    kombu, cut into thin strips
juice of 1 lemon
4 oz/115 g green beans, tips
    removed
1 quantity freshly cooked
    sushi rice
2 oz/55 g lotus root, thinly
    sliced
4 tbsp salmon roe
4 shiso leaves, to garnish
Japanese soy sauce, pickled
    gingerroot, and wasabi
    paste, to serve

method

1 Insert a thin wooden skewer along the underside of each shrimp to prevent it from curling during cooking. Place 1 inch/2.5 cm of water in a large pan and add a little salt and the sake. Bring to a boil, add the skewered shrimp, and let simmer for 2 minutes or until they turn pink. Drain and let cool.

2 Peel each shrimp, cut along the back of the body, and scrape out the intestinal thread. Deepen the incision and carefully open the shrimp into a flat butterfly-shape. Sprinkle with the rice vinegar and place in the refrigerator until needed.

3 Slice the salmon into 1/3-inch/8-mm thick strips, using a wet, very sharp knife and cutting across the grain. Wipe your knife on a damp cloth between each cut. Place in a bowl with the kombu strips and lemon juice. Let stand for 15 minutes, turning the fish once.

4 Drop the green beans into boiling salted water for 1 minute to blanch, then plunge into ice-cold water. Drain, then cut into strips.

5 Divide the sushi rice between 4 serving bowls. To each bowl, add a quarter of the salmon, 2 cooked shrimp, a quarter of the sliced green beans and lotus root, and 1 tbsp of the salmon roe. Garnish with a shiso leaf and serve with soy sauce, pickled gingerroot, and wasabi paste alongside.

classic sushi boat with salmon roe

ingredients

MAKES 8 PIECES

1/3 quantity freshly cooked
sushi rice

2 sheets of toasted nori, each
cut into 4 strips lengthwise

wasabi paste

8 tbsp salmon, trout, or flying
fish roe

soy sauce and pickled
gingerroot, to serve

method

1 Divide the rice into 8 equal batches. Wet your hands to stop the rice from sticking, then shape each batch of rice into an oval. Carefully wrap a strip of nori around each oval of rice and trim off any excess. Place a drop of vinegared water on the underside of the join to seal it.

2 Dab a little wasabi on top of each sushi boat and top with 1 tbsp of the salmon roe. Repeat with the rest of the ingredients. Serve with soy sauce, pickled gingerroot, and more wasabi paste on the side.

seared salmon sashimi with sesame & black pepper

ingredients

SERVES 4

2 oz/55 g daikon (long white radish)

3 oz/85 g white sesame seeds

black pepper

14 oz/400 g sashimi-grade salmon

2 tsp peanut oil

4 shiso leaves

ponzu dipping sauce, to serve

method

1 Shred the daikon using the finest setting on a mandolin. Alternatively, cut it into long thin slices and then cut each slice along its length as finely as possible. Rinse, drain, and then place in the refrigerator until needed.

2 Crush the sesame seeds in a mortar and pestle and spread over a large plate. Grind over plenty of black pepper and stir to mix.

3 Trim the salmon fillet into a neat rectangle. Heat the oil in a skillet until very hot. Sear the salmon for 1 minute on both sides and the edges, then remove from the pan.

4 Lay the salmon on the sesame and pepper mixture, and turn to coat evenly. Use a wet, very sharp knife to cut the seared salmon into 1/3-inch/8-mm thick oblongs, slicing across the grain. Wipe your knife on a damp cloth between each cut.

5 Arrange the slices on 4 serving plates. Place a shiso leaf on each plate and top with a quarter of the shredded daikon. Serve with the ponzu dipping sauce.

wraps with fresh tuna, salmon roe & shiso leaves

ingredients

MAKES 6 PIECES

4 oz/115 g sashimi-grade tuna

3 sheets of toasted nori

1/4 quantity freshly cooked
   sushi rice

wasabi paste

6 shiso leaves, finely chopped

2 tbsp salmon roe

Japanese soy sauce, pickled
   gingerroot, and wasabi
   paste, to serve

method

1 Trim the tuna and cut it into strips about 1/3 inch/8 mm thick, using a wet, very sharp knife and slicing across the grain. Wipe your knife on a damp cloth between each cut.

2 Fold a sheet of nori in half lengthwise, press along the fold, and then tear it into 2 pieces. Put the half you are not using straight away back into the package or cover it with plastic wrap so that it does not dry out.

3 Lay the half-sheet of nori smooth-side down on a work surface and place a heaping tbsp of rice on the left-hand side. Dab the rice with a little wasabi paste. Top with a sixth of the tuna, then add a sixth of the chopped shiso leaves.

4 Fold the bottom left-hand corner of the nori over the rice and filling, so that the folded edge forms a right angle with the bottom edge. Continue folding along that line to make a cone with a sharp point at the bottom. Place a drop of vinegared water on the underside of the join to seal it.

5 Put 1 tsp of the salmon roe in the cone to garnish. Repeat with the rest of the ingredients to make 6 cones in total. Serve with soy sauce, pickled gingerroot, and wasabi paste on the side.

salmon, cucumber & pickled radish wraps

ingredients

MAKES 6 PIECES

4 oz/115 g sashimi-grade salmon

3 sheets of toasted nori

1/4 quantity freshly cooked sushi rice

wasabi paste

1/3 English cucumber, seeded and cut into thin strips

2 oz/55 g takuan (pickled radish), cut into thin strips

Japanese soy sauce, pickled gingerroot, and wasabi paste, to serve

method

1 Trim the salmon and cut into strips about 1/3 inch/8 mm thick, using a wet, very sharp knife and slicing across the grain. Wipe your knife on a damp cloth between each cut.

2 Fold a nori sheet in half lengthwise, press along the fold, and then tear it into 2 pieces. Put the half you are not using straight away back into the package or cover it with plastic wrap so that it does not dry out.

3 Lay a half-sheet of nori smooth-side down on a work surface and place a heaping tbsp of rice on the left-hand side. Dab the rice with a little wasabi paste. Top with a sixth of the salmon strips, then add a sixth of the cucumber and takuan strips.

4 Fold the bottom left-hand corner of the nori over the rice and filling, so that the folded edge forms a right angle with the bottom edge. Continue folding along that line to make a cone with a sharp point at the bottom. Place a drop of vinegared water on the underside of the join to seal it.

5 Repeat with the rest of the ingredients to make 6 cones in total. Serve with soy sauce, pickled gingerroot, and wasabi paste.

salmon & scallops with cilantro & lime

ingredients

SERVES 4

6 tbsp peanut oil

10 oz/280 g salmon steak, skinned and cut into 1-inch/2.5-cm chunks

8 oz/225 g scallops

3 carrots, sliced thinly

2 celery stalks, cut into 1-inch/2.5-cm pieces

2 orange bell peppers, sliced thinly

6 oz/175 g oyster mushrooms, sliced thinly

1 clove garlic, crushed

6 tbsp chopped fresh cilantro

3 shallots, sliced thinly

2 limes, juiced

1 tsp lime zest

1 tsp dried red pepper flakes

3 tbsp dry sherry

3 tbsp soy sauce

cooked noodles, to serve

method

1 In a wok or large skillet, heat the oil over medium heat. Add the salmon and scallops, and stir-fry for 3 minutes. Remove from the pan, then set aside and keep warm.

2 Add the carrots, celery, bell peppers, mushrooms, and garlic to the wok and stir-fry for 3 minutes. Add the cilantro and shallots, and stir.

3 Add the lime juice and zest, dried red pepper flakes, sherry, and soy sauce and stir. Return the salmon and scallops to the wok and stir-fry carefully for another minute.

4 Serve immediately on a bed of cooked noodles.

sweet chili salmon hand rolls

ingredients

MAKES 6 PIECES

5 1/2-oz/150-g piece of salmon
    fillet, skin on
salt and black pepper
1 tbsp vegetable oil
3 sheets of toasted nori
1/4 quantity freshly cooked
    sushi rice
2 scallions, halved lengthwise
    and shredded
4 tbsp Japanese mayonnaise
2 tbsp sweet chili sauce, plus
    extra to serve
thin cucumber sticks, to serve

method

1 Season the salmon with the salt and pepper. Heat the oil in a skillet until it is very hot, then add the salmon skin-side down. Cook over high heat for 2 minutes, until the skin is crisp. Reduce the heat to medium and cook for 2 more minutes, then turn the salmon over and cook for an additional minute or until the fish is cooked through. Let cool, then flake it, keeping some pieces attached to the skin.

2 Fold a nori sheet in half lengthwise, press along the fold, and tear it into 2 pieces. Lay a half-sheet smooth-side down on a work surface and place a heaping tbsp of rice on the left. Lay a sixth of the flaked salmon and shredded scallion on the rice. Spoon 2/3 tbsp of the mayonnaise over the top and dot on 1 tsp sweet chili sauce.

3 Fold the bottom left-hand corner of the nori over the rice and filling, so that the folded edge forms a right angle with the bottom edge. Continue folding along that line to make a cone with a sharp point at the bottom. Place a drop of vinegared water on the underside of the join to seal it.

4 Repeat with the rest of the ingredients to make 6 cones in total. Serve with cucumber sticks and extra sweet chili sauce.

salmon with red curry in banana leaves

ingredients

SERVES 4

4 salmon steaks, about
    6 oz/175 g each
2 banana leaves, halved
1 garlic clove, crushed
1 tsp grated fresh gingerroot
1 tbsp Thai red curry paste
1 tsp brown sugar
1 tbsp Thai fish sauce
2 tbsp lime juice

to garnish
lime wedges
whole fresh red chiles
finely chopped fresh red chile

method

1 Preheat the oven to 425°F/220°C. Place a salmon steak in the center of each half banana leaf. Mix the garlic, gingerroot, curry paste, sugar, and fish sauce together, then spread over the surface of the fish. Sprinkle with lime juice.

2 Carefully wrap the banana leaves around the fish, tucking in the sides as you go to make neat, compact pockets.

3 Place the pockets seam-side down on a baking sheet. Bake in the preheated oven for 15–20 minutes, or until the fish is cooked and the banana leaves are beginning to brown.

4 Serve garnished with lime wedges, whole chiles, and finely chopped chile.

pan-fried spiced salmon

ingredients

SERVES 4

1-inch/2.5-cm piece fresh
gingerroot, grated

1 tsp coriander seeds,
crushed

1/4 tsp chili powder

1 tbsp lime juice

1 tsp sesame oil

4 salmon fillet pieces with
skin, about 5 1/2 oz/
150 g each

2 tbsp vegetable oil

stir-fried vegetables and
freshly cooked rice,
to serve

cilantro leaves, to garnish

method

1 Mix the gingerroot, crushed coriander, chili powder, lime juice, and sesame oil together in a bowl.

2 Place the salmon on a wide, nonmetallic plate or dish and spoon the mixture over the flesh side of the fillets, spreading it to coat each piece of salmon evenly.

3 Cover the dish with plastic wrap and let chill in the refrigerator for 30 minutes.

4 Heat a wide, heavy-bottom skillet or ridged grill pan with the vegetable oil over high heat. Place the salmon in the hot skillet, skin-side down, and cook for 4–5 minutes, without turning, until the salmon is crusty underneath and the flesh flakes easily.

5 Serve the salmon immediately, with freshly cooked rice, garnished with cilantro leaves, and stir-fried vegetables.

chargrilled tuna with chile salsa

ingredients

SERVES 4

4 tuna steaks, about
6 oz/175 g each
grated rind and juice of 1 lime
2 tbsp olive oil
salt and pepper
green salad, to serve

chile salsa
2 orange bell peppers
1 tbsp olive oil
juice of 1 lime
juice of 1 orange
2–3 fresh red chiles, seeded
and chopped
pinch of cayenne pepper

method

1 Rinse the tuna thoroughly under cold running water and pat dry with paper towels, then place in a large shallow nonmetallic dish. Sprinkle the lime rind and juice and the oil over the fish. Season with salt and pepper, cover with plastic wrap, and let marinate in the refrigerator for up to 1 hour.

2 Preheat the grill. To make the salsa, brush the bell peppers with the olive oil and cook over hot coals, turning frequently, for 10 minutes, or until the skin is blackened and charred. Remove from the grill and let cool slightly, then peel off the skins and discard the seeds. Place the bell peppers in a food processor with the remaining salsa ingredients and process to a puree. Transfer to a bowl and season with salt and pepper.

3 Cook the tuna over hot coals for 4–5 minutes on each side until golden. Transfer to plates, and serve immediately with the green salad and the salsa.

marinated tuna chirashi sushi

ingredients

SERVES 4

12 oz/350 g sashimi-grade
  tuna
juice of 2 lemons
1 tbsp soy sauce
1 quantity freshly cooked
  sushi rice
4 tbsp finely chopped chives
4 tbsp pickled gingerroot
2 tsp wasabi paste
4 shiso leaves, to garnish
4 tsp white sesame seeds,
  toasted

method

1 Put the tuna into a bowl and pour the lemon juice and soy sauce over the top. Turn the tuna to coat, then place in the refrigerator and let marinate for 30 minutes.

2 Remove the tuna from the marinade and slice into 1/3-inch/8-mm thick strips, using a wet, very sharp knife and cutting across the grain. Wipe your knife on a damp cloth between each cut to keep your tuna strips neat.

3 Divide the sushi rice between 4 serving bowls. Arrange the tuna slices on the rice and sprinkle the chives over the top.

4 Add 1 tbsp pickled gingerroot and 1/2 teaspoon wasabi paste to each bowl, garnish with a shiso leaf, and sprinkle with the toasted sesame seeds.

tuna tataki hand rolls

ingredients

MAKES 6 PIECES

1 tsp freshly ground black
pepper

1 tbsp shredded fresh
gingerroot

1 tbsp white sesame seeds

5$^{1}/_{2}$ oz/150 g very fresh
tuna fillet

salt

2 tbsp vegetable oil

3 sheets of toasted nori

$^{1}/_{4}$ quantity freshly cooked
sushi rice

$^{1}/_{2}$ English cucumber, seeded
and cut into thin sticks

4 tbsp Japanese mayonnaise

wasabi paste

method

1 Mix together the black pepper, shredded gingerroot, and sesame seeds. Rub the mixture all over the tuna, pressing the seeds on firmly. Season the tuna lightly with salt.

2 Heat the oil in a skillet until it is very hot. Cook the tuna for 4 minutes on each side, or until just cooked through. Remove from the skillet, let cool, then cut into thin slices.

3 Fold a nori sheet in half lengthwise, press along the fold, and then tear it into 2 pieces. Lay a half-sheet smooth-side down on a work surface and place a heaping tbsp of rice on the left. Lay a sixth of the tuna strips and cucumber sticks on the rice, then spoon over $^{2}/_{3}$ tbsp of the mayonnaise and dot a little wasabi paste on top.

4 Fold the bottom left-hand corner of the nori over the rice and filling, so that the folded edge forms a right angle with the bottom edge. Continue folding along that line to make a cone with a sharp point at the bottom. Place a drop of vinegared water on the underside of the join to seal it.

5 Repeat with the rest of the ingredients to make 6 cones in total.

spiced tuna in sweet-&-sour sauce

ingredients

SERVES 4

4 fresh tuna steaks, about
   1 lb 2 oz/500 g in total

1/4 tsp pepper

2 tbsp peanut oil

1 onion, diced

1 small red bell pepper,
   seeded and cut into short
   thin sticks

1 garlic clove, crushed

1/2 cucumber, seeded and cut
   into short thin sticks

2 pineapple slices, diced

1 tsp finely chopped fresh
   gingerroot

1 tbsp brown sugar

1 tbsp cornstarch

1 1/2 tbsp lime juice

1 tbsp Thai fish sauce

1 cup fish stock

lime slices and cucumber
   slices, to garnish

method

1 Sprinkle the tuna steaks with pepper on both sides. Heat a heavy-bottom skillet or ridged grill pan and brush with a little of the oil. Arrange the tuna steaks in the skillet and cook for 8 minutes, turning them over once.

2 Meanwhile, heat the remaining oil in a separate skillet. Add the onion, bell pepper, and garlic and cook gently for 3–4 minutes to soften.

3 Remove the skillet from the heat and stir in the cucumber, pineapple, gingerroot, and sugar.

4 Blend the cornstarch with the lime juice and fish sauce, then stir into the stock and add to the skillet. Stir over medium heat until boiling, then cook for 1–2 minutes, or until thickened and clear.

5 Spoon the sauce over the tuna and serve immediately, garnished with slices of lime and cucumber.

white fish hand rolls with tartar sauce

ingredients

MAKES 6 PIECES

1¹/₃ oz/38 g prepared tempura
  mix

vegetable oil, for deep frying

6 oz/175 g skinless white fish,
  cut into ¹/₂-inch/5-mm
  thick strips about 2 inch/
  5 cm long

3 sheets of toasted nori

¹/₄ quantity freshly cooked
  sushi rice

3 tbsp tartar sauce, plus extra
  to serve

3 scallions, halved lengthwise
  and shredded

method

1 Blend the tempura batter with water according to the package instructions. The batter should be lumpy with plenty of air bubbles. Heat the oil in a deep-fryer to 350–375°F/180–190°C, or until a cube of bread browns in 30 seconds.

2 Dip the fish strips in the batter and add to the deep-fryer 3 at a time. Fry for 2–3 minutes, until the batter is golden brown and the fish is cooked. Drain on paper towels and let cool.

3 Fold a nori sheet in half lengthwise, press along the fold, and then tear it into 2 pieces. Lay a half-sheet smooth-side down on a work surface and place a heaping tablespoon of the rice on the left. Spread ¹/₂ tbsp tartar sauce over the rice and then top with 2 battered fish strips. Sprinkle with a sixth of the shredded scallion.

4 Fold the bottom left-hand corner of the nori over the rice and filling, so that the folded edge forms a right angle with the bottom edge. Continue folding along that line to make a cone with a sharp point at the bottom. Place a drop of vinegared water on the underside of the seam to seal it.

5 Repeat with the rest of the ingredients to make 6 cones in total. Serve with extra tartar. Sauce for dipping.

baked cod with a curry crust

ingredients

SERVES 4

1/2 tsp sesame oil

4 cod fillet pieces, about
5 1/2 oz/150 g each

1 1/2 cups fresh white
breadcrumbs

2 tbsp blanched almonds,
chopped

2 tsp Thai green curry paste

finely grated rind of 1/2 lime,
plus extra thinly pared rind
to garnish

salt and pepper

lime slices, to garnish

boiled new potatoes and
mixed salad greens,
to serve

method

1 Preheat the oven to 400°F/200°C. Brush the oil over the bottom of a wide, shallow ovenproof dish or pan, then arrange the cod pieces in a single layer.

2 Mix the breadcrumbs, almonds, curry paste, and grated lime rind together in a bowl, stirring well to blend thoroughly and evenly. Season to taste with salt and pepper.

3 Carefully spoon the crumb mixture over the fish pieces, pressing lightly with your hand to hold it in place.

4 Bake the dish, uncovered, in the preheated oven for 35–40 minutes, or until the fish is cooked through and the crumb topping is golden brown.

5 Serve the dish hot, garnished with lime slices and rind and accompanied by boiled new potatoes and mixed salad greens.

monkfish with lime & chile sauce

ingredients

SERVES 4

4 monkfish fillets, 4 oz/115 g
    each

1/4 cup rice flour or cornstarch

6 tbsp vegetable or peanut oil

4 garlic cloves, crushed

2 large fresh red chiles,
    seeded and sliced

2 tsp jaggery or soft light
    brown sugar

juice of 2 limes

grated rind of 1 lime

boiled rice, to serve

method

1 Toss the fish in the flour, shaking off any excess. Heat the oil in a wok and cook the fish on all sides until browned and cooked through, taking care when turning not to break it up.

2 Lift the fish out of the wok and keep warm. Add the garlic and chiles and stir-fry for 1–2 minutes, until they have softened.

3 Add the sugar, the lime juice and rind, and 2–3 tablespoons of water and bring to a boil. Let simmer gently for 1–2 minutes, then spoon the mixture over the fish. Serve immediately with rice.

monkfish stir-fry

ingredients

SERVES 4

2 tsp sesame oil

1 lb/450 g monkfish steaks, cut into 1 inch/2.5 cm chunks

1 red onion, sliced thinly

3 cloves garlic, chopped finely

1 tsp grated fresh gingerroot

8 oz/225 g fine tip asparagus

6 oz/185 g mushrooms, sliced thinly

2 tbsp soy sauce

1 tbsp lemon juice

lemon wedges, to garnish

cooked noodles, to serve

method

1 Heat the oil in a wok over a medium–high heat. Add the fish, onion, garlic, gingerroot, asparagus, and mushrooms. Stir-fry for 2–3 minutes.

2 Stir in the soy sauce and lemon juice and cook for another minute. Remove from the heat and transfer to warm serving dishes.

3 Garnish with lemon wedges and serve immediately on a bed of cooked noodles.

spicy thai seafood stew

ingredients

SERVES 4

7 oz/200 g squid, cleaned and
tentacles discarded

1 lb 2 oz/500 g firm white fish
fillet, preferably monkfish
or halibut

1 tbsp corn oil

4 shallots, finely chopped

2 garlic cloves, finely chopped

2 tbsp Thai green curry paste

2 small lemongrass stems,
finely chopped

1 tsp shrimp paste

generous 2 cups coconut milk

7 oz/200 g jumbo shrimp,
shelled and deveined

12 clams in shells, cleaned

8 fresh basil leaves, finely
shredded

fresh basil leaves, to garnish

freshly cooked rice, to serve

method

1 Using a sharp knife, cut the squid body cavities into thick rings and the white fish into bite-size chunks.

2 Heat the oil in a large preheated wok. Add the shallots, garlic, and curry paste and stir-fry for 1–2 minutes. Add the lemongrass and shrimp paste, then stir in the coconut milk and bring to a boil.

3 Reduce the heat until the liquid is simmering gently, then add the white fish, squid, and shrimp to the wok and simmer for 2 minutes.

4 Add the clams and simmer for an additional 1 minute, or until the clams have opened. Discard any clams that remain closed.

5 Sprinkle the shredded basil leaves over the stew. Transfer to serving plates, then garnish with whole basil leaves and serve immediately with rice.

udon noodle stir-fry with fish cake & gingerroot

ingredients

SERVES 2

11 oz/300 g ready-to-wok udon noodles

1 leek, shredded

1¹/₃ cups bean sprouts

8 shiitake mushrooms, finely sliced

2 pieces Japanese fish cake, sliced

12 shrimp, shelled and deveined

2 eggs, beaten

oil, for stir-frying

2 tbsp shoyu (Japanese soy sauce)

3 tbsp mirin

2 tbsp chopped fresh cilantro leaves

chili oil

sesame oil

2 scallions, finely sliced

2 tbsp shredded beni-shoga (red gingerroot), to serve

method

1 Rinse the noodles under cold running water to remove any oil and tip into a bowl.

2 Add the leek, bean sprouts, mushrooms, fish cake, shrimp, and eggs to the noodles and mix well to combine.

3 Preheat a wok over high heat. Add a little oil and heat until very hot. Add the noodle mixture and stir-fry until golden, and the shrimp have turned pink and are cooked through.

4 Add the soy sauce, mirin, and cilantro and toss together. Divide the noodles between 2 bowls, drizzle with the chili and sesame oils, and sprinkle over the scallions and beni-shoga. Serve immediately.

sea bass with chile oil

ingredients

SERVES 4

2 oz/55 g daikon (long white radish)

1 small fresh sea bass, scaled and filleted

small handful of baby salad greens

2 tsp chili oil

Japanese soy sauce, pickled gingerroot, and wasabi paste, to serve

method

1 Shred the daikon using the finest setting on a mandolin. Alternatively, cut it into long thin slices and then cut each slice along its length as finely as possible. Rinse, drain, and then place in the refrigerator until needed.

2 Trim the sea bass fillets into neat rectangles, and place skinned-side up on a chopping board. Cut each fillet into oblongs 1/3 inch/ 8 mm thick, using a wet, very sharp knife and slicing across the grain. Wipe your knife on a damp cloth between each cut.

3 Place a few baby salad greens on 4 serving plates and top with a heap of shredded daikon. Arrange the sea bass slices so that they overlap slightly in a fan shape, and drizzle with the chili oil. Serve with soy sauce, pickled gingerroot, and wasabi.

sweet-&-sour sea bass

ingredients

SERVES 2

2¼ oz/60 g bok choy, shredded
1½ oz/40 g bean sprouts
1½ oz/40 g shiitake mushrooms, sliced
1½ oz/40 g oyster mushrooms, torn
scant ¼ cup scallion
1 tsp finely grated gingerroot
1 tbsp finely sliced lemongrass
2 sea bass fillets, 3 ¼ oz/90 g each, skinned and boned
generous 1 tbsp sesame seeds, toasted

sweet-&-sour sauce
scant ½ cup unsweetened pineapple juice
1 tbsp sugar
1 tbsp red wine vinegar
2 star anise, crushed
3 fl oz/90 ml tomato juice
1 tbsp cornstarch, blended with a little cold water

method

1 Preheat the oven to 400°F/200°C. Cut 2 pieces of parchment paper to make 15-inch/38-cm squares and 2 pieces of aluminum foil to make 15-inch/38-cm squares.

2 To make the sauce, heat the pineapple juice, sugar, red wine vinegar, star anise, and tomato juice. Let simmer for 1–2 minutes, then thicken with the cornstarch and water mixture, whisking continuously. Pass through a fine strainer into a small bowl to cool.

3 In a separate large bowl, mix together the bok choy, bean sprouts, mushrooms, and scallion, then add the gingerroot and lemongrass. Toss all the ingredients together.

4 Put a square of greaseproof paper on top of a square of foil and fold into a triangle. Open up and place half the vegetable mix in the center, pour half the sweet and sour sauce over the vegetables, and place the sea bass on top. Sprinkle with a few sesame seeds. Close the triangle over the mixture and, starting at the top, fold the right corner and crumple the edges together to form an airtight triangular bag. Repeat to make another bag.

5 Place on a cookie sheet and cook in the preheated oven for 10 minutes, until the foil bags puff with steam. To serve, place on individual plates and snip open at the table.

chirashi sushi with smoked mackerel

ingredients

SERVES 4

8 snow peas

2-inch/5-cm piece of daikon (long white radish)

1 quantity freshly cooked sushi rice

juice and zest of 1 lemon

2 scallions, finely chopped

2 smoked mackerel, skin removed and cut into diagonal strips

1/2 English cucumber, peeled and cut into slices

1 sheet of toasted nori, cut into thin strips

4 tbsp pickled gingerroot

2 tsp wasabi paste

method

1 Drop the snow peas into boiling, salted water for 1 minute to blanch, then plunge into ice-cold water to stop the cooking. Drain well.

2 Shred the daikon using the finest setting on a mandolin or a very sharp knife. If you are using a knife, then cut the daikon into long, thin slices and cut each slice along its length as finely as you can. Rinse and then drain.

3 Mix the sushi rice with the lemon juice and lemon zest.

4 Divide the lemony rice between 4 serving bowls and sprinkle the scallions over the top. Arrange the mackerel, cucumber, snow peas, and daikon on top of the rice. Garnish with nori strips, and add 1 tbsp of pickled gingerroot and 1/2 tsp wasabi paste to each bowl.

vegetarian

From stuffed vegetables to rolled omelets and from spicy curries to crisp noodles, the vegetarian dishes of Asia are wonderfully imaginative, tasty, and distinctive. The range of ingredients is extensive—all kinds of vegetables are used, including sprouts, beans, and mushrooms, alongside nuts, rice, noodles, eggs, and bean curd. As a result, meals are not only delicious but also healthy and nutritious. However, as with other types of dishes, each country has its own culinary style and vegetarian specialties—classic Chinese stir-fries, vibrant Thai curries, and piquant Japanese pickles, for example.

Most ingredients will be familiar to Western cooks and are widely available in supermarkets, but you may need to find more specialist suppliers for a few, such as the small pickled umeboshi plums and the Japanese herb shiso. While it is certainly fun to experiment with unfamiliar ingredients, these exciting recipes with more mundane items, such as carrots or broccoli, will still prove to be a taste revelation and are sure to expand the repertoire of the keen vegetarian cook.

Bean curd, also known as tofu, is a soy product that is very widely used in China and Japan and also features in the cuisines of some other Asian countries, such as Indonesia and Korea. Chinese bean curd tends to be

firmer in texture than Japanese, which is sometimes crumbled before cooking. High in protein and low in fat, it is a versatile ingredient that can be cooked in many different ways. It tastes fairly neutral but readily absorbs the flavors of other ingredients, whether aromatics, hot spices, seasoned broths, or sauces.

avocado, watercress & pickle wraps

ingredients

MAKES 6 PIECES

3 sheets of toasted nori

¼ quantity freshly cooked
    sushi rice

wasabi paste

6 sprigs of watercress

¼ English cucumber, seeded
    and cut into sticks

1 ripe green-skinned avocado,
    pitted, peeled, and cut into
    12 slices

2 oz/55 g Japanese pickle
    such as sakurazuke or
    shibazuke

18 long chives, trimmed

Japanese soy sauce, pickled
    gingerroot, and wasabi
    paste, to serve

method

1 Fold the nori in half lengthwise, press along the fold, and then tear the sheet into 2 pieces. Put the half you are not using straight away back into the package or cover it with plastic wrap so that it does not dry out.

2 Lay a half-sheet of nori, smooth-side down, on a work surface and place a heaping tbsp of rice on the left-hand side. Dab a little wasabi over the rice. Arrange 1 sprig of watercress, a sixth of the cucumber sticks, 2 avocado slices, and a sixth of the pickle on top. Garnish with 3 long chives.

3 Fold the bottom left-hand corner of the nori over the rice and filling, so that the folded edge forms a right angle with the bottom edge. Continue folding along that line to make a cone with a sharp point at the bottom. Place a drop of vinegared water on the underside of the join to seal it.

4 Repeat with the rest of the ingredients to make 6 cones in total. Serve with soy sauce, pickled gingerroot, and wasabi paste.

omelet wraps with pickled radish & shiso

ingredients

MAKES 6 PIECES

¼ quantity freshly cooked
    sushi rice
wasabi paste
2 oz/55 g takuan (pickled
    radish), cut into thin strips
6 shiso leaves

omelet wrappings
4 eggs
1 tsp superfine sugar
2 tsp mirin
1 tsp Japanese soy sauce
¼ tsp salt
3 tsp vegetable oil

method

1 First make the omelet. Gently whisk the eggs with the sugar, mirin, soy sauce, and salt, taking care not to create large air bubbles. Strain into a pitcher.

2 Pour 1 tsp of the oil into a tamago pan or skillet, then heat over low–medium heat. Pour in ⅓ of the omelet mixture, tilting the pan to coat the bottom. When the omelet is almost set, flip it over and cook the other side. Turn it out onto a plate lined with paper towels and let cool. If using a round skillet, trim to make a square shape. Cut the omelet in half to make 2 wrappings.

3 Place 1 piece of omelet on your chopping board. Spoon a heaping tbsp of sushi rice onto the left-hand side. Dab a little wasabi over the rice. Place a sixth of the takuan strips and 1 shiso leaf over the rice.

4 Fold the bottom left-hand corner of the omelet over the rice and filling, so that the folded edge forms a right angle with the bottom edge. Continue folding along that line to make a cone that ends in a point.

5 Serve straight away while you use the rest of the ingredients to make the remaining rolls.

omelet pouches with mushroom

ingredients

MAKES 6 PIECES

1 tbsp butter

8 oz/225 g fresh mushrooms such as oyster or shiitake, sliced

1/4 quantity freshly cooked sushi rice

1 tbsp finely chopped flat-leaf parsley

pinch of cayenne pepper

6 long chives

Japanese soy sauce, pickled gingerroot, and wasabi paste, to serve

omelet wrappings

4 eggs

1 tsp superfine sugar

2 tsp mirin

1 tsp Japanese soy sauce

1/4 tsp salt

4 tsp vegetable oil

method

1 Melt the butter in a small pan. When it is sizzling, add the sliced mushrooms and cook over high heat for 3–4 minutes until browned and reduced by half in volume.

2 Remove the mushrooms with a slotted spoon and chop finely. Mix with the rice, chopped parsley, and cayenne pepper.

3 Now make the omelet wrappings. Gently whisk the eggs with the sugar, mirin, soy sauce, and salt, taking care not to produce any large air bubbles. Strain into a pitcher.

4 Pour 2/3 tsp of the oil into a 6-inch/15-cm skillet, then heat over low-medium heat. Pour in a sixth of the omelet mixture, tilting the pan to coat the bottom. When the omelet is almost set, flip it over and cook the other side. Turn out onto a plate lined with paper towels and let cool.

5 Transfer 1 omelet to your work surface and place a sixth of the mushroom and rice mixture in the center. Gather up the 4 corners of the omelet and tie them together using a long chive. Serve with soy sauce, pickled gingerroot, and wasabi paste.

asparagus & omelet rolls

ingredients

MAKES 6–8 PIECES

8 thin asparagus spears

4 eggs

1 tbsp water

1 tbsp mirin

1 tsp soy sauce

1/2 tbsp vegetable oil

ponzu dipping sauce, to serve

method

1 Lay the asparagus spears flat in a skillet filled with simmering water and cook for 3 minutes or until tender. Cut into 3 1/2-inch/9-cm lengths and let cool.

2 Whisk the eggs with the water, mirin, and soy sauce. Heat the oil in a nonstick skillet and pour in the egg mixture. Cook on one side until the top is just set, then lay the asparagus lengths in neat lines at one end of the skillet.

3 Shake the skillet to loosen the omelet, then tip the pan away from you so that the omelet slides up the side. Using 2 chopsticks, fold the omelet over the asparagus and then continue folding to make a roll.

4 Lay a sheet of plastic wrap over a rolling mat. Tip the omelet out onto the plastic wrap. Roll it up in the mat and plastic wrap and let cool. This helps it to set in shape.

5 Transfer the roll to a chopping board, seam-side down. Trim the ends and then cut the roll into 3/4-inch/2-cm pieces with a wet, very sharp knife. Turn the pieces on end and arrange them on a serving plate. Serve with the ponzu dipping sauce.

omelet rolls with cream cheese & bell pepper

ingredients

MAKES 24 PIECES

1 quantity freshly cooked
    sushi rice
4 sheets of toasted nori
wasabi paste
3 oz/85 g cream cheese
2 red bell peppers, quartered
    and seeded, then broiled
    until the skin blackens,
    skinned, and sliced
20 chives, left whole

omelet wraps
6 eggs
1 tsp superfine sugar
2 tsp mirin
1 tsp Japanese soy sauce
1/4 tsp salt
4 tsp vegetable oil

method

1 First make the omelet. Gently whisk the eggs with the sugar, mirin, soy sauce, and salt, taking care not to create large air bubbles. Strain into a pitcher.

2 Heat 1 tsp of the oil in a tamago pan or skillet. Pour in a quarter of the egg mixture, tilting the pan to coat the bottom. Cook over low–medium heat until the omelet is almost set, then flip it over and cook the other side. Turn it out onto a plate lined with paper towels and let cool. If you have used a skillet, trim the omelet to make a square shape.

3 Place a sheet of plastic wrap on a rolling mat. Lay the omelet on top. With wet hands, spread a quarter of the sushi rice over the omelet. Lay the nori on top, trimming to fit.

4 Dab a line of wasabi paste across the rice at the end nearest to you. Spread with a layer of cream cheese and top with the roasted bell pepper slices and 5 chives. Carefully roll the mat to wrap the omelet around the filling, using gentle, even pressure.

5 Transfer the roll to a chopping board, seam-side down. Cut it into 6 equal pieces using a wet, very sharp knife. Transfer the roll to a serving dish, keeping it seam-side down. Repeat with the remaining ingredients.

cucumber rolls with sesame

ingredients

MAKES 24 PIECES

2 sheets of toasted nori

1/2 quantity freshly cooked sushi rice

wasabi paste

4 tsp white sesame seeds, toasted

1/3 English cucumber, seeded and cut into sticks about 1/4 in/5 mm square

Japanese soy sauce and pickled gingerroot, to serve

method

1 Fold a nori sheet in half lengthwise, press all along the fold, and tear it into 2 equal pieces. Place a half-sheet smooth-side down on a sushi rolling mat so that one of the long edges is directly in front of you.

2 With wet hands, spread a quarter of the rice over the nori, leaving a 1/2-inch/1-cm clear border along the furthest edge.

3 Dab a small amount of wasabi in a line across the rice at the end nearest to you. Sprinkle with 1 tsp of the sesame seeds and top with strips of cucumber, arranged in a continuous line.

4 Pick up the nearest edge of the rolling mat. Slowly roll the mat away from you to wrap the nori around the filling. Use gentle, even pressure and lift the mat out of the way as you go. Press the roll onto the uncovered border of the nori to seal it.

5 Transfer the roll to a chopping board, seam-side down. Cut it in half and then cut each half into 3 equal pieces using a wet, very sharp knife. Make 3 more rolls with the remaining ingredients. Serve with soy sauce, pickled gingerroot, and more wasabi paste.

pickled radish & kampyo rolls

ingredients

MAKES 24 PIECES

2 sheets of toasted nori

1/2 quantity freshly cooked sushi rice

4 strips of takuan (pickled radish), 1/2 inch/1 cm square and 8 inch/20 cm long

Japanese soy sauce, pickled gingerroot, and wasabi paste, to serve

spiced kampyo

1/2 oz/15 g kampyo (dried gourd)

salt, for rubbing

3/4 cup dashi stock

1 tbsp superfine sugar

1 tbsp Japanese soy sauce

method

1 Gently rub the kampyo with salt under running water to soften. Rinse, then soak for 2 hours in fresh water. Place in a small pan, cover with water, and let simmer for 10 minutes. Drain, then return to the pan with the seasoning ingredients. Bring to a boil, then let simmer for 15 minutes or until the ribbons are soft. Let cool, then cut 4 pieces to 8 inches/20 cm long.

2 Fold a nori sheet in half lengthwise, press all along the fold, and tear it into 2 equal pieces. Place a half-sheet smooth-side down on a sushi rolling mat so that one of the long edges is directly in front of you.

3 With wet hands, spread a quarter of the rice over the nori, leaving a 1/2-inch/1-cm clear border along the furthest edge. Place a strip of takuan across the rice at the end nearest to you. Top with a ribbon of kampyo.

4 Slowly roll the mat to wrap the nori around the filling, using even pressure. Press the roll onto the uncovered border to seal it. Transfer the roll to a chopping board. Cut it in half and then cut each half into 3 equal pieces using a wet, very sharp knife. Repeat with the rest of the ingredients. Serve with soy sauce, pickled gingerroot, and wasabi paste.

asparagus & bell pepper rolls with tahini sauce

ingredients

MAKES 24 PIECES

1/2 red bell pepper

4 very thin spears of
  asparagus

2 sheets of toasted nori

1/2 quantity freshly cooked
  sushi rice

tahini sauce

4 tsp tahini

1 tsp sugar

1 tsp Japanese soy sauce

1 tsp sake

method

1 Put the ingredients for the tahini sauce into a small bowl. Stir until the sugar dissolves.

2 Place the bell pepper skin-side up under a hot broiler until the skin blackens. Let cool in a sealed plastic bag or box, then remove the skin and cut the flesh into thin strips. Blanch the asparagus spears in boiling water for 1–2 minutes, then dip into ice-cold water to stop the cooking. Drain.

3 Fold a nori sheet in half lengthwise, press along the fold, and tear the sheet in half. Place a half-sheet smooth-side down on a rolling mat with one of the long sides toward you. With wet hands, spread a quarter of the rice over the nori, leaving a 1/2-inch/1-cm clear border along the furthest edge.

4 Spread a line of tahini sauce across the rice at the end nearest to you. Top with a sixth of the bell pepper and add 1 asparagus spear.

5 Pick up the nearest edge of the rolling mat. Slowly roll the mat away from you to wrap the nori around the filling. Press onto the clear border of nori to seal it. Transfer the roll to a chopping board and cut into 6 equal pieces using a wet, sharp knife. Repeat with the rest of the ingredients. Serve with the tahini sauce.

pinwheel rolls with mushroom & spinach

ingredients

MAKES 24 PIECES

7 oz/200 g spinach, stalks
   removed
1/2 tsp sesame oil
4 sheets of toasted nori
1 quantity freshly cooked
   sushi rice
wasabi paste
4 tsp pine nuts, toasted
Japanese soy sauce, pickled
   gingerroot, and wasabi
   paste, to serve

spiced mushrooms

1 oz/25 g dried shiitake
   mushrooms, soaked in
   hot water for 30 minutes,
   then chopped finely, stems
   discarded
3/4 cup dashi stock
1 tbsp mirin

method

1 First prepare the mushrooms. Place them in a pan with the dashi stock, bring to a boil, and let simmer for 15 minutes. Stir in the mirin and let cool in the pan. Drain well.

2 Wash the spinach and place in a pan with just the water that is clinging to the leaves. Cook for 2 minutes over medium heat to wilt. Press in a colander to squeeze out the water. Chop finely, then mix with the sesame oil.

3 Place a nori sheet smooth-side down on a rolling mat so that one of the shorter sides is toward you. With wet hands, spread a quarter of the rice over the nori, leaving a 1/2-inch/1-cm clear border along the furthest edge.

4 Dab a line of wasabi across the rice at the end nearest to you. Top with a quarter of the spiced mushrooms and place some of the sesame spinach alongside. Sprinkle with 1 tsp of the pine nuts.

5 Slowly roll the mat to wrap the nori tightly around the filling, creating a pinwheel effect. Press the roll onto the uncovered border of the nori to seal it. Transfer the roll to a chopping board and cut it into 6 equal pieces using a wet, very sharp knife. Repeat with the rest of the ingredients. Serve with soy sauce, pickled gingerroot, and wasabi.

umeboshi plum rolls

ingredients

MAKES 24 PIECES

2 sheets nori

1/2 quantity freshly cooked
sushi rice

20 umeboshi plums, pitted
and chopped

5 shiso leaves, finely chopped

Japanese soy sauce, pickled
gingerroot, and wasabi
paste, to serve

method

1 Fold a sheet of nori in half lengthwise, press all along the fold, and then tear into 2 pieces. Place a half-sheet smooth-side down on a rolling mat so that it lies with one of the long sides directly in front of you.

2 With wet hands, spread a quarter of the rice over the nori, leaving a 1/2-inch/1-cm clear border along the furthest edge.

3 Arrange a line of the chopped plums across the rice at the end nearest to you. Top with a sixth of the chopped shiso leaves.

4 Pick up the nearest edge of the rolling mat and slowly roll the mat away from you to wrap the nori around the filling. Use gentle, even pressure and lift the mat out of the way as you go. Press the roll onto the uncovered border of the nori to seal it.

5 Transfer the roll to a chopping board, seam-side down. Cut it in half and then cut each half into 3 equal pieces using a wet, very sharp knife. Make 3 more rolls with the remaining ingredients. Serve with soy sauce, pickled gingerroot, and wasabi paste.

rice noodle rolls with snow pea sprouts

ingredients

MAKES 24 PIECES

4 oz/115 g thin dried rice
    noodles

1/2 red bell pepper

2 tsp rice vinegar

1 tsp sugar

pinch of salt

2 scallions, green parts finely
    chopped (white parts
    discarded)

4 sheets of toasted nori

wasabi paste

1/2 English cucumber, seeded
    and cut into thin sticks

1/2 large carrot, cut into thin
    sticks

1 oz/30 g snow pea or mung
    bean sprouts

gingerroot and sesame dipping
    sauce, to serve

method

1 Cook the noodles according to the package instructions. Rinse, drain, and pat dry with paper towels. Put the bell pepper under a hot broiler until the skin blackens. Let cool in a plastic bag or box, then remove the skin and cut the flesh into thin strips.

2 Put the rice vinegar, sugar, and salt into a large bowl, and stir until the sugar dissolves. Add the cooked noodles and chopped scallions and turn to coat.

3 Place a nori sheet on a rolling mat so that one of the long sides is directly in front of you. Spread a quarter of the noodle mixture over the bottom third of the nori.

4 Dab a line of wasabi across the noodles. Top with a quarter of the roasted bell pepper strips, then add a line of cucumber sticks and a line of carrot sticks. Sprinkle the filling with a quarter of the sprouts.

5 Slowly roll the mat to wrap the nori around the filling. Press the roll onto the uncovered border of the nori to seal it. Transfer the roll to a chopping board, seam-side down. Cut it into 6 equal pieces using a wet, very sharp knife. Repeat with the remaining ingredients. Serve with the gingerroot and sesame sauce.

inside-out rolls with avocado & shibazuke

ingredients

MAKES 24 PIECES

4 sheets of toasted nori

1 quantity freshly cooked
   sushi rice

1/2 English cucumber, seeded
   and cut into thin sticks

1 ripe green-skinned avocado,
   pitted, peeled, and cut into
   strips

4 oz/115 g shibazuke (pickled
   aubergine) or other
   Japanese pickle

20 whole chives, trimmed

2 tbsp black sesame seeds,
   toasted

2 tbsp white sesame seeds,
   toasted

Japanese soy sauce, pickled
   gingerroot, and wasabi
   paste, to serve

method

1 Put a sheet of nori, smooth-side down, on a rolling mat so that it lies with one of the short ends in front of you. With wet hands, spread a quarter of the rice evenly over the nori.

2 Lay a sheet of plastic wrap over the rice, then turn the whole thing over so that the plastic is under the rice and the seaweed side is facing upward.

3 Place a line of cucumber sticks across the nori at the end nearest to you. Arrange a line of avocado strips next to the cucumber and a line of shibazuke, or other pickle if using, next to that. Add 5 whole chives.

4 Pick up the nearest edge of the rolling mat and slowly roll the mat away from you to wrap the rice-covered nori tightly around the filling, creating a pinwheel effect. Lift the mat and plastic wrap out of the way as you go. Spread the toasted black and white sesame seeds over a plate and roll the sushi in them to coat the rice-covered nori.

5 Transfer the roll to a chopping board. Cut it in half and then cut each half into 3 equal pieces using a wet, very sharp knife. Repeat with the remaining ingredients. Serve with soy sauce, pickled gingerroot, and wasabi.

avocado sushi with tapenade

ingredients

MAKES 10 PIECES

1/2 sheet of toasted nori

1/2 quantity freshly cooked sushi rice

1 ripe avocado, pitted, peeled, and cut into thin slices

2 tsp tapenade

pickled gingerroot and wasabi paste, to serve

method

1 Cut the half-sheet of nori into 10 strips about 1/2 inch/1 cm wide and 3 inches/7.5 cm long.

2 Wet a finger sushi mold. Fill each section with sushi rice, working the rice into the corners without pressing too hard. Press down with the lid, then remove it, and turn the neat blocks out onto a chopping board. Repeat so that you have 10 blocks.

3 Alternatively, shape the rice by hand. Take a golfball-sized amount of rice in the palm of one hand, then gently press it into an oblong, using your palm and the fingers of your other hand. The block should be 2 inches/5 cm long and 3/4 inch/2 cm wide. Repeat to make 10 blocks, and place on a chopping board.

4 Place a couple of slices of avocado lengthwise on each rice block. Secure with a nori strip, tucking the ends under the rice block. Put a dab of tapenade on the center of the nori strip. Serve with pickled gingerroot and wasabi paste alongside.

sesame-bean curd chirashi sushi

ingredients

SERVES 4

1 block firm bean curd

2 red bell peppers, quartered and seeded

1 sheet of toasted nori

1 quantity freshly cooked sushi rice

4 tbsp pickled gingerroot

2 tsp wasabi paste

2 tbsp finely chopped scallions, green parts only, to garnish

pickled gingerroot and wasabi paste, to serve

sesame marinade

1/4 tsp sesame oil

1 garlic clove, crushed

3/4-inch/2-cm piece gingerroot, peeled and shredded

3 tbsp Japanese soy sauce

4 tbsp sake

1 tsp dark brown sugar

1 tsp red chili flakes

method

1 Wrap the bean curd in kitchen towels and place on a small chopping board. Put another chopping board on top and let stand for 30 minutes to squeeze out the excess water. Then cut the bean curd into slices about 1/3 inch/8 mm thick, cutting crosswise across the block. Transfer the bean curd slices to a small bowl.

2 Place all the ingredients for the marinade into a bowl or pitcher, and stir until the sugar dissolves. Pour the marinade over the bean curd slices and carefully turn to coat. Place in the refrigerator for 20 minutes to marinate.

3 Put the quartered bell peppers skin-side up under a hot broiler until the skin blackens. Let cool in a sealed plastic bag or box, then peel off the skin and cut the flesh into strips.

4 Cut the nori sheet into 1/2-inch/1-cm squares.

5 Divide the sushi rice between 4 serving bowls. Arrange the bean curd slices on the rice and spoon a little of the marinade on top. Add a quarter of the pepper strips to each bowl, along with a few nori squares, 1 tbsp pickled gingerroot, and 1/2 tsp wasabi paste. Garnish with the chopped scallions, and serve with pickled gingerroot and wasabi paste.

oyster mushroom & fried bean curd chirashi sushi

ingredients

SERVES 4

2 sheets of abura-age (deep-fried bean curd)

2^1/$_4$ cups dashi stock

4 tbsp sake

2 tbsp sugar

4 tbsp Japanese soy sauce

2 tbsp vegetable oil

1 lb/450 g fresh oyster or shiitake mushrooms, thinly sliced

1 quantity freshly cooked sushi rice

2 tsp white sesame seeds, toasted

Japanese soy sauce, pickled gingerroot, and wasabi paste, to serve

method

1 Cut the fried bean curd sheets into thin strips. Place the dashi stock, sake, sugar, and the soy sauce in a pan, stir, then add the bean curd strips. Cook over low heat for 15 minutes, uncovered, until the liquid has reduced by half. Drain well.

2 Heat the oil in a skillet. Add the mushrooms and cook, stirring, over medium-high heat for 2 minutes, until soft.

3 Divide the rice between 4 serving bowls. Top with the seasoned fried bean curd and the cooked mushrooms, and sprinkle with the toasted sesame seeds. Serve with soy sauce, pickled gingerroot, and wasabi paste alongside.

chirashi sushi with feta & sunblush tomatoes

ingredients

SERVES 4

6 oz/175 g feta cheese

3 oz/85 g sunblush tomatoes
  in oil

handful of basil leaves,
  shredded, plus a few whole
  leaves to garnish

1 quantity freshly cooked
  sushi rice

2 oz/55 g of baby spinach
  greens

method

1 Drain the feta and cut it into small cubes. Slice the sunblush tomatoes into thin strips and pat with paper towels to remove any excess oil. Mix carefully into the feta with the shredded basil.

2 Divide the sushi rice between 4 serving bowls. Arrange a quarter of the baby spinach greens on each serving, and top with a mound of the feta and tomato mixture. Garnish each serving with a couple of whole basil leaves.

chirashi sushi with omelet & mushrooms

ingredients

SERVES 4

16 thin asparagus spears
12 snow peas
1 quantity freshly cooked
    sushi rice
1 English cucumber, seeded
    and cut into thin 2-inch/
    5-cm long sticks
1 sheet of nori, cut into shreds
4 tbsp pickled gingerroot
2 tsp wasabi

spiced mushrooms
1 oz/25 g dried shiitake
    mushrooms
3/4 cup dashi stock
1 tbsp mirin

Japanese omelet
3 eggs
1/2 tsp superfine sugar
1 tsp mirin
1/2 tsp Japanese soy sauce
1/8 tsp salt
2 tsp vegetable oil

method

1 First prepare the spiced mushrooms. Soak the mushrooms in hot water for 30 minutes. Cut them into thin slices, discard the stems, and place in a pan with the dashi stock. Simmer for 15 minutes, take off the heat, and stir in the mirin. Let cool, then drain well.

2 Make the omelet mixture: Gently whisk the eggs with the sugar, mirin, soy sauce, and salt, taking care not to create large air bubbles. Strain into a pitcher.

3 Pour 1 tsp of the oil into a tamago pan or skillet, then heat over low-medium heat. Pour in half of the omelet mixture, tilting the pan to coat the bottom. When the omelet is almost set, flip it over and cook the other side. Turn out onto a plate lined with paper towels and let cool. Repeat to make another omelet. Cut the omelets into fine shreds and set aside.

4 Place the asparagus spears and snow peas in boiling water for 1–2 minutes to blanch. Remove and plunge into ice-cold water.

5 Divide the sushi rice between serving bowls. Top with a quarter of the spiced mushroom slices and cucumber sticks, 4 asparagus spears, and 3 snow peas. Sprinkle with the omelet shreds and nori. Add 1 tablespoon of the pickled gingerroot and 1/2 tsp wasabi paste to each bowl.

green bean sushi boats

ingredients

MAKES 8 PIECES

20 green beans, trimmed and
finely sliced

1 tbsp sesame oil

1 tbsp white sesame seeds,
toasted

salt and black pepper

1 tsp grated lemon zest

1/3 quantity freshly cooked
sushi rice

2 sheets of toasted nori, each
cut into 4 strips lengthwise

wasabi paste

soy sauce and pickled
gingerroot, to serve

method

1 Put the green beans in a pan with a little water and bring to a boil. Cook for 2 minutes, then drain and toss with the sesame oil and toasted sesame seeds. Season with salt and pepper to taste, and mix in the lemon zest.

2 Divide the rice into 8 equal batches. Wet your hands to stop the rice from sticking, then shape each batch into an oval using your hands. Carefully wrap a strip of nori around each oval of rice, trimming off any excess. Place a drop of vinegared water on the underside of the seam to seal it.

3 Dab a little wasabi on top of each sushi boat and top with the green beans. Repeat with the rest of the ingredients. Serve with soy sauce, pickled gingerroot, and more wasabi paste.

green bean & tomato chirashi sushi

ingredients

SERVES 4

5 oz/140 g very thin green beans

5 oz/140 g tomatoes on the vine

1 yellow bell pepper

1 quantity freshly cooked sushi rice

4 tsp white sesame seeds, toasted

Japanese soy sauce, pickled gingerroot, and wasabi paste, to serve

method

1 Drop the beans into a pan of boiling water for 1–2 minutes to blanch. Plunge into ice-cold water to stop the cooking, then drain.

2 Cut the tomatoes into thin slices, discarding the seeds.

3 Cut the bell pepper into quarters, remove and discard the seeds, and cut into thin strips.

4 Divide the sushi rice between 4 serving bowls. Arrange the blanched green beans, sliced tomatoes, and pepper strips on the rice. Scatter the toasted sesame seeds over the top. Serve with soy sauce, pickled gingerroot, and wasabi paste alongside.

sweet rolled omelet sushi

ingredients

MAKES 10 PIECES

1/2 sheet of toasted nori
1/2 quantity freshly cooked
   sushi rice
Japanese soy sauce, pickled
   gingerroot, and wasabi
   paste, to serve

rolled omelet

6 eggs
1 tsp superfine sugar
2 tsp mirin
1 tsp Japanese soy sauce
1/4 tsp salt
1–2 tsp vegetable oil

method

1 First make the omelet. Gently beat the eggs together with sugar, mirin, soy sauce, and salt, taking care not to create large air bubbles. Strain into a pitcher.

2 Heat a tamago pan or skillet over medium heat. Use a brush or folded piece of paper towel to oil the pan. Add a third of the egg mixture to the pan and tilt the pan to cover the bottom evenly. When the omelet has just set, fold it 4 times lengthwise toward you, using a wooden spatula. Set aside, trimming it into an oblong if you have used a round skillet.

3 Repeat with another third of the egg mixture, placing the first folded omelet on top of the omelet in the pan before you wrap it up. Do the same for the rest of the egg mixture, so that you end up with 1 thick roll. Let cool, then cut crosswise into 10 slices.

4 Cut the half-sheet of nori into 10 strips about 1/2 inch/1 cm wide and 3 inches/7.5 cm long.

5 Make 10 rice blocks using a finger sushi mold or by hand and place them on a chopping board.

6 Place a slice of rolled omelet onto each rice block. Wrap a nori strip neatly around each one, tucking the ends under the rice block to secure. Serve with soy sauce, pickled gingerroot, and wasabi paste.

asparagus & red bell pepper sushi

ingredients

MAKES 10 PIECES

2 red bell peppers, quartered and seeded

30 baby asparagus

1/2 sheet of toasted nori

1/2 quantity freshly cooked sushi rice

Japanese soy sauce, pickled gingerroot, and wasabi paste, to serve

method

1 Place the quartered bell peppers skin-side up under a hot broiler until the skin blackens. Let cool in a sealed plastic bag or box, peel off the skin, and cut the flesh into strips. Drop the asparagus into boiling water for 1–2 minutes to blanch, then dip into ice-cold water to stop the cooking.

2 Cut the half-sheet of nori into 10 strips about 1/2 inch/1 cm wide and 3 inches/7.5 cm long.

3 Wet a sushi mold to stop the rice from sticking. Arrange a layer of pepper strips over the bottom, leaving no gaps. Top with half of the sushi rice, and press down with the lid.

4 Lift off the sides of the sushi mold, holding down the lid with your thumbs as you do so. Turn the sushi out onto a chopping board so that the peppers are on top, and slice into 5 equal pieces using a wet, very sharp knife. Repeat, to make 10 pieces in total.

5 Place 3 asparagus tips lengthwise across the center of the pepper, and secure with a strip of nori, tucking the ends under the rice block to keep it neatly in place. Serve with soy sauce, pickled gingerroot, and wasabi paste.

spiced carrot sushi

ingredients

MAKES 10 PIECES

1/2 quantity freshly cooked
    sushi rice
1 tsp shredded gingerroot,
    squeezed to remove excess
    water, to garnish
2 tsp finely chopped scallion,
    green parts only, to garnish
Japanese soy sauce, pickled
    gingerroot, and wasabi
    paste, to serve

spiced carrot

1/2 cup dashi stock
2 tsp superfine sugar
2 tsp Japanese soy sauce
1 large carrot, peeled and cut
    into large thin slices

method

1 First prepare the spiced carrot. Put the dashi stock, sugar, and soy sauce into a small pan and set over low heat. Add the carrot slices and cook for 5–6 minutes, until tender but still retaining a little bite. Drain and let cool.

2 Wet the sushi mold to stop the rice from sticking. Cover the bottom with a layer of the spiced carrot. Top with half the sushi rice, then press down with the lid.

3 Lift off the sides of the sushi mold, holding down the lid with your thumbs as you do so. Turn the sushi out onto a chopping board so that the carrot layer is on top, and slice into 5 equal pieces. Repeat with the rest of the ingredients to make 10 pieces in total.

4 Top each sushi bar with a little shredded gingerroot and scallion. Serve with soy sauce, pickled gingerroot, and wasabi paste on the side.

mediterranean pressed sushi

ingredients

MAKES 10 PIECES

2 red bell peppers, quartered
and seeded
3¹/₂ oz/100 g mozzarella,
cut into thin slices
handful of small basil leaves
4 sundried tomatoes in oil,
drained and cut into strips
olive oil, for brushing
¹/₂ quantity freshly cooked
sushi rice

method

1 Place the quartered bell peppers skin-side up under a hot broiler until the skin blackens. Let cool in a sealed plastic bag or box, peel off the skin, and cut the flesh into strips.

2 Wet the sushi mold to prevent the rice from sticking. Arrange the grilled bell pepper and mozzarella in wide, diagonal strips over the bottom of the sushi press, placing thinner strips of basil leaves and sundried tomatoes in-between. Brush with oil, then cover with half of the sushi rice. Press down with the lid.

3 Lift off the sides of the sushi mold, holding down the lid with your thumbs as you do so. Turn the sushi out onto a chopping board so that the layer of mozzarella and pepper is on top. Slice into 5 equal pieces using a wet, very sharp knife. Wipe your knife on a damp cloth between cuts to keep your sushi neat. Repeat, so that you have 10 pieces in total.

fresh shiitake mushroom sushi

ingredients

MAKES 10 PIECES

1 tbsp Japanese soy sauce

10 fresh shiitake mushrooms, stems removed

1/2 sheet of toasted nori

1/2 quantity freshly cooked sushi rice

Japanese soy sauce, pickled gingerroot, and wasabi paste, to serve

method

1 Brush the soy sauce on the mushrooms, and cook under a hot broiler for 1–2 minutes on each side, or until tender.

2 Cut the half-sheet of nori into 10 strips about 1/2 inch/1 cm wide and 3 inches/7.5 cm long.

3 Wet a finger sushi mold. Fill each section with sushi rice, working the rice into the corners without pressing too hard. Press down with the lid, then remove it and turn the neat blocks out onto a chopping board. Repeat so that you have 10 blocks.

4 Alternatively, shape the rice by hand. Take a golfball-sized amount of rice in the palm of one hand, then gently press it into an oblong, using your palm and the fingers of your other hand. The block should be 2 inches/5 cm long and 3/4 inch/2 cm wide. Repeat to make 10 blocks, and place on a chopping board.

5 Place 1 broiled mushroom, skin-side down, on each rice block. Secure with a nori strip, tucking the ends under the rice block. Serve with soy sauce, pickled gingerroot, and wasabi paste on the side.

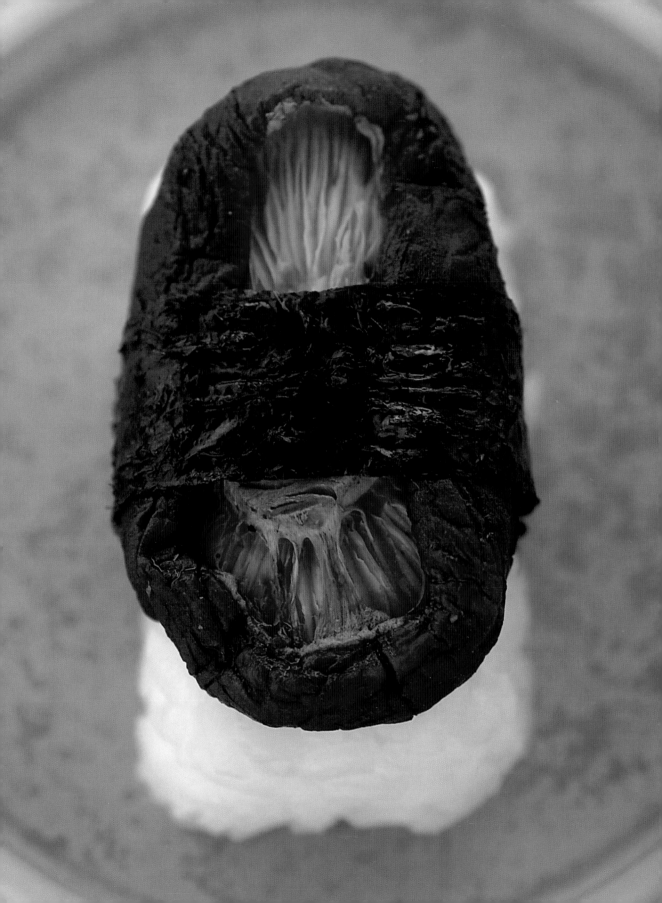

bean curd sushi with gingerroot & scallion

ingredients

MAKES 10 PIECES

1/2 block firm bean curd

1/2 sheet of toasted nori

1/2 quantity freshly cooked
   sushi rice

10 long chives, trimmed

1 tsp shredded gingerroot,
   pressed to remove
   excess water

method

1 Wrap the bean curd in paper towels and place on a small chopping board. Place another chopping board on top to help squeeze out the excess water. Let stand for 30 minutes.

2 Cut the drained bean curd into 10 slices about 1/4 inch/5 mm thick, cutting crosswise across the block. Reserve any remaining bean curd for another recipe. Cut the 1/2-sheet of nori into 10 strips about 1/2 inch/1 cm wide and 3 inches/7.5 cm long.

3 Wet a finger sushi mold. Fill each section with sushi rice, working the rice into the corners. Press down with the lid, remove it, and turn the neat blocks out onto a chopping board. Repeat so that you have 10 blocks.

4 Alternatively, shape the rice by hand. Take a golfball-sized amount of rice in the palm of one hand, then gently press it into an oblong, using your palm and the fingers of your other hand. The block should be 2 inches/5 cm long and 3/4 inch/2 cm wide. Repeat to make 10 blocks, and place on a chopping board.

5 Lay a slice of bean curd lengthwise across each rice block. Wrap a nori strip neatly around each one, tucking the ends under the rice block to secure. Knot a chive around each sushi to secure the bean curd, and garnish with shredded gingerroot.

eggplant sushi with sweet soy sauce

ingredients

MAKES 10 PIECES

2 Japanese eggplants

olive oil, for brushing

1/2 quantity freshly cooked
　　sushi rice

2 tsp white sesame seeds,
　　toasted

sweet soy sauce

1/2 cup Japanese soy sauce

1 1/2 tbsp superfine sugar

1/2 cup mirin

method

1 Cut the eggplants into 1/4-inch/5-mm thick slices. They should be 1 3/4 inches wide and 3 inches/7.5 cm long so that they can be draped over the smaller rice blocks. Brush with a little olive oil and place under a medium-high broiler for 6–8 minutes or until tender, turning once.

2 Place all the ingredients for the dipping sauce in a small pan, stir, and bring to a boil. Cook until reduced by half, then let cool.

3 Wet a finger sushi mold. Fill each section with sushi rice, working the rice into the corners without pressing too hard. Press down with the lid, then remove it, and turn the neat blocks out onto a chopping board. Repeat so that you have 10 blocks.

4 Alternatively, shape the rice by hand. Take a golfball-sized amount of rice in the palm of one hand, then gently press it into an oblong, using your palm and the fingers of your other hand. The block should be 2 inches/5 cm long and 3/4 inch/2 cm wide. Repeat to make 10 blocks, and place on a chopping board.

5 Place one slice of eggplant on each rice block and scatter a few sesame seeds over the top. Serve with the sweet soy sauce.

sweet bean curd pouches

ingredients

MAKES 8 PIECES

4 abura-age (deep-fried bean
    curd)

3/4 cup dashi stock

3 tbsp soy sauce

2 tbsp superfine sugar

1 tbsp sake

1 tbsp sesame seeds, toasted

1/4 quantity freshly cooked
    sushi rice

method

1 Put the bean curd into a bowl and pour boiling water over it to remove any excess oil. Drain and let cool. Cut each piece in half and gently open out each half into a bag.

2 Place the dashi stock, soy sauce, sugar, and sake in a pan, stir, and bring to a boil. Add the bean curd bags, and let simmer for 10–15 minutes until almost all the liquid has been absorbed. Remove from the heat, drain, and let cool. Press any remaining liquid out of the bags with a clean dish towel (the bags should be moist but not wet).

3 Gently mix the toasted sesame seeds with the sushi rice. Fill the bags with the rice mixture and fold over the tops to enclose them. Serve at room temperature.

seasoned bean curd

ingredients

SERVES 2

10½ oz/300 g silken bean
 curd, drained
4 tbsp vegetable oil
2 scallions, finely sliced
½ fresh red chile, finely sliced
1 tbsp Japanese soy sauce
1 tsp sesame oil

method

1 Place the bean curd on a heatproof serving plate. Cut the block into cubes, but keep it intact.

2 Heat the oil in a small pan over high heat until hot. Add the sliced scallions and chile and wait until they begin to sizzle.

3 Pour the hot oil mixture over the bean curd, then sprinkle with the soy sauce and sesame oil. Serve as a block.

stuffed eggplants

ingredients

SERVES 4

8 small eggplants

2 tbsp vegetable or peanut oil

4 shallots, chopped finely

2 garlic cloves, crushed

2 fresh red chiles, seeded and
    chopped

1 zucchini, chopped coarsely

4 oz/115 g block creamed
    coconut, chopped

few Thai basil leaves, chopped

small handful of fresh cilantro,
    chopped

4 tbsp Thai soy sauce

rice with chopped scallions,
    to serve

sweet chili sauce, to serve

method

1 Preheat the oven to 400°F/200°C. Put the eggplants in a roasting pan and cook for 8–10 minutes, until just softened. Cut in half and scoop out the flesh, reserving the shells.

2 Heat the oil in a wok or large skillet and sauté the shallots, garlic, and chile for 2–3 minutes before adding the zucchini and eggplant flesh. Add the creamed coconut, the herbs, and soy sauce, and let simmer for 3–4 minutes.

3 Divide the mixture between the eggplant shells.

4 Return to the oven for 5–10 minutes, until hot and serve immediately with rice and sweet chili sauce.

eggplant & mushroom stuffed omelet

ingredients

SERVES 4

3 tbsp vegetable oil

1 garlic clove, finely chopped

1 small onion, finely chopped

1 small eggplant, diced

1/2 small green bell pepper, seeded and chopped

1 large dried shiitake mushroom, soaked, drained, and sliced

1 tomato, diced

1 tbsp light soy sauce

1/2 tsp sugar

1/4 tsp pepper

2 large eggs

salad greens, tomato wedges and cucumber slices, to garnish

dipping sauce, to serve

method

1 Heat half the oil in a large skillet. Add the garlic and cook over high heat for 30 seconds. Add the onion and the eggplant and continue to stir-fry until golden.

2 Add the bell pepper and stir-fry for an additional 1 minute to soften. Stir in the mushroom, tomato, soy sauce, sugar, and pepper. Remove from the skillet and keep hot.

3 Beat the eggs together lightly. Heat the remaining oil in a clean skillet, swirling to coat a wide area. Pour in the egg and swirl to set around the skillet.

4 When the egg is set, spoon the filling into the center. Fold in the sides of the omelet to form a square package.

5 Slide the omelet carefully on to a warmed dish and garnish with salad greens, tomato wedges, and cucumber slices. Serve with a dipping sauce.

eggplant & bean curry

ingredients

SERVES 4

2 tbsp vegetable or peanut oil

1 onion, chopped

2 garlic cloves, crushed

2 fresh red chiles, seeded and
chopped

1 tbsp Thai red curry paste

1 large eggplant, cut into
chunks

4 oz/115 g pea or small
eggplants

generous 1 cup baby fava
beans

4 oz/115 g fine green beans

1½ cups vegetable stock

2 oz/55 g block creamed
coconut, chopped

3 tbsp Thai soy sauce

1 tsp jaggery or soft light
brown sugar

3 kaffir lime leaves, torn
coarsely

4 tbsp chopped fresh cilantro

method

1 Heat the oil in a wok or large skillet and sauté the onion, garlic, and chiles for 1–2 minutes. Stir in the curry paste and cook for 1–2 minutes.

2 Add the eggplants and cook for 3–4 minutes, until starting to soften. (You may need to add a little more oil as eggplants soak it up quickly.) Add all the beans and stir-fry for 2 minutes.

3 Pour in the stock and add the creamed coconut, soy sauce, sugar, and lime leaves. Bring gently to a boil and cook until the coconut has dissolved. Stir in the cilantro and serve hot.

bean curd & green vegetable curry

ingredients

SERVES 4

vegetable or peanut oil, for
    deep-frying
8 oz/225 g firm bean curd,
    drained and cut into cubes
2 tbsp vegetable or peanut oil
1 tbsp chili oil
2 fresh green chiles, seeded
    and sliced
2 garlic cloves, crushed
6 scallions, sliced
2 medium zucchini, cut into
    sticks
1/2 cucumber, peeled, seeded,
    and sliced
1 green bell pepper, seeded
    and sliced
1 small head broccoli, cut into
    florets
2 oz/55 g fine green beans,
    halved
scant 1/2 cup frozen peas,
    thawed
1 1/4 cups vegetable stock
2 oz/55 g block creamed
    coconut, chopped
2 tbsp Thai soy sauce
1 tsp jaggery or soft light
    brown sugar
4 tbsp chopped fresh parsley,
    to garnish

method

1 Heat the oil for deep-frying in a skillet and carefully lower in the bean curd cubes, in batches, and cook for 2–3 minutes, until golden brown. Remove with a slotted spoon and drain on paper towels.

2 Heat the other oils in a wok and stir-fry the chiles, garlic, and scallions for 2–3 minutes. Add the zucchini, cucumber, green bell pepper, broccoli, and green beans, and stir-fry for an additional 2–3 minutes.

3 Add the peas, stock, coconut, soy sauce, and sugar. Cover and let simmer for 2–3 minutes, until all the vegetables are tender and the coconut has dissolved.

4 Stir in the bean curd and serve immediately, sprinkled with the parsley.

spiced cashew nut curry

ingredients

SERVES 4

1²/3 cups unsalted cashew
  nuts
1 tsp coriander seeds
1 tsp cumin seeds
2 cardamom pods, crushed
1 tbsp corn oil
1 onion, finely sliced
1 garlic clove, crushed
1 small fresh green chile,
  seeded and chopped
1 cinnamon stick
¹/2 tsp ground turmeric
4 tbsp coconut cream
1¹/4 cups hot vegetable stock
3 dried kaffir lime leaves,
  crumbled
cilantro leaves, to garnish
freshly cooked jasmine rice,
  to serve

method

1 Place the cashew nuts in a bowl, then cover with cold water and let soak overnight. Drain thoroughly. Crush the seeds and cardamom pods in a mortar using a pestle.

2 Heat the oil in a large skillet. Add the onion and garlic and stir-fry for 2–3 minutes to soften but not brown. Add the chile, crushed spices, cinnamon stick, and turmeric and stir-fry for an additional 1 minute.

3 Add the coconut cream and the hot stock to the skillet. Bring to a boil, then add the cashew nuts and lime leaves.

4 Cover the skillet, then reduce the heat and simmer for 20 minutes. Serve hot with jasmine rice garnished with cilantro leaves.

zucchini & cashew curry

ingredients

SERVES 4

2 tbsp vegetable or peanut oil

6 scallions, chopped

2 garlic cloves, chopped

2 fresh green chiles, seeded
   and chopped

1 lb/450 g zucchini, cut into
   thick slices

4 oz/115 g shiitake
   mushrooms, halved

1/2 cup bean sprouts

1/2 cup cashews, toasted or
   dry-fried

few Chinese chives, chopped

4 tbsp Thai soy sauce

1 tsp fish sauce

rice or noodles, to serve

method

1 Heat the oil in a wok or large skillet and sauté the scallions, garlic, and chiles for 1–2 minutes, until softened but not browned.

2 Add the zucchini and mushrooms and cook for 2–3 minutes until tender.

3 Add the bean sprouts, nuts, chives, and both sauces and stir-fry for 1–2 minutes.

4 Serve hot with rice or noodles.

vegetable & coconut curry

ingredients

SERVES 4

2 lb 4 oz/1 kg mixed
    vegetables

1 onion, coarsely chopped

3 garlic cloves, thinly sliced

1-inch/2.5-cm piece fresh
    gingerroot, thinly sliced

2 fresh green chiles, seeded
    and finely chopped

1 tbsp vegetable oil

1 tsp ground turmeric

1 tsp ground coriander

1 tsp ground cumin

7 oz/200 g creamed coconut

2$\frac{1}{2}$ cups boiling water

salt and pepper

2 tbsp chopped cilantro,
    to garnish

freshly cooked rice, to serve

method

1 Cut the mixed vegetables into chunks. Place the onion, garlic, gingerroot, and chiles in a food processor and process until almost smooth.

2 Heat the oil in a large, heavy-bottom skillet. Add the onion mixture and cook for 5 minutes.

3 Add the turmeric, coriander, and cumin and cook for 3–4 minutes, stirring. Add the mixed vegetables and stir to coat in the spice paste.

4 Mix the creamed coconut and boiling water together in a pitcher. Stir until the coconut has dissolved. Add the coconut milk to the vegetables, then cover and simmer for 30–40 minutes, or until the vegetables are tender.

5 Season to taste with salt and pepper, then garnish with the chopped cilantro and serve with rice.

potato & spinach yellow curry

ingredients

SERVES 4

2 garlic cloves, finely chopped

1¼-inch/3-cm piece fresh galangal, finely chopped

1 lemongrass stem, finely chopped

1 tsp coriander seeds

3 tbsp vegetable oil

2 tsp Thai red curry paste

½ tsp ground turmeric

generous ¾ cup coconut milk

9 oz/250 g potatoes, cut into ¾-inch/2-cm cubes

scant ½ cup vegetable stock

7 oz/200 g fresh young spinach leaves

1 small onion, thinly sliced

method

1 Place the garlic, galangal, lemongrass, and coriander seeds in a mortar and, using a pestle, grind to a smooth paste.

2 Heat 2 tablespoons of the oil in a skillet or preheated wok. Stir in the garlic paste mixture and stir-fry for 30 seconds. Stir in the curry paste and turmeric, then add the coconut milk and bring to a boil.

3 Add the potatoes and stock. Return to a boil, then reduce the heat and simmer, uncovered, for 10–12 minutes, or until the potatoes are almost tender.

4 Stir in the spinach and simmer until the leaves are wilted.

5 Meanwhile, heat the remaining oil in a separate skillet. Add the onion and cook until crisp and golden brown. Place the fried onions on top of the curry just before serving.

carrot & pumpkin curry

ingredients

SERVES 4

²/₃ cup vegetable stock

1-inch piece fresh galangal,
    sliced

2 garlic cloves, chopped

1 lemongrass stalk (white part
    only), chopped finely

2 fresh red chiles, seeded and
    chopped

4 carrots, peeled and cut into
    chunks

8 oz/225 g pumpkin, peeled,
    seeded, and cut into cubes

2 tbsp vegetable or peanut oil

2 shallots, chopped finely

3 tbsp Thai yellow curry paste

1³/₄ cups coconut milk

4–6 sprigs fresh Thai basil

2 tbsp toasted pumpkin seeds,
    to garnish

method

1 Pour the stock into a large pan and bring to a boil. Add the galangal, half the garlic, the lemongrass, and chiles, and let simmer for 5 minutes. Add the carrots and pumpkin and let simmer for 5–6 minutes, until tender.

2 Meanwhile, heat the oil in a wok or skillet and stir-fry the shallots and the remaining garlic for 2–3 minutes. Add the curry paste and stir-fry for 1–2 minutes.

3 Stir the shallot mixture into the pan and add the coconut milk and basil. Let simmer for 2–3 minutes. Serve hot, sprinkled with the toasted pumpkin seeds.

onion, potato & red bell pepper curry

ingredients

SERVES 4

2 tbsp vegetable or peanut oil

2 red onions, sliced

2 garlic cloves, chopped finely

2-inch piece fresh gingerroot,
   chopped finely

1 fresh red chile, seeded and
   chopped

1 tbsp Thai red curry paste

8 oz/225 g potatoes,
   cut into cubes, boiled for
   5 minutes, and drained

2 red bell peppers, seeded
   and diced

1^1/$_4$ cups vegetable stock

1 tsp salt

4 tbsp chopped fresh cilantro

method

1 Heat the oil in a wok and stir-fry the onions, garlic, gingerroot, and chile for 2–3 minutes. Add the curry paste and stir-fry over low heat for 2–3 minutes.

2 Add the potatoes, bell peppers, stock, and salt, and cook for 3–4 minutes, until all the vegetables are tender. Stir in the cilantro and serve immediately.

chickpea curry

ingredients

SERVES 4

6 tbsp vegetable oil

2 onions, sliced

1 tsp finely chopped fresh
    gingerroot

1 tsp ground cumin

1 tsp ground coriander

1 tsp fresh garlic, crushed

1 tsp chili powder

2 fresh green chiles

2–3 tbsp fresh cilantro leaves

$2/3$ cup water

1 large potato

14 oz/400 g canned
    chickpeas, drained

1 tbsp lemon juice

method

1 Heat the vegetable oil in a large, heavy-bottom pan. Add the onions and cook, stirring occasionally, until golden. Reduce the heat, add the gingerroot, ground cumin, ground coriander, garlic, chili powder, fresh green chiles, and fresh cilantro leaves and stir-fry for 2 minutes.

2 Add the water to the mixture in the pan and stir to mix.

3 Using a sharp knife, cut the potato into dice, then add, with the chickpeas, to the pan. Cover and let simmer, stirring occasionally, for 5–7 minutes.

4 Sprinkle the lemon juice over the curry. Transfer the chickpea curry to serving dishes and serve hot.

mixed vegetable curry with chickpea pancakes

ingredients

SERVES 4

4 medium carrots

10¹/₂ oz/300 g potatoes

2 tbsp vegetable oil

1¹/₂ tsp cumin seeds

seeds from 5 green cardamom
    pods

1¹/₂ tsp mustard seeds

2 onions, grated

1 tsp ground turmeric

1 tsp ground coriander

1¹/₂ tsp chili powder

1 bay leaf

1 tbsp grated fresh gingerroot

2 large garlic cloves, crushed

generous 1 cup strained
    tomatoes

scant 1 cup vegetable stock

1 cup frozen peas

4 oz/115 g frozen spinach
    leaves

chickpea pancakes

1¹/₂ cups chickpea flour

1 tsp salt

¹/₂ tsp baking soda

1³/₄ cups water

vegetable oil, for cooking

method

1 To make the pancakes, sift the flour, salt, and baking soda into a large mixing bowl. Make a well in the center and add the water. Using a balloon whisk, gradually mix the flour into the water to form a smooth batter. Let stand for 15 minutes.

2 Heat enough oil to cover the bottom of a skillet over medium heat. Add a small quantity of batter to the skillet, and cook for 3 minutes on one side, then turn over and cook the other side until golden. Keep warm while you repeat with the remaining batter to make 8 pancakes.

3 Meanwhile, cut the carrots into chunks and the potatoes into fourths. Place in a steamer and steam until just tender.

4 Heat the oil in a large pan over medium heat and fry the cumin, cardamom, and mustard seeds until they start to sizzle. Add the onions, partially cover, and cook over medium-low heat, stirring frequently, until soft and golden.

5 Add the other spices, bay leaf, gingerroot, and garlic and cook, stirring, for 1 minute. Add the strained tomatoes, stock, carrots, and potatoes, partially cover, and cook for 10–15 minutes, or until the vegetables are tender. Add the peas and spinach, then cook for 2–3 minutes. Serve with the warm pancakes.

thai yellow vegetable curry with brown basmati rice

ingredients

SERVES 4

1/2 medium yellow bell pepper, seeded
1 celery stalk
13/4 oz/50 g baby corn
1/2 small leek
1/2 large sweet potato
31/2 oz/100 g bok choy
1/2 small zucchini
13/4 oz/50 g snow peas
11/4 cups pineapple juice
scant 1 cup water
3 tbsp lime juice
2 tbsp cornstarch
4 tbsp low-fat plain yogurt
4 tbsp chopped fresh cilantro
3 cups cooked brown basmati rice

spice mix
1 tsp finely chopped garlic
1/4 tsp ground turmeric
1 tsp ground coriander
1 tsp finely chopped lemongrass
3 kaffir lime leaves
1 tsp finely chopped green chile

method

1 To make the spice mix, pound all the spices to a fine paste using a mortar and pestle.

2 To prepare the vegetables, cut the yellow bell pepper into 1/2-inch/1-cm squares, cut the celery, baby corn, and leek into 1/4-inch/5-mm lengths, and cut the sweet potato into 1/2-inch/1-cm cubes. Shred the bok choy. Cut the zucchini into 1/4-inch/5-mm cubes and slice the snow peas into thin strips.

3 Put the pepper, celery, baby corn, leek, sweet potato, pineapple juice, water, and the spice mix into a large pan with a lid and bring to a boil. Reduce the heat and skim the froth from the surface with a metal spoon. Cover and let simmer for 15 minutes.

4 Add the bok choy, zucchini, and snow peas and cook for 2 minutes. Add the lime juice, then gradually add the cornstarch blended with a little cold water. Cook, stirring constantly, until thickened to the required consistency.

5 Remove the curry from the heat and let cool for 2–3 minutes. Stir in the yogurt. (Do not boil once the yogurt has been added or the curry will separate.) Stir in the fresh cilantro and serve the curry with the rice.

rice noodles with mushrooms & bean curd

ingredients

SERVES 4

8 oz/225 g rice stick noodles

2 tbsp vegetable oil

1 garlic clove, finely chopped

3/4-inch/2-cm piece fresh
   gingerroot, finely chopped

4 shallots, thinly sliced

1¼ cups sliced shiitake
   mushrooms

3½ oz/100 g firm bean curd
   (drained weight), cut
   into ½-inch/1.5-cm dice
   shapes

2 tbsp light soy sauce

1 tbsp rice wine or dry sherry

1 tbsp Thai fish sauce

1 tbsp smooth peanut butter

1 tsp chili sauce

2 tbsp toasted peanuts,
   chopped

shredded fresh basil leaves

method

1 Place the rice noodles in a bowl, then cover with hot water and let soak for 15 minutes, or according to the package directions. Drain well.

2 Heat the oil in a large skillet. Add the garlic, gingerroot, and shallots and stir-fry for 1–2 minutes, or until softened and lightly browned.

3 Add the mushrooms and stir-fry for an additional 2–3 minutes. Stir in the bean curd and toss gently to brown lightly.

4 Mix the soy sauce, rice wine, fish sauce, peanut butter, and chili sauce together in a small bowl, then stir into the skillet.

5 Stir in the rice noodles and toss to coat evenly in the sauce. Sprinkle with peanuts and shredded basil leaves and serve hot.

vegetables with bean curd & spinach

ingredients

SERVES 4

vegetable or peanut oil,
    for deep-frying

8 oz/225 g firm bean curd,
    drained and cut into cubes

2 tbsp vegetable or peanut oil

2 onions, chopped

2 garlic cloves, chopped

1 fresh red chile, seeded
    and sliced

3 celery stalks, sliced
    diagonally

8 oz/225 g mushrooms,
    sliced thickly

4 oz/115 g baby corn,
    cut in half

1 red bell pepper, seeded and
    cut into strips

3 tbsp Thai red curry paste

1³/₄ cups coconut milk

1 tsp jaggery or soft light
    brown sugar

2 tbsp Thai soy sauce

5 cups baby spinach leaves

method

1 Heat the oil in a skillet and deep-fry the bean curd cubes, in batches, for 4–5 minutes, until crisp and browned. Remove with a slotted spoon and drain on paper towels.

2 Heat 2 tablespoons of the oil in a wok or skillet and stir-fry the onions, garlic, and chile for 1–2 minutes, until they start to soften. Add the celery, mushrooms, corn, and red bell pepper, and stir-fry for 3–4 minutes, until they soften.

3 Stir in the curry paste and coconut milk and gradually bring to a boil. Add the sugar and soy sauce and then the spinach. Cook, stirring constantly, until the spinach has wilted. Serve immediately, topped with the bean curd.

asian vegetables with yellow bean sauce

ingredients

SERVES 4

1 eggplant

salt

2 tbsp vegetable oil

3 garlic cloves, crushed

4 scallions, chopped

1 small red bell pepper, seeded and thinly sliced

4 baby corn cobs, halved lengthwise

scant 1 cup snow peas

7 oz/200 g green bok choy, coarsely shredded

$14^{1}/_{2}$ oz/425 g canned straw mushrooms, drained

generous $^{3}/_{4}$ cup fresh bean sprouts

2 tbsp rice wine or dry sherry

2 tbsp yellow bean sauce

2 tbsp dark soy sauce

1 tsp chili sauce

1 tsp sugar

$^{1}/_{2}$ cup chicken or vegetable stock

1 tsp cornstarch

2 tsp water

method

1 Cut the eggplant into 2-inch/5-cm long thin sticks. Place in a colander, then sprinkle with salt and let stand for 30 minutes. Rinse in cold water and dry with paper towels.

2 Heat the oil in a skillet or preheated wok. Add the garlic, scallions, and bell pepper and stir-fry over high heat for 1 minute. Stir in the eggplant pieces and stir-fry for an additional 1 minute, or until softened.

3 Stir in the corn cobs and snow peas and stir-fry for 1 minute. Add the bok choy, mushrooms, and bean sprouts and stir-fry for 30 seconds.

4 Mix the rice wine, yellow bean sauce, soy sauce, chili sauce, and sugar together in a bowl, then add to the skillet with the stock. Bring to a boil, stirring constantly.

5 Slowly blend the cornstarch with the water to form a smooth paste, then stir quickly into the skillet and cook for an additional 1 minute. Serve immediately.

egg-fried rice with vegetables & crispy onions

ingredients

SERVES 4

4 tbsp vegetable or peanut oil

2 garlic cloves, chopped finely

2 fresh red chiles, seeded and
    chopped

4 oz/115 g mushrooms, sliced

2 oz/55 g snow peas, halved

2 oz/55 g baby corn, halved

3 tbsp Thai soy sauce

1 tbsp jaggery or soft light
    brown sugar

few Thai basil leaves

3 cups cooked and cooled rice

2 eggs, beaten

2 onions, sliced

method

1 Heat half the oil in a wok or large skillet and sauté the garlic and chiles for 2–3 minutes.

2 Add the mushrooms, snow peas, and corn, and stir-fry for 2–3 minutes before adding the soy sauce, sugar, and basil. Stir in the rice.

3 Push the mixture to one side of the wok and add the eggs to the bottom. Stir until lightly set before combining into the rice mixture.

4 Heat the remaining oil in another skillet and sauté the onions until crispy and brown. Serve the rice topped with the onions.

stir-fried gingerroot mushrooms

ingredients

SERVES 4

2 tbsp vegetable oil

3 garlic cloves, crushed

1 tbsp Thai red curry paste

1/2 tsp ground turmeric

15 oz/425 g canned straw
    mushrooms, drained and
    halved

3/4-inch/2-cm piece fresh
    gingerroot, finely shredded

scant 1/2 cup coconut milk

1 1/2 oz/40 g dried shiitake
    mushrooms, soaked,
    drained, and sliced

1 tbsp lemon juice

1 tbsp light soy sauce

2 tsp sugar

1/2 tsp salt

8 cherry tomatoes, halved

7 oz/200 g firm bean curd
    (drained weight)

cilantro leaves, for sprinkling

freshly cooked Thai fragrant
    rice, to serve

scallion curls, to garnish

method

1 Heat the oil in a preheated wok or large skillet. Add the garlic and cook for 1 minute, stirring. Stir in the curry paste and turmeric and cook for an additional 30 seconds.

2 Stir in the straw mushrooms and gingerroot and stir-fry for 2 minutes. Stir in the coconut milk and bring to a boil.

3 Stir in the shiitake mushrooms, lemon juice, soy sauce, sugar, and salt and heat thoroughly. Add the tomatoes and bean curd and toss gently to heat through.

4 Sprinkle the cilantro over the mixture and serve hot with freshly cooked fragrant rice garnished with scallion curls.

egg fu yung

ingredients

SERVES 4–6

2 eggs

1/2 tsp salt

pinch of white pepper

1 tsp melted butter

2 tbsp vegetable or peanut oil

1 tsp finely chopped garlic

1 small onion, finely sliced

1 green bell pepper,
  finely sliced

1 lb/450 g cooked rice, chilled

1 tbsp light soy sauce

1 tbsp finely chopped scallions

5 oz/150 g bean sprouts,
  trimmed

2 drops of sesame oil

method

1 Beat the eggs with the salt and pepper. Heat the butter in a pan and pour in the eggs. Cook as an omelet, until set, then remove from the pan and cut into slivers.

2 In a preheated wok or deep pan, heat the oil and stir-fry the garlic until fragrant. Add the onion and stir-fry for 1 minute, then add the green bell pepper and stir-fry for an additional 1 minute. Stir in the rice and when the grains are separated, stir in the light soy sauce and cook for 1 minute.

3 Add the scallions and egg strips and stir well, then finally add the bean sprouts and sesame oil. Stir-fry for 1 minute and serve.

sichuan noodles

ingredients

SERVES 4

1 large carrot

9 oz/250 g dried thick Chinese
egg noodles

2 tbsp peanut or corn oil

2 large garlic cloves, very
finely chopped

1 large red onion, cut in half
and thinly sliced

1/2 cup vegetable stock
or water

2 tbsp bottled chili bean sauce

2 tbsp Chinese sesame paste

1 tbsp dried Sichuan
peppercorns, roasted and
ground

1 tsp light soy sauce

2 small bok choy or other
Chinese cabbage,
cut into fourths

method

1 Peel the carrot and cut off both ends, then grate it lengthwise on the coarsest side of a grater to make long, thin strips. Set the carrot strips aside.

2 Cook the noodles in a pan of boiling water for 4 minutes, or according to the package instructions, until soft. Drain and rinse with cold water to stop the cooking, then set aside.

3 Heat a wok or large skillet over high heat. Add the oil and heat until it shimmers. Add the garlic and onion and stir-fry for 1 minute. Add the vegetable stock, chili bean sauce, sesame paste, ground Sichuan peppercorns, and soy sauce and bring to a boil, stirring to blend the ingredients together. Add the bok choy fourths and carrot strips and continue stir-frying for 1–2 minutes, until they are just wilted. Add the noodles and continue stir-frying, using 2 forks to mix all the ingredients together. Serve the noodles when they are hot.

hot-&-sour noodle salad

ingredients

SERVES 4

12 oz/350 g dried rice
    vermicelli noodles

4 tbsp sesame oil

3 tbsp soy sauce

juice of 2 limes

1 tsp sugar

4 scallions, finely sliced

1–2 tsp hot chili sauce

2 tbsp chopped fresh cilantro

method

1 Prepare the noodles according to the package instructions. Drain, put in a bowl, and toss with half the oil.

2 Mix the remaining oil, soy sauce, lime juice, sugar, scallions, and chili sauce together in a bowl. Stir into the noodles.

3 Stir in the cilantro and serve.

sweet-&-sour vegetables on noodle pancakes

ingredients

SERVES 4

4 oz/115 g dried thin cellophane noodles

6 eggs

4 scallions, sliced diagonally

2¹/₂ tbsp peanut or corn oil

2 lb/900 g selection of vegetables, such as carrots, baby corn, cauliflower, broccoli, snow peas, and onions, peeled as necessary and chopped into same-size pieces

3¹/₂ oz/100 g canned bamboo shoots, drained

scant 1 cup sweet-and-sour sauce

salt and pepper

method

1 Soak the noodles in enough lukewarm water to cover and let stand for 20 minutes, or according to the package instructions, until soft. Drain them well and use scissors to cut into 3-inch/7.5-cm pieces, then set aside.

2 Beat the eggs, then stir in the noodles, the scallions, salt, and pepper. Heat an 8-inch/ 20-cm skillet over high heat. Add 1 tablespoon oil and swirl it around. Pour in a fourth of the egg mixture and tilt the skillet so it covers the bottom. Lower the heat to medium and cook for 1 minute, or until the thin pancake is set. Flip it over and add a little extra oil, if necessary. Continue cooking until beginning to color. Keep warm in a low oven while you make 3 more pancakes.

3 After you've made 4 pancakes, heat a wok or large, heavy-bottom skillet over high heat. Add 1¹/₂ tablespoons oil and heat until it shimmers. Add the thickest vegetables, such as carrots, first and stir-fry for 30 seconds. Gradually add the remaining vegetables and bamboo shoots. Stir in the sauce and stir-fry until all the vegetables are tender and the sauce is hot. Spoon the vegetables and sauce over the pancakes.

egg-fried rice with peas

ingredients

SERVES 4

5^1/$_2$ oz/150 g long-grain rice

3 eggs, beaten

2 tbsp vegetable oil

2 garlic cloves, crushed

4 scallions, chopped

generous 1 cup cooked peas

1 tbsp light soy sauce

pinch of salt

shredded scallions, to garnish

method

1 Cook the rice in a pan of boiling water for 10–12 minutes until almost cooked, but not soft. Drain well, rinse under cold running water and drain thoroughly.

2 Place the beaten eggs in a nonstick pan and cook over low heat, stirring constantly, until softly scrambled. Remove the pan from the heat and set aside.

3 Preheat a wok over medium heat. Add the oil and swirl it around to coat the sides of the wok. When the oil is hot, add the garlic, scallions, and peas and sauté, stirring occasionally, for 1–2 minutes.

4 Stir the rice into the mixture in the wok, mixing to combine. Add the eggs, soy sauce, and salt to the wok and stir to mix in the eggs thoroughly.

5 Transfer to serving dishes and serve garnished with the shredded scallions.

spicy bean curd

ingredients

SERVES 4

9 oz/250 g firm bean curd,
    rinsed and drained
    thoroughly and cut into
    $1/2$-inch/1-cm cubes
4 tbsp peanut oil
1 tbsp grated fresh gingerroot
3 garlic cloves, crushed
4 scallions, sliced thinly
1 head of broccoli,
    cut into florets
1 carrot, cut into batons
1 yellow bell pepper,
    sliced thinly
9 oz/250 g shiitake
    mushrooms, sliced thinly
steamed rice, to serve

m a r i n a d e
5 tbsp vegetable stock
2 tsp cornstarch
2 tbsp soy sauce
1 tbsp superfine sugar
pinch of chile flakes

method

1 Combine all the ingredients for the marinade in a large bowl. Add the bean curd and toss well to cover in the marinade. Set aside to marinate for 20 minutes.

2 In a large skillet or wok, heat 2 tablespoons of the peanut oil and stir-fry the bean curd with its marinade until brown and crispy. Remove from the skillet and set aside.

3 Heat the remaining 2 tablespoons of peanut oil in the skillet and stir-fry the gingerroot, garlic, and scallions for 30 seconds. Add the broccoli, carrot, yellow bell pepper, and mushrooms to the skillet and cook for 5–6 minutes. Return the bean curd to the skillet and stir-fry to reheat. Serve immediately over steamed rice.

a firepot of mushrooms & bean curd

ingredients

SERVES 4

2 oz/55 g dried Chinese
  mushrooms
4 oz/115 g firm bean curd,
  drained
2 tbsp sweet chili sauce
2 tbsp peanut or corn oil
2 large garlic cloves, chopped
1/2-inch/1-cm piece fresh
  gingerroot, peeled and
  finely chopped
1 red onion, sliced
1/2 tbsp Sichuan peppercorns,
  lightly crushed
2 oz/55 g canned straw
  mushrooms, drained
  weight, rinsed
vegetable stock or water
1 star anise
pinch of sugar
soy sauce, to taste
4 oz/115 g dried thin
  cellophane noodles

method

1 Soak the mushrooms in enough boiling water to cover for 20 minutes, or until soft. Cut the bean curd into bite-size chunks and coat with the chili sauce, then let marinate.

2 Just before you are ready to start cooking, strain the soaked mushrooms through a strainer lined with a paper towel, reserving the soaking liquid. Heat the oil in a medium-size ovenproof casserole or large skillet with a lid. Add the garlic and gingerroot and stir them around for 30 seconds. Add the onion and peppercorns and keep stirring until the onion is almost tender. Add the bean curd, the soaked mushrooms, and canned mushrooms and stir carefully so the bean curd doesn't break up.

3 Add the reserved mushroom soaking liquid to the wok with just enough vegetable stock or water to cover. Stir in the star anise and a pinch of sugar with several dashes of soy sauce. Bring to a boil, then reduce the heat to the lowest setting, cover, and let simmer for 5 minutes. Add the noodles, re-cover and simmer for an additional 5 minutes, or until the noodles are tender. The noodles should be covered with liquid, so add extra stock at this point, if necessary. Use a fork or wooden spoon to stir the noodles into the other ingredients. Add more soy sauce, if liked.

broccoli & snow pea stir-fry

ingredients

SERVES 4

2 tbsp vegetable or peanut oil

dash of sesame oil

1 garlic clove, finely chopped

1 medium-large head broccoli,
  cut into small florets

4 oz/115 g snow peas,
  trimmed

8 oz/225 g Chinese cabbage,
  chopped into 1/2-inch/1-cm
  slices

5–6 scallions, finely chopped

1/2 tsp salt

2 tbsp light soy sauce

1 tbsp Shaoxing rice wine

1 tsp sesame seeds, lightly
  toasted

method

1 In a preheated wok or deep pan, heat the oils, then add the garlic and stir-fry vigorously. Add all the vegetables and salt and stir-fry over high heat, tossing rapidly, for about 3 minutes.

2 Pour in the light soy sauce and Shaoxing and cook for an additional 2 minutes.

3 Sprinkle with the sesame seeds and serve hot.

garlic spinach stir-fry

ingredients

SERVES 4

6 tbsp vegetable oil

6 garlic cloves, crushed

2 tbsp black bean sauce

3 tomatoes, coarsely chopped

2 lb/900 g spinach, tough
    stalks removed, coarsely
    chopped

1 tsp chili sauce, or to taste

2 tbsp fresh lemon juice

salt and pepper

method

1 Heat the oil in a preheated wok or large skillet over high heat, add the garlic, black bean sauce, and tomatoes and stir-fry for 1 minute.

2 Stir in the spinach, chili sauce, and lemon juice and mix well. Cook, stirring frequently, for 3 minutes, or until the spinach is just wilted. Season with salt and pepper. Remove from the heat and serve immediately.

spicy vegetarian stir-fry

ingredients

SERVES 4

3 tbsp vegetable oil

$1/2$ tsp turmeric

8 oz/225 g potatoes, cut into
$1/2$ inch/1 cm cubes

3 shallots, chopped finely

1 bay leaf

$1/2$ tsp ground cumin

1 tsp finely grated fresh
gingerroot

$1/4$ tsp chili powder

4 tomatoes, chopped coarsely

$10^1/2$ oz/300 g spinach,
trimmed and chopped
coarsely

generous 1 cup fresh or or
frozen peas

1 tbsp lemon juice

salt and pepper

cooked basmati rice, to serve

method

1 In a wok, heat 2 tablespoons of the oil and add the turmeric and a pinch of salt. Carefully add the potatoes, stirring continuously to coat in the turmeric. Stir-fry for 5 minutes, then remove from the wok and set aside.

2 Heat the remaining tablespoon of oil and stir-fry the shallots for 1–2 minutes. Mix in the bay leaf, cumin, gingerroot, and chili powder, then add the tomatoes and stir-fry for 2 minutes.

3 Add the spinach, mixing well to combine all the flavors. Cover and simmer for 2–3 minutes. Return the potatoes to the wok and add the peas and lemon juice. Cook for 5 minutes, or until the potatoes are tender.

4 Remove the wok from the heat and discard the bay leaf, then season with salt and pepper. Serve with cooked basmati rice.

crispy noodle & vegetable stir-fry

ingredients

SERVES 4

peanut or sunflower oil,
 for deep-frying
4 oz/115 g rice vermicelli,
 broken into 3-inch/7.5-cm
 lengths
4 oz/115 g green beans,
 cut into short lengths
2 carrots, cut into thin sticks
2 zucchini, cut into thin sticks
4 oz/115 g shiitake
 mushrooms, sliced
1-inch/2.5-cm piece fresh
 gingerroot, shredded
1/2 small head Napa cabbage,
 shredded
4 scallions, shredded
3 oz/85 g bean sprouts
2 tbsp dark soy sauce
2 tbsp Chinese rice wine
large pinch of sugar
2 tbsp coarsely chopped fresh
 cilantro

method

1 Fill a wok or deep, heavy-bottom skillet halfway with oil. Heat to 350–375°F/180–190°C, or until a cube of bread browns in 30 seconds.

2 Add the noodles, in batches, and cook for 1 1/2–2 minutes, or until crisp and puffed up. Remove and drain on paper towels. Pour off all but 2 tablespoons of oil from the wok.

3 Heat the remaining oil over high heat. Add the green beans and stir-fry for 2 minutes. Add the carrot and zucchini sticks, sliced mushrooms, and gingerroot and stir-fry for an additional 2 minutes.

4 Add the shredded Napa cabbage, scallions, and bean sprouts and stir-fry for an additional 1 minute. Add the soy sauce, rice wine, and sugar and cook, stirring constantly, for 1 minute.

5 Add the chopped cilantro and toss well. Serve immediately, with the noodles.

agedashi bean curd

ingredients

SERVES 2

$^2/_3$ cup water

2 tsp dashi granules

2 tbsp shoyu (Japanese
soy sauce)

2 tbsp mirin

vegetable oil, for deep-frying

$10^1/_2$ oz/300 g silken bean
curd, drained on paper
towels and cut into 4 cubes

2 tbsp all-purpose flour

1 tsp grated fresh gingerroot

2 tsp grated daikon

$^1/_4$ tsp kezuri-bushi shavings

method

1 Put the water in a pan with the dashi granules and bring to a boil. Add the shoyu and mirin and cook for 1 minute. Keep warm.

2 Preheat a wok, then fill one-third full with oil, or use a deep-fryer. Heat the oil to 350–375°F/180–190°C, or until a cube of bread browns in 30 seconds. Meanwhile, dust the bean curd cubes with the flour.

3 Add the bean curd to the oil, in batches, and cook until lightly golden in color. Remove, drain on paper towels, and keep hot while you cook the remaining bean curd cubes.

4 Put 2 pieces of bean curd in each of 2 bowls and divide the dashi stock between them. Top with gingerroot, daikon, and kezuri-bushi.

chinese vegetables & bean sprouts with noodles

ingredients

SERVES 4

5 cups vegetable stock

1 garlic clove, crushed

1/2-inch/1-cm piece fresh
gingerroot, finely chopped

8 oz/225 g dried medium
egg noodles

1 red bell pepper, seeded
and sliced

3/4 cup frozen peas

1/2 cup broccoli florets

3 oz/85 g shiitake mushrooms,
sliced

2 tbsp sesame seeds

8 oz/225 g canned water
chestnuts, drained and
halved

8 oz/225 g canned bamboo
shoots, drained

10 oz/280 g Napa cabbage,
sliced

scant 1 cup bean sprouts

3 scallions, sliced

1 tbsp dark soy sauce

pepper

method

1 Bring the stock, garlic, and gingerroot to a boil in a large pan. Stir in the noodles, red bell pepper, peas, broccoli, and mushrooms and return to a boil. Reduce the heat, cover, and let simmer for 5–6 minutes, or until the noodles are tender.

2 Meanwhile, preheat the broiler to medium. Spread the sesame seeds out in a single layer on a cookie sheet and toast under the preheated broiler, turning to brown evenly— watch constantly because they brown very quickly. Tip the sesame seeds into a small dish and set aside.

3 Once the noodles are tender, add the water chestnuts, bamboo shoots, Napa cabbage, bean sprouts, and scallions to the pan. Return the stock to a boil, stir to mix the ingredients, and let simmer for an additional 2–3 minutes to heat through thoroughly.

4 Carefully drain off 1 1/4 cups of the stock into a small heatproof pitcher and set aside. Drain and discard any remaining stock and turn the noodles and vegetables into a warmed serving dish. Quickly mix the soy sauce with the reserved stock and pour over the noodles and vegetables. Season with pepper and serve at once.

oyster mushrooms & vegetables with peanut chili sauce

ingredients

SERVES 4

1 tbsp sesame oil

4 scallions, sliced finely

1 carrot, cut into batons

1 zucchini, cut into batons

1/2 head of broccoli, cut into
    florets

1 lb/450 g oyster mushrooms,
    sliced thinly

2 tbsp coarse peanut butter

1 tsp chili powder, or to taste

3 tbsp water

cooked rice or noodles,
    to serve

wedges of lime, to garnish

method

1 Heat the oil in a skillet or wok until almost smoking. Stir-fry the scallions for 1 minute. Add the carrot and zucchini and stir-fry for an additional 1 minute. Then add the broccoli and cook for 1 minute more.

2 Stir in the mushrooms and cook until they are soft and at least half the liquid they produce has evaporated. Add the peanut butter and stir well. Season with the chili powder. Finally, add the water and cook for an additional 1 minute.

3 Serve over rice or noodles and garnish with wedges of lime.

spicy noodles with mushroom egg rolls

ingredients

SERVES 4

2 tbsp vegetable or peanut oil

1 small onion, chopped finely

8 oz/225 g mushrooms,
    chopped

1 tbsp Thai red curry paste

1 tbsp Thai soy sauce

1 tbsp fish sauce

8 square egg roll skins

vegetable or peanut oil,
    for deep-frying

8 oz/225 g quick-cook noodles

1 garlic clove, chopped

6 scallions, chopped

1 red bell pepper, seeded and
    chopped

1 tbsp ground coriander

1 tbsp ground cumin

method

1 Heat 1 tablespoon of the oil in a wok and stir-fry the onion and mushrooms until crisp and browned. Add the curry paste, soy sauce, and fish sauce, and stir-fry for 2–3 minutes. Remove the wok from the heat.

2 Spoon an eighth of the mixture across one of the egg roll skins and roll up, folding the sides over the filling to enclose it.

3 Heat the oil for deep-frying in a wok and deep-fry the egg rolls, 4 at a time, until crisp and browned. Drain on paper towels and keep warm.

4 Meanwhile, put the noodles in a bowl, cover with boiling water, and let swell.

5 Heat the remaining oil in the wok and stir-fry the garlic, scallions, and red bell pepper for 2–3 minutes. Stir in the coriander and cumin, then drain the noodles and add them to the wok. Toss together and serve topped with the egg rolls.

almonds
    baked cod with a curry crust 574
    shrimp & rice salad 74
angler fish
    fish curry 534
    fish curry with rice noodles 536
    steamed yellow fish fillets 544
    stir-fried rice noodles with marinated
        fish 538
asparagus
    asparagus & bell pepper rolls with tahini
        sauce 608
    asparagus & omelet rolls 600
    asparagus & red bell pepper sushi 634
    beef noodles with oyster sauce 306
    chirashi sushi with omelet &
        mushrooms 626
    crab, asparagus & shiitake rolls 240
    monkfish stir-fry 578
    salmon, asparagus & mayonnaise rolls 234
    stir-fried scallops with asparagus 454
    tempura 216
avocados
    avocado sushi with tapenade 618
    avocado, watercress & pickle wraps 594
    California rolls 248
    chirashi sushi with lobster & wasabi
        mayonnaise 512
    chirashi sushi with shrimp, crab &
        avocado 460
    inside-out rolls with avocado &
        shibazuke 616
    pepper-wrapped shrimp rolls 238
    shrimp & avocado skewers 244

bamboo shoots
    bamboo shoots with bean curd 132
    beef chop suey 286
    beef stir-fry 290
    Chinese vegetables & bean sprouts with
        noodles 710
    crispy egg rolls 152
    five-willow fish 500
    fried fish with pine nuts 494
    gingerroot chicken with noodles 416
    hot-&-sour soup 44
    soft-wrapped pork & shrimp rolls 150
    spring rolls 146
    stir-fried scallops with asparagus 454
    sweet-&-sour noodles with chicken 388
    sweet-&-sour vegetables on noodle
        pancakes 692
    turkey with bamboo shoots & water
        chestnuts 428
    whole chicken soup 40
bean curd 592
    agedashi bean curd 708
    bamboo shoots with bean curd 132
    bean curd & bean sprout soup 20
    bean curd & green vegetable curry 656
    bean curd sushi with gingerroot &
        scallion 642
    buckwheat noodle salad with smoked bean
        curd 96
    Chinese vegetable soup 26
    firepot of mushrooms & bean curd 698
    hot-&-sour soup 44
    julienne vegetable salad 94
    ma po doufu 304
    miso soup 56
    monk's soup 32
    oyster mushroom & fried bean curd
        chirashi sushi 622

rice noodles with bean curd soup 18
rice noodles with mushrooms & bean
    curd 676
seasoned bean curd 648
sesame-bean curd chirashi sushi 620
shredded chile chicken pouches 366
soft-wrapped pork & shrimp rolls 150
spicy bean curd 696
stir-fried gingerroot mushrooms 684
sweet bean curd pouches 646
Thai bean curd cakes with chili dip 206
vegetable & bean curd tempura 218
vegetables with bean curd & spinach 678
vegetarian spring rolls 148
bean sprouts
    Asian vegetables with yellow bean
        sauce 680
    bean curd & bean sprout soup 20
    beef chow mein 308
    beef stir-fry 290
    chicken chow mein 392
    Chinese chicken rice 418
    Chinese fried rice 260
    Chinese shrimp salad 72
    Chinese vegetables & bean sprouts with
        noodles 710
    classic stir-fried vegetables 102
    crab fried rice 264
    crispy egg rolls 152
    crispy noodle & vegetable stir-fry 706
    egg fu yung 686
    julienne vegetable salad 94
    pad Thai 344
    peppered beef salad 76
    pork lo mein 330
    pork with vegetables 346
    salmon & shrimp spring rolls with plum
        sauce 154
    shrimp laksa 480
    spring rolls 146
    stir-fried bean sprouts 134
    stir-fried beef with bean sprouts 294
    sweet-&-sour sea bass 586
    Thai chicken-coconut soup 22
    udon noodle stir-fry with fish cake &
        gingerroot 582
    vegetable & noodle soup 30
    yaki soba 420
    zucchini & cashew curry 660
beef
    beef chop suey 286
    beef chow mein 308
    beef with fresh noodles 318
    beef noodles with oyster sauce 306
    beef with onions & broccoli 302
    beef satay with peanut sauce 168
    beef stir-fry 290
    broiled beef salad 78
    chirashi sushi with soy-glazed steak 322
    dan dan mian 320
    egg-fried rice with seven-spice beef 316
    gingerroot beef with yellow bell peppers 296
    ground beef & cilantro soup 36
    hot beef & coconut curry 314
    hot sesame beef 288
    inside-out rolls with beef teriyaki 252
    ma po doufu 304
    marinated beef with vegetables 284
    Mussaman curry 298
    peppered beef salad 76
    red-hot beef with cashew nuts 312
    rice sticks with beef in black bean
        sauce 310

roast beef wraps with wasabi
    mayonnaise 282
spicy beef & noodle soup 34
spicy beef with potato 300
stir-fried beef with bean sprouts 294
stir-fried beef with broccoli &
    gingerroot 292
bell peppers
    Asian vegetables with yellow bean
        sauce 680
    asparagus & bell pepper rolls with tahini
        sauce 608
    asparagus & red bell pepper sushi 634
    bean curd & green vegetable curry 656
    beef with fresh noodles 318
    beef stir-fry 290
    broiled beef salad 78
    chargrilled tuna with chile salsa 564
    chicken chow mein 392
    chicken & green vegetables 390
    chicken noodle soup 42
    Chinese chicken rice 418
    Chinese fried rice 260
    Chinese vegetables & bean sprouts with
        noodles 710
    chunky potatoes with cilantro leaves 122
    classic stir-fried vegetables 102
    corn fritters 204
    duck with mixed bell peppers 432
    duck with scallion soup 48
    egg fu yung 686
    eggplant with red bell peppers 126
    five-spice crispy pork with egg-fried
        rice 352
    five-willow fish 500
    fried fish with pine nuts 494
    gingered chicken & vegetable salad 82
    gingered chicken kebabs 370
    gingerroot beef with yellow bell
        peppers 296
    green bean & tomato chirashi sushi 630
    hot sesame beef 288
    hot-&-sour vegetable salad 98
    julienne vegetable salad 94
    Malaysian-style coconut noodles with
        shrimp 478
    Mediterranean pressed sushi 638
    mixed vegetables with quick-fried basil 138
    noodles with shrimp & green bell
        peppers 470
    omelet rolls with cream cheese &
        pepper 602
    onion, potato & red bell pepper curry 668
    pepper-wrapped shrimp rolls 238
    peppered beef salad 76
    pork with bell peppers 348
    pork lo mein 330
    pork with vegetables 346
    red curry pork with bell peppers 342
    red lamb curry 360
    rice noodles with bean curd soup 18
    rice sticks with beef in black bean
        sauce 310
    salmon & scallops with cilantro & lime 556
    sesame-bean curd chirashi sushi 620
    Sichuan-style pork & pepper 326
    sour-&-spicy pork 334
    spareribs in a sweet-&-sour sauce 354
    spiced tuna in sweet-&-sour sauce 570
    spicy bean curd 696
    spicy noodles with mushroom egg rolls 714
    spicy Sichuan pork 324
    squid & red bell peppers 520

squid & red onion stir-fry 522
stir-fried beef with bean sprouts 294
stir-fried green beans with red bell
    pepper 108
sweet chile squid 516
sweet-&-sour chicken 378
sweet-&-sour noodles with chicken 388
tempura 216
Thai red chicken curry 402
Thai yellow vegetable curry with brown
    basmati rice 674
tuna rice 266
turkey with bamboo shoots & water
    chestnuts 428
vegetable & bean curd tempura 218
vegetables with bean curd & spinach 678
Xinjiang lamb casserole 358
yaki soba 420
bok choy
    Asian vegetables with yellow bean
        sauce 680
    bamboo shoots with bean curd 132
    chicken with vegetables & cilantro rice 408
    Chinese mushroom soup 24
    crispy seaweed 214
    Malaysian-style coconut noodles with
        shrimp 478
    red chicken salad 80
    Sichuan noodles 688
    stir-fried squid with hot black bean
        sauce 518
    sweet-&-sour sea bass 586
    sweet-&-sour vegetables with cashew
        nuts 106
    Thai yellow vegetable curry with brown
        basmati rice 674
broccoli
    bean curd & green vegetable curry 656
    beef chop suey 286
    beef with onions & broccoli 302
    broccoli & snow pea stir-fry 700
    chicken & green vegetables 390
    classic stir-fried vegetables 102
    gingerroot chicken with toasted sesame
        seeds 386
    hot sesame beef 288
    stir-fried beef with broccoli & gingerroot 292
    stir-fried broccoli 114
    sweet-&-sour vegetables with cashew
        nuts 106

cabbage
    buckwheat noodle salad with smoked bean
        curd 96
    classic stir-fried vegetables 102
    hot-&-sour cabbage 120
    pork & gingerroot dumplings 160
    red chicken salad 80
    shrimp, snow peas & cashew nuts 464
    soft-wrapped pork & shrimp rolls 150
    somen noodles with shrimp 488
    vegetarian spring rolls 148
carrots
    carrot & pumpkin curry 666
    pickled daikon & carrot 208
    spiced carrot sushi 636
cashew nuts
    broiled beef salad 78
    cauliflower & beans with cashew nuts 140
    chicken with cashew nuts 384
    red-hot beef with cashew nuts 312
    shrimp, snow peas & cashew nuts 464
    spiced cashew nut curry 658

sweet-&-sour noodles with chicken 388
sweet-&-sour vegetables with cashew
    nuts 106
zucchini & cashew curry 660
cauliflower
    cauliflower & beans with cashew nuts 140
    gingerroot chicken with toasted sesame
        seeds 386
cheese
    chirashi sushi with feta & sunblush
        tomatoes 624
    crab soufflé 490
    Mediterranean pressed sushi 638
    omelet rolls with cream cheese &
        pepper 602
chicken
    bang bang chicken 382
    chicken with cashew nuts 384
    chicken chow mein 392
    chicken chow mein baskets 394
    chicken fried rice 376
    chicken & green vegetables 390
    chicken noodle soup 42
    chicken & peanut curry 398
    chicken satay 176
    chicken steamed with rice in lotus
        leaves 410
    chicken teriyaki rolls 246
    chicken with vegetables & cilantro rice 408
    chicken with water chestnuts and plum
        sauce 426
    chicken with yellow curry sauce 404
    Chinese chicken rice 418
    chirashi sushi with teriyaki chicken 374
    clear soup with mushrooms & chicken 38
    cross the bridge noodles 396
    egg-fried rice with chicken 414
    gingered chicken & vegetable salad 82
    gingered chicken kebabs 370
    gingerroot chicken with noodles 416
    gingerroot chicken with toasted sesame
        seeds 386
    gong bao chicken 380
    green chicken curry 400
    ground chicken skewers 372
    Hainan chicken rice 412
    kara-age chicken 172
    lemongrass chicken skewers 174
    noodle baskets with chicken lime salad 424
    red chicken salad 80
    shredded chile chicken pouches 366
    soy chicken wings 170
    spiced cilantro chicken 406
    sweet-&-sour chicken 378
    sweet-&-sour noodles with chicken 388
    teriyaki chicken with sesame noodles 422
    Thai chicken-coconut soup 22
    Thai red chicken curry 402
    Thai-style chicken chunks 368
    whole chicken soup 40
    yaki soba 420
chickpeas
    chickpea curry 670
    mixed vegetable curry with chickpea
        pancakes 672
Chinese cabbage
    broccoli & snow pea stir-fry 700
    cabbage & cucumber in a vinegar
        dressing 104
    daikon & cucumber salad 92
    salmon & shrimp spring rolls with plum
        sauce 154
    Sichuan noodles 688

Singapore noodles 332
whole chicken soup 40
Chinese greens
    stir-fried Chinese greens 116
    see also Chinese cabbage; choi sum;
        Napa cabbage
choi sum
    choi sum in oyster sauce 118
    cross the bridge noodles 396
clams
    clams in black bean sauce 446
    spicy Thai seafood stew 580
coconut
    Asian coconut rice 268
    fish in coconut 540
    hot beef & coconut curry 314
    Malaysian-style coconut noodles with
        shrimp 478
    shrimp with coconut rice 474
    Thai chicken-coconut soup 22
    vegetable & coconut curry 662
cod
    baked cod with a curry crust 574
    fish curry with rice noodles 536
    stir-fried rice noodles with marinated
        fish 538
corn
    Asian vegetables with yellow bean
        sauce 680
    chicken fried rice 376
    chicken with yellow curry sauce 404
    classic stir-fried vegetables 102
    corn fritters 204
    crab & corn soup 54
    egg-fried rice with vegetables & crispy
        onions 682
    gingered chicken & vegetable salad 82
    gingerroot beef with yellow bell
        peppers 296
    hot-&-sour vegetable salad 98
    lettuce wraps 198
    mixed vegetables with quick-fried basil 138
    pork with vegetables 346
    shrimp & haddock with rice 498
    shrimp, snow peas & cashew nuts 464
    sour-&-spicy pork 334
    spicy Thai soup with shrimp 52
    stir-fried lamb with mint 364
    Thai yellow vegetable curry with brown
        basmati rice 674
    tuna rice 266
    vegetables with bean curd & spinach 678
    wontons 190
crabmeat
    California rolls 248
    chirashi sushi with shrimp, crab &
        avocado 460
    crab, asparagus & shiitake rolls 240
    crab & cilantro salad 62
    crab & corn soup 54
    crab fried rice 264
    crab parcels 186
    crab soufflé 490
    crispy crab wontons 192
    lemon pepper crab sushi boats 506
    pork & crab meatballs 166
    stir-fried fresh crab with gingerroot 510
    Thai-style chirashi sushi with crabmeat 492
cucumber
    cabbage & cucumber in a vinegar
        dressing 104
    cucumber rolls with sesame 604
    daikon & cucumber salad 92

duck salad 86
pickled baby cucumbers 200
pickled cucumber 202
salmon, cucumber & pickled radish
wraps 554

daikon
chirashi sushi with smoked mackerel 588
chirashi sushi with soy-glazed steak 322
daikon & cucumber salad 92
mixed sashimi 444
pickled daikon & carrot 208
roast beef wraps with wasabi
mayonnaise 282
sea bass with chili oil 584
seared salmon sashimi with sesame &
black pepper 550
seared swordfish salad 70
dipping sauces 272-77
duck
Chinese crispy duck 434
duck breasts with chile & lime 438
duck & hoisin hand rolls 430
duck with mixed bell peppers 432
duck salad 86
duck with scallion soup 48
Peking duck 436

eggplants
Asian vegetables with yellow bean
sauce 680
eggplant & bean curry 654
eggplant with miso 128
eggplant & mushroom stuffed omelet 652
eggplant & onion salad 90
eggplant with red bell peppers 126
eggplant sushi with sweet soy sauce 644
gingered chicken kebabs 370
inside-out rolls with avocado &
shibazuke 616
Sichuan fried eggplant 124
stuffed eggplants 650
Thai red chicken curry 402
vegetable & bean curd tempura 218
eggs
asparagus & omelet rolls 600
chicken fried rice 376
Chinese fried rice 260
chirashi sushi with omelet &
mushrooms 626
corn fritters 204
crab fried rice 264
crab soufflé 490
curried egg salad 100
egg-fried rice 256
egg-fried rice with chicken 414
egg-fried rice with peas 694
egg-fried rice with seven-spice beef 316
egg-fried rice with vegetables & crispy
onions 682
eggplant & mushroom stuffed omelet 652
egg fu yung 686
five-spice crispy pork with egg-fried
rice 352
katsudon 338
omelet pouches with mushroom 598
omelet rolls 156
omelet rolls with cream cheese &
pepper 602
omelet wraps with pickled radish &
shiso 596
onion pancakes 194
shrimp fu yung 484

sweet rolled omelet sushi 632
sweet-&-sour vegetables on noodle
pancakes 692
tea-scented eggs 196

fish & seafood
chiles stuffed with fish paste 448
chirashi sushi with lobster & wasabi
mayonnaise 512
congee with fish fillet 528
cross the bridge noodles 396
deep-fried river fish with chili bean
sauce 504
fish cakes 188
fish in coconut 540
fried fish with pine nuts 494
mixed sashimi 444
rice with seafood & squid 526
seafood tempura 220
seared swordfish salad 70
spiced steamed fish 542
spicy Thai seafood stew 580
steamed sole with black bean sauce 502
steamed yellow fish fillets 544
udon noodle stir-fry with fish cake &
gingerroot 582
white fish hand rolls with tartar sauce 572
whitebait with green chile 178
see also angler fish; clams; crabmeat;
mackerel; monkfish; mussels; salmon;
scallops; sea bass; shrimp; squid; tuna

gingerroot
gingerroot & sesame dipping sauce 272
home-made pickled gingerroot 210
green beans
bean curd & green vegetable curry 656
chicken & green vegetables 390
crispy noodle & vegetable stir-fry 706
eggplant & bean curry 654
fish cakes 188
green bean & tomato chirashi sushi 630
green bean sushi boats 628
green beans with sesame dressing 112
monk's soup 32
Singapore noodles 332
spicy green beans 110
stir-fried green beans with red bell
pepper 108
vegetable & bean curd tempura 218

lamb
lamb with lime leaves 362
red lamb curry 360
stir-fried lamb with mint 364
Xinjiang lamb casserole 358
Xinjiang rice pot with lamb 356
lettuce
lettuce wraps 198
shrimp tempura & lettuce wraps 458

mackerel
chirashi sushi with smoked mackerel 588
mixed sashimi 444
mangoes
Chinese shrimp salad 72
sea bass & mango salad 68
shrimp & rice salad 74
miso
eggplant with miso 128
miso soup 56
monkfish
monkfish with lime & chile sauce 576

monkfish stir-fry 578
spicy Thai seafood stew 580
mushrooms
baby squid stuffed with pork &
mushrooms 514
braised straw mushrooms 130
Chinese mushroom soup 24
chirashi sushi with omelet &
mushrooms 626
clear soup with mushrooms & chicken 38
crab, asparagus & shiitake rolls 240
curried noodles with shrimp & straw
mushrooms 466
eggplant & mushroom stuffed omelet 652
firepot of mushrooms & bean curd 698
fresh shiitake mushroom sushi 640
gingerroot shrimp with oyster
mushrooms 462
mushroom & noodle soup 16
omelet pouches with mushroom 598
oyster mushroom & fried bean curd
chirashi sushi 622
oyster mushrooms & vegetables with
peanut chili sauce 712
pinwheel rolls with mushroom &
spinach 610
rice noodles with mushrooms & bean
curd 676
shrimp with scallions & straw
mushrooms 476
spicy noodles with mushroom egg rolls 714
stir-fried gingerroot mushrooms 684
sweet-&-sour vegetables with cashew
nuts 106
mussels
mixed seafood curry 532
Thai fisherman's catch 482

Napa cabbage
Chinese vegetable soup 26
Chinese vegetables & bean sprouts with
noodles 710
crispy noodle & vegetable stir-fry 706
red chicken salad 80
tuna & tomato salad with gingerroot
dressing 64
noodles
ants climbing a tree 328
beef chow mein 308
beef with fresh noodles 318
beef noodles with oyster sauce 306
buckwheat noodle salad with smoked bean
curd 96
chicken chow mein 392
chicken chow mein baskets 394
chicken & green vegetables 390
chicken noodle soup 42
Chinese mushroom soup 24
Chinese shrimp salad 72
Chinese vegetables & bean sprouts with
noodles 710
crispy noodle & vegetable stir-fry 706
cross the bridge noodles 396
curried noodles with shrimp & straw
mushrooms 466
gingered chicken & vegetable salad 82
gingerroot chicken with noodles 416
hoisin pork with garlic noodles 336
hot-&-sour noodle salad 690
julienne vegetable salad 94
lettuce wraps 198
Malaysian-style coconut noodles with
shrimp 478

monk's soup 32
mushroom & noodle soup 16
noodle baskets with chicken lime salad 424
noodles with shrimp & green bell
      peppers 470
pad Thai 344
pork lo mein 330
pork with vegetables 346
rice noodle rolls with snow pea sprouts 614
rice noodles with bean curd soup 18
rice noodles with mushrooms & bean
      curd 676
seafood chow mein 530
shrimp laksa 480
shrimp with noodles 472
Sichuan noodles 688
Singapore noodles 332
soba noodle rolls 158
somen noodles with shrimp 488
sour-&-spicy pork 334
spicy beef & noodle soup 34
spicy noodles with mushroom egg rolls 714
stir-fried beef with bean sprouts 294
stir-fried rice noodles with marinated
      fish 538
sweet-&-sour noodles with chicken 388
sweet-&-sour vegetables on noodle
      pancakes 692
teriyaki chicken with sesame noodles 422
Thai chicken-coconut soup 22
udon noodle stir-fry with fish cake &
      gingerroot 582
vegetable & noodle soup 30
vegetarian spring rolls 148
yaki soba 420

onion pancakes 194

papayas: shrimp & papaya salad 60
peanuts
      beef satay with peanut sauce 168
      chicken & peanut curry 398
      chicken noodle soup 42
      chicken satay 176
      dan dan mian 320
      gong bao chicken 380
      lettuce wraps 198
      Malaysian-style coconut noodles with
            shrimp 478
      Mussaman curry 298
      oyster mushrooms & vegetables with
            peanut chili sauce 712
      pad Thai 344
      Thai red chicken curry 402
peas
      bean curd & green vegetable curry 656
      chicken fried rice 376
      chicken noodle soup 42
      Chinese fried rice 260
      Chinese vegetables & bean sprouts with
            noodles 710
      egg-fried rice with peas 694
      egg-fried rice with seven-spice beef 316
      eggplant & bean curry 654
      five-spice crispy pork with egg-fried
            rice 352
      mixed vegetable curry with chickpea
            pancakes 672
      spicy vegetarian stir-fry 704
      Thai-style chirashi sushi with crabmeat 492
      vegetable parcels 212
pineapple
      chicken & peanut curry 398

duck salad 86
shrimp & pineapple curry 468
spareribs in a sweet-&-sour sauce 354
spiced tuna in sweet-&-sour sauce 570
ponzu dipping sauce 274
pork
      ants climbing a tree 328
      baby squid stuffed with pork &
            mushrooms 514
      bean curd & bean sprout soup 20
      chicken steamed with rice in lotus
            leaves 410
      chunky potatoes with cilantro leaves 122
      crispy pork dumplings 164
      dumplings in a cold spicy sauce 162
      five-spice crispy pork with egg-fried
            rice 352
      fried rice with pork & shrimp 340
      hoisin pork with garlic noodles 336
      hot-&-sour soup 44
      katsudon 338
      pad Thai 344
      pork & crab meatballs 166
      pork & gingerroot dumplings 160
      pork & romaine lettuce in egg & lemon
            sauce 508
      pork with bell peppers 348
      pork lo mein 330
      pork tonkatsu rolls 250
      pork with vegetables 346
      red curry pork with bell peppers 342
      Sichuan-style pork & pepper 326
      Singapore noodles 332
      soft-wrapped pork & shrimp rolls 150
      sour-&-spicy pork 334
      spareribs in a sweet-&-sour sauce 354
      spicy fried ground pork 350
      spicy Sichuan pork 324
      spring rolls 146
      whole chicken soup 40
      wonton soup 46
potatoes
      chunky potatoes with cilantro leaves 122
      onion, potato & red bell pepper curry 668
      potato & spinach yellow curry 664
      scallop, potato & sesame rolls 242
      spicy beef with potato 300
pumpkin
      carrot & pumpkin curry 666
      Sichuan pumpkin soup 28

radishes
      Chinese shrimp salad 72
      daikon & cucumber salad 92
      lettuce wraps 198
      omelet wraps with pickled radish &
            shiso 596
      pickled radish & kampyo rolls 606
      salmon, cucumber & pickled radish
            wraps 554
rice
      Asian coconut rice 268
      chicken fried rice 376
      chicken steamed with rice in lotus
            leaves 410
      chicken with vegetables & cilantro rice 408
      Chinese chicken rice 418
      Chinese fried rice 260
      congee with fish fillet 528
      crab fried rice 264
      egg-fried rice 256
      egg-fried rice with chicken 414
      egg-fried rice with peas 694

egg-fried rice with seven-spice beef 316
egg-fried rice with vegetables & crispy
      onions 682
egg fu yung 686
five-spice crispy pork with egg-fried
      rice 352
fried rice with pork & shrimp 340
golden rice 262
Hainan chicken rice 412
jasmine rice with lemon & basil 270
perfect sushi rice 258
rice & turkey salad 84
rice with seafood & squid 526
rice sticks with beef in black bean
      sauce 310
shrimp with coconut rice 474
shrimp & haddock with rice 498
shrimp & rice salad 74
steamed white rice 254
tuna rice 266
Xinjiang rice pot with lamb 356

salmon
      chirashi sushi with salmon 546
      classic sushi boat with salmon roe 548
      fish curry 534
      fish curry with rice noodles 536
      mixed sashimi 444
      mixed seafood curry 532
      pan-fried spiced salmon 562
      rice with seafood & squid 526
      salmon & arugula rolls with pesto 226
      salmon, asparagus & mayonnaise rolls 234
      salmon, cucumber & pickled radish
            wraps 554
      salmon with red curry in banana leaves 560
      salmon & scallops with cilantro & lime 556
      salmon & shrimp spring rolls with plum
            sauce 154
      salmon, spinach & wasabi mash rolls 230
      seared salmon sashimi with sesame &
            black pepper 550
      seven-spiced salmon rolls 232
      smoked salmon sushi balls 228
      stir-fried rice noodles with marinated
            fish 538
      sweet chili salmon hand rolls 558
      wraps with fresh tuna, salmon roe & shiso
            leaves 552
scallops
      chirashi sushi on scallop shells 450
      mixed sashimi 444
      salmon & scallops with cilantro & lime 556
      scallop, potato & sesame rolls 242
      seafood chow mein 530
      seafood tempura 220
      simple stir-fried scallops 452
      spicy scallops with lime & chile 456
      stir-fried scallops with asparagus 454
      Thai shrimp & scallop soup 58
      Thai-style seafood soup 50
sea bass
      five-willow fish 500
      sea bass & mango salad 68
      sea bass with chili oil 584
      sweet-&-sour sea bass 586
      whole deep-fried fish with soy &
            gingerroot 496
seaweed salad 66
shrimp
      chicken steamed with rice in lotus
            leaves 410
      Chinese shrimp salad 72

chirashi sushi with salmon 546
chirashi sushi with shrimp, crab & avocado 460
crisp sesame shrimp 184
crispy wrapped shrimp 182
curried noodles with shrimp & straw mushrooms 466
fish in coconut 540
fried rice with pork & shrimp 340
gingerroot shrimp with oyster mushrooms 462
Malaysian-style coconut noodles with shrimp 478
mixed seafood curry 532
noodles with shrimp & green bell peppers 470
pad Thai 344
pepper-wrapped shrimp rolls 238
salmon & shrimp spring rolls with plum sauce 154
seafood chow mein 530
seafood tempura 220
shrimp & avocado skewers 244
shrimp with coconut rice 474
shrimp fu yung 484
shrimp & haddock with rice 498
shrimp laksa 480
shrimp with noodles 472
shrimp & papaya salad 60
shrimp & pineapple curry 468
shrimp & rice salad 74
shrimp with scallions & straw mushrooms 476
shrimp, snow peas & cashew nuts 464
shrimp tempura & lettuce wraps 458
shrimp toasts 180
Singapore noodles 332
soft-wrapped pork & shrimp rolls 150
somen noodles with shrimp 488
spicy Thai seafood stew 580
spicy Thai soup with shrimp 52
spring rolls 146
steamed shrimp rolls with lime dipping sauce 236
Thai fisherman's catch 482
Thai shrimp & scallop soup 58
Thai-style seafood soup 50
udon noodle stir-fry with fish cake & gingerroot 582
wok-fried jumbo shrimp in spicy sauce 486
wonton soup 46
yaki soba 420
snow peas
beef chop suey 286
broccoli & snow pea stir-fry 700
rice noodle rolls with snow pea sprouts 614
shrimp, snow peas & cashew nuts 464
stir-fried squid with hot black bean sauce 518
soybeans: edamame 136
spinach
garlic spinach stir-fry 702
pinwheel rolls with mushroom & spinach 610
potato & spinach yellow curry 664
salmon, spinach & wasabi mash rolls 230
vegetables with bean curd & spinach 678
spring rolls 146
salmon & shrimp spring rolls with plum sauce 154
vegetarian spring rolls 148
squash: vegetable & bean curd tempura 218

squid
baby squid stuffed with pork & mushrooms 514
fish in coconut 540
mixed seafood curry 532
rice with seafood & squid 526
salt & pepper squid wraps 524
seafood chow mein 530
seafood tempura 220
spicy Thai seafood stew 580
squid & red bell peppers 520
squid & red onion stir-fry 522
stir-fried squid with hot black bean sauce 518
sweet chile squid 516
sushi rice
asparagus & bell pepper rolls with tahini sauce 608
asparagus & red bell pepper sushi 634
avocado sushi with tapenade 618
avocado, watercress & pickle wraps 594
bean curd sushi with gingerroot & scallion 642
California rolls 248
chicken teriyaki rolls 246
chirashi sushi with feta & sunblush tomatoes 624
chirashi sushi with lobster & wasabi mayonnaise 512
chirashi sushi with omelet & mushrooms 626
chirashi sushi with salmon 546
chirashi sushi on scallop shells 450
chirashi sushi with shrimp, crab & avocado 460
chirashi sushi with smoked mackerel 588
chirashi sushi with soy-glazed steak 322
chirashi sushi with teriyaki chicken 374
classic sushi boat with salmon roe 548
classic tuna nori rolls 222
crab, asparagus & shiitake rolls 240
cucumber rolls with sesame 604
eggplant sushi with sweet soy sauce 644
fresh shiitake mushroom sushi 640
green bean & tomato chirashi sushi 630
green bean sushi boats 628
inside-out rolls with avocado & shibazuke 616
inside-out rolls with beef teriyaki 252
lemon pepper crab sushi boats 506
marinated tuna chirashi sushi 566
Mediterranean pressed sushi 638
omelet pouches with mushroom 598
omelet rolls with cream cheese & pepper 602
omelet wraps with pickled radish & shiso 596
oyster mushroom & fried bean curd chirashi sushi 622
perfect sushi rice 258
pickled radish & kampyo rolls 606
pinwheel rolls with mushroom & spinach 610
pork tonkatsu rolls 250
salmon & arugula rolls with pesto 226
salmon, asparagus & mayonnaise rolls 234
salmon, cucumber & pickled radish wraps 554
sesame-bean curd chirashi sushi 620
seven-spiced salmon rolls 232
shrimp & avocado skewers 244
smoked salmon sushi balls 228
spiced carrot sushi 636
sweet bean curd pouches 646
sweet chili salmon hand rolls 558

sweet rolled omelet sushi 632
Thai-style chirashi sushi with crabmeat 492
tuna tataki hand rolls 568
umeboshi plum rolls 612
white fish hand rolls with tartar sauce 572
wraps with fresh tuna, salmon roe & shiso leaves 552
sweet potatoes
spicy Thai soup with shrimp 52
tempura 216
Thai yellow vegetable curry with brown basmati rice 674
vegetable & bean curd tempura 218

tempura 216
seafood tempura 220
shrimp tempura & lettuce wraps 458
vegetable & bean curd tempura 218
teriyaki dipping sauce 276
tomatoes
Chinese tomato salad 88
chirashi sushi with feta & sunblush tomatoes 624
green bean & tomato chirashi sushi 630
Mediterranean pressed sushi 638
tuna & tomato salad with gingerroot dressing 64
tuna
chargrilled tuna with chile salsa 564
classic tuna nori rolls 222
marinated tuna chirashi sushi 566
mixed sashimi 444
mixed seafood curry 532
soba noodle rolls 158
spiced tuna in sweet-&-sour sauce 570
tuna rice 266
tuna sesame blocks 224
tuna tataki hand rolls 568
tuna & tomato salad with gingerroot dressing 64
wraps with fresh tuna, salmon roe & shiso leaves 552
turkey
rice & turkey salad 84
turkey with bamboo shoots & water chestnuts 428

umeboshi plum rolls 612

water chestnuts
baby squid stuffed with pork & mushrooms 514
beef chop suey 286
chicken with water chestnuts and plum sauce 426
Chinese crispy duck 434
Chinese vegetables & bean sprouts with noodles 710
classic stir-fried vegetables 102
crispy crab wontons 192
mixed vegetables with quick-fried basil 138
red lamb curry 360
turkey with bamboo shoots & water chestnuts 428
wonton soup 46
wontons 190
crispy crab wontons 192

zucchini
bean curd & green vegetable curry 656
julienne vegetable salad 94
sweet-&-sour vegetables with cashew nuts 106
zucchini & cashew curry 660